The Politics of Migration in Italy

Migration represents one of the key issues in both Italian and European politics, and it has triggered EU-wide debates and negotiations, alongside alarmist and often sensationalist news reporting on the activities of government, party and social movement actors.

The Politics of Migration in Italy explores what happens when previously undiscussed issues become central to political agendas and are publicly debated in the mass media. Examining how political actors engage with the issue of migration in electoral campaigning, this book highlights how complex policy issues are addressed selectively by political entrepreneurs and how the responses of political actors are influenced by strategic incentives and ongoing events. This book studies the dynamics of the politicization of the immigration issue across three local contexts in Italy – Prato, Milan and Rome – which differ systematically with respect to crucial economic, cultural and security dimensions of immigration.

Offering an innovative exploration of party competition and migration in Italy, as well as providing the conceptual and analytical tools to understand how these dynamics play out beyond the Italian case, this book is essential reading for students, scholars and policymakers working in the areas of migration studies, agenda-setting and European politics more generally.

Pietro Castelli Gattinara holds a PhD in Political Science from the European University Institute, and is currently a postdoctoral researcher at the Centre for Social Movement Studies (COSMOS), Scuola Normale Superiore of Florence, Italy.

Routledge Studies in Extremism and Democracy
Series Editors: Roger Eatwell, *University of Bath*, and Matthew
Goodwin, *University of Nottingham.*
Founding Series Editors: Roger Eatwell, *University of Bath*
and Cas Mudde, *University of Antwerp-UFSIA.*

This new series encompasses academic studies within the broad fields of 'extremism'
and 'democracy'. These topics have traditionally been considered largely in isolation
by academics. A key focus of the series, therefore, is the (inter-)*relation* between
extremism and democracy. Works will seek to answer questions such as to what
extent 'extremist' groups pose a major threat to democratic parties, or how democracy can respond to extremism without undermining its own democratic credentials.

The books encompass two strands:

Routledge Studies in Extremism and Democracy includes books with an intro-
ductory and broad focus which are aimed at students and teachers. These books
will be available in hardback and paperback. Titles include:

Understanding Terrorism in America
From the Klan to al Qaeda
Christopher Hewitt

**New British Fascism: Rise of the
British National Party**
Matthew Goodwin

Fascism and the Extreme Right
Roger Eatwell

The End of Terrorism?
Leonard Weinberg

**Racist Extremism in Central and
Eastern Europe**
Edited by Cas Mudde

**Mapping the Extreme Right in
Contemporary Europe:
From Local to
Transnational**
*Edited by Andrea Mammone,
Emmanuel Godin
and Brian Jenkins*

**Political Parties and Terrorist
Groups (2nd Edition)**
*Leonard Weinberg, Ami Pedahzur and
Arie Perliger*

**The New Extremism in 21st Century
Britain**
*Edited by Roger Eatwell and Matthew
Goodwin*

**Varieties of Right-Wing
Extremism in Europe**
*Edited by Andrea Mammone,
Emmanuel Godin
and Brian Jenkins*

Right-Wing Radicalism Today
Perspectives from Europe and the US
Edited by Sabine von Mering and
Timothy Wyman McCarty

Revolt on the Right
Explaining support for the radical
right in Britain
Robert Ford and Matthew Goodwin

Routledge Research in Extremism and Democracy offers a forum for innovative new research intended for a more specialist readership. These books will be in hardback only. Titles include:

The Politics of Migration in Italy

Perspectives on local debates and party competition

Pietro Castelli Gattinara

Routledge
Taylor & Francis Group

LONDON AND NEW YORK

First published 2016
by Routledge
2 Park Square, Milton Park, Abingdon, Oxon OX14 4RN

and by Routledge
711 Third Avenue, New York, NY 10017

Routledge is an imprint of the Taylor & Francis Group, an informa business

British Library Cataloguing-in-Publication Data
A catalogue record for this book is available from the British Library

Library of Congress Cataloging-in-Publication Data
Names: Castelli Gattinara, Pietro, author.
Title: The politics of migration in Italy : perspectives on local debates and
    party competition / Pietro Castelli Gattinara.
Description: New York, NY : Routledge, 2016. | Series: Routledge studies
    in extremism and democracy
Identifiers: LCCN 2015046786 | ISBN 9781138642560 (hardback) |
    ISBN 9781315628677 (e-book)
Subjects: LCSH: Italy—Emigration and immigration—Political aspects. |
    Italy—Emigration and immigration—Government policy. | Local
    government—Italy. | Political campaigns—Italy.
Classification: LCC JV8133 .C38 2016 | DDC 325.45—dc23
LC record available at http://lccn.loc.gov/2015046786

ISBN: 978-1-138-64256-0 (hbk)
ISBN: 978-1-315-62867-7 (ebk)

Typeset in Times New Roman
by Apex CoVantage, LLC

MIX
Paper from
responsible sources
FSC   FSC® C013056
www.fsc.org

Printed and bound in Great Britain by
TJ International Ltd, Padstow, Cornwall

For Giovi, because you can't read just comics forever.
And for my little Petros, though you truly do not care.
Yet.

This book has been published with a financial subsidy
from the European University Institute.

Contents

Figures

Tables

Acknowledgements

This book stems from the doctoral research project that I have developed, from 2010 to 2014, at the Department of Political and Social Sciences of the European University Institute, in Florence. When I first discovered that I would move to Tuscany for my PhD, I was four and a half years younger than I am now. I was living on the other side of Europe. Gianni Alemanno was the mayor of Rome. I had more hair and cleaner lungs. I was voting the wrong party. I spoke Turkish. I thought I would have gone back to Rome. I cycled but I did not play football. I was working in a pizzeria and spending my holidays in a place called Terschelling. I could barely distinguish the Alps from the Apennines. I did not have a gin tonic problem. I did not know the meaning of 'humongous'. I thought *Prezzemolo* was a herb. I had never been to Calabria. I had never met a CasaPound member. I thought I would never go to the U.S. I did not know the *marc de champagne*. I had never lived in Paris. I did not know Carmela, Francesca, Pantaleone, Giusy and Libera. The concept of migration had a completely different meaning for me. I considered myself a quantitative sociologist. I had a positive impression of people in Tuscany. I had round sunglasses. I had never spent Easter in Crete. I had a scooter. I was thoroughly non-violent. Ballantines was not Ballantines. I did not know the Leicestershire. I hated anarchists. None of my friends had babies. I was about to get married. I did not understand Irish. I thought Berlusconi was the worse it could happen. I believed in miracles. I was a Euro-enthusiast. I thought Totti would retire soon. I was considerably more self-confident. I did not know queer theory. I was considerably less cynical. I did not know Caterina and my cat was not yet born.

In four years, with respect to some of these and many other aspects, I have changed. This book embodies only one dimension of this change. What is sure is that 60 months ago I knew much less than I do now, for which I should primarily thank Hanspeter Kriesi, without whom this book would have simply not been possible. Beyond conventional formulas, it is true that his never-ending attention to my work and progress, his availability and understanding, his experience and his criticism contributed in a fundamental way not only to this work, but more generally to what I've learnt as a PhD student. I am also grateful to Laura Morales, Ruud Koopmans and Rainer Baubock for their comments on earlier versions of this book, and I wish to thank the many other – official and unofficial – supervisors that I had over the past years. Those who helped me in the initial stages of this endeavour, with whom I had to struggle and negotiate the first chaotic and wild versions of this work. Those who adopted me (Donatella), in many ways, within their community, for reasons that are still unclear (excluding maybe the normal motivations of *buon vicinato*). And those others who perceived that the ways of supervision are inscrutable, supporting with their curiosity and persistence the completion of this volume.

The usual suspects contributed, in different ways, to my experience of thinking, developing and writing. At various stages the support and solidarity of my grandparents, parents and brothers and sisters has helped me figure out solutions to problems that seemed insuperable but were not. As always, Di Foggia and Ruggero assisted me when I was in most need. At *Pigmalione,* I shared with them not only the complaints and frustration but also the amusement and challenges of the PhD life, being well aware that a glass of Lucano is mightier than a bivariate table. My colleagues in Leicester and my friends in Paris witnessed the most critical moments in the revision of this manuscript, for which I apologize. I also wish to thank the nutrias of Arno for relentlessly triggering my imagination and the several friends that supported me in my complaints about Florence. My neighbours in via del Campuccio and Danilo kept me busy when I was alone, and my cat Minik Aslan has been the silent observer of most years of my PhD. He is the mute witness of the worse secrets and compromises of my work.

The most important person in these last years is also the one I don't need to thank, since Caterina knows already that without her I would be somewhere else, I would be doing something else, I would be someone else. *Grazie,* anyways. Instead, I'd like to offer official thanks to Herman and Wolfgang for giving me good reasons to stay in Florence. I am grateful to Antonella, Fiamma and Cinzia for their everyday genuine support, to Maureen for her priceless kindness and empathy, to Gabriella despite our not infrequent disputes, and to my personal semiologist Alberto Caselli for making me fully enjoy these Florentine years. More broadly, I must acknowledge the essential contribution of one type of animal within the variegated fauna of my friends and colleagues: the lunatics. Markos, Myrssini and Robocop, their Trotskyist baby, Frank and Shachi, Cocotto, Zamponi, Donagh, Albanese, Tomek, Sarah and Elina, Kuffner, Maja, Marco, Mazzamauro, Semih, the Kutmanalianev family, Felicetti, Helge, Pedro, Francisco, Leonidas, Bogna, Nick and Frank, Jerome, Cini, Eliska, Daniela, Hugo, Virginia, Luc, and the extended community of monkeys, founding mothers and new generations of *Prezzemoli.* These are the people with whom I shared the main lesson that I will retain from this dulling and entertaining chunk of life: to call every truth false which was not accompanied by at least one laugh.

1   Introduction

Migration has reshaped considerably European societies over the last three decades. Despite the end of the guest-workers programmes of the 1960s and 1970s, countries like Britain, France, Germany and the Netherlands have been experiencing new inflows of migrants in recent years, mainly originating from areas affected by humanitarian crises and from within Europe. Similarly, states that were traditional senders of migrants – in the southern border of the continent, Greece, Italy, Spain, Portugal – progressively transformed into new destination countries. With the global refugee crisis of 2014–2015, large numbers of migrants and asylum seekers have streamed into European countries from the Middle East and Africa, making the Mediterranean the world's most dangerous sea to cross, and transforming immigration and migrants' integration into two of the most pressing challenges for contemporary policy-makers in Europe.

Immigration has the potential to reshape the domestic landscape of receiving countries in many ways. Yet, the extent to which it affects democratic politics depends primarily on the attitudes of native-born majorities and therefore on the way in which political actors and the mass media represent migration as a policy issue. National governments, local authorities and supranational organizations are involved in the process of politicization of migration, developing policies for migration control and for the incorporation of foreign residents. Domestic electorates express support or opposition to such policy initiatives, whilst political parties construct their own rhetoric and understanding of it, and the mass media determine the visibility of anti-immigration actors, xenophobic right-wing parties, and pro-migrant movements and organizations.

The combination of these situations has made it necessary to study the causes and consequences of the politicization of immigration at different levels of governance, and the nature of public attitudes toward migrants in European societies. When studying immigration, however, scholars of party politics and political behaviour have mainly focused on the exceptional features of the issue, whether in terms of its disruptive consequences for West European party systems, or in terms of protest, xenophobia and radicalism. The impressive scholarly and normative interest in these aspects has tended to overshadow the extent to which immigration debates, once marginal to electoral campaigning, have stabilized within party competition. The aim of this book, by contrast, is to assess the role played by immigration in electoral campaigning once it was normalized within party systems. This in turn implies evaluating the process by which previously non-salient issues are integrated in the public sphere, and become stable features of electoral debates and party competition.

In doing so, this book advances hypotheses important to the understanding of a real-world phenomenon of crucial significance for democracy in the EU, as demonstrated by the reactions to the ongoing refugee crisis by European leaders and political representatives. My focus is on Italy, a setting where large-scale migration has been sudden and its politicization relatively recent. In the following pages, I will provide an in-depth analysis of six electoral campaigns in three cities: Rome, Milan and Prato. At the same time, this book seeks to contribute to the literature explaining the politicization of migration. On the one hand, I shall build upon previous theories and hypotheses in order to advance our understanding of these dynamics. On the other, I shall broaden the scope of investigation of the politicization of migration to address local politics and patterns of electoral competition. The remainder of this chapter will accordingly introduce the crucial features of the scientific contribution of the present volume, discussing the main research questions and innovative aspects of the research and, subsequently, discuss the research design and methodology of the study.

Competing on migration at the local level

This book focuses on the dynamics of electoral competition on the immigration issue in local electoral campaigns. Immigration provides good grounds on which to test and improve theories on party competition and electoral campaigning for at least three reasons. First, as mentioned above, the immigration issue only became salient in European political systems relatively recently. Rather than as a single issue, however, my claim is that immigration has penetrated electoral debates as a bundle of multiple aspects and issues conditionally and strategically framed by the actors involved in competition. In addition, its relative novelty seems to have paved the way to a variety of party politicization strategies, ranging from attempts to exclude it from public agendas to direct efforts to challenge the radical parties that contributed to its emergence. This offers a crucial opportunity to analyze the different dimensions and framing strategies structuring party competition. Third and most importantly, the immigration issue has been described in previous literature as cross-cutting the traditional divide between economic and cultural issues, since it simultaneously contains economic, cultural and identity features. As a prototypical example of a multidimensional issue, immigration provides a good opportunity to observe the mechanisms of electoral campaigning across different dimensions and frames.

Based on these considerations, I set out to investigate two aspects that have not received sufficient attention in previous literature on this subject: the multidimensional nature of policy issues in electoral campaigning and the importance of local factors in determining electoral debates on immigration. By investigating these two aspects jointly, and by empirically assessing the campaigning strategies of political actors at the local level, I suggest an understanding of electoral competition based on the breakdown of policy problems along constitutive issue dimensions. To this goal, I develop an innovative approach to understanding the supply side of electoral competition, by focusing on the inherently multidimensional structure of complex policy issues. So far, both saliency and spatial models have tended to focus on one-dimensional policy issues, which parties can either endorse or reject as a whole. This research, contrarily, emphasizes their multidimensional and thematic nature, and looks at the role played by issue dimensions in the politicization strategies and framing choices of competing electoral actors.

In this respect, my main claim in this book is that saliency and positional strategies of issue competition are not sufficient to account for the dynamics of electoral campaigning on contentious policy issues. Instead, one must also account for framing strategies and issue-specific constitutive dimensions. Once the immigration issue is salient at the party-system level in fact, electoral actors lose their capacity to dismiss the issue altogether, and have to set up their electoral campaigns on the basis of alternative interpretations of the same issue. Rather than competing over different issues, they compete over directing attention to and away from different aspects of the same social reality.

On this basis, I shall look at whether political actors in election campaigns consider certain dimensions of the immigration issue more important than others, and whether they adopt different positions depending on the aspect of immigration. Parties are selective with respect to the dimensions of immigration they choose to highlight, emphasizing the aspects on which they have a strategic advantage whilst trying to conceal others. In order to disentangle the process of agenda setting competition in electoral campaigns on immigration, this study offers a close examination of political parties' priorities and approaches with respect to the subcategories of complex policy issues.

The concept of dimensionality builds on the idea that complex political issues involve a large amount of dimensions of choice that could matter to citizens while making up their minds. Yet people generally process information in a selective manner and therefore take in consideration only some of these many dimensions. Since there are little rewards for discussing all the dimensions of a policy issue, political actors have additional incentives to represent policy problems in a partial and incomplete way. Recognizing the thematic nature of policy issues enables understanding which aspects are important in setting up public agendas in electoral times. When new dimensions of the issue become important, or when alternative understandings emerge, agendas may be reshaped, since emerging actors may challenge the ones that enjoyed an advantage in the public definition of an issue at a previous point in time.

This is why the study of electoral campaigning must focus on the way in which messages are crafted. In line with previous literature, I define a 'frame' as a central organizing idea that attracts attention to certain aspects of an issue, while directing it away from others (Gamson, 2004). Given that frames promote 'a particular problem definition, causal interpretation, moral evaluation, and/or treatment recommendation for the item described' (Entman, 1993, p. 52), framing strategies refer to the active effort of an actor to construct a certain meaning for a given reality or phenomenon (Entman, 1993; Hänggli and Kriesi, 2010). This is done by emphasizing certain aspects on which to fix the public's attention while obscuring alternative ones.

On the basis of these premises, the main question motivating the research proposed here can be spelled out: how do political actors politicize an issue like immigration, which used to be 'novel' but is by now established in electoral campaign dynamics, which is cross-cutting and multidimensional in nature, and which is differently embedded in local contexts? I investigate immigration in order to explore the nature of campaigning on complex policy issues and the framing choices that accompany party strategies, with the goal of improving traditional spatial and saliency understandings of electoral competition. In so doing, I aim at explaining the set of constraints and opportunities that determine the discursive choices of strategic actors in electoral campaigning. What is the role played by the different attributes of the immigration issue in electoral competition? Which dimensions of immigration emerge in local electoral debates? What is the role of local factors, and to what extent do politicization strategies depend on the fact that immigration is differently embedded across local contexts? To what extent do parties compete using these alternative issue dimensions and frames? Does uncertainty in actors' strategies of politicization persist?

In order to answer these questions and to assess the dimensionality of electoral competition, I address immigration debates from three interrelated angles. First, I look at immigration debates across three Italian cities, considering whether and to what extent local factors and characteristics of electoral campaigns influence framing and dimensional choices in politicizing immigration. Second, I investigate whether political actors develop strategies of competition based on issue dimensions rather than on the immigration issue as a whole. This implies that parties do not differ from one another in terms of *whether* they discuss the immigration issue or not, but rather on *how* they discuss it. Third, I explore the role the mass media play as a transmission belt in the construction of electoral agendas, assessing the news value of the multiple aspects of the immigration issue and comparing the way in which political actors deal with them across different channels of communication.

Research design and methodology

My study is a comparative investigation of the politicization of the issue of migration across six electoral campaigns in three Italian cities: Milan, Rome and Prato. In recent years, scholars have increasingly recognized the importance of immigration in local political contexts. Although most of the actual policy competence on immigration affairs lies with national institutions, in fact, local political actors have important competences in the field of migrants' integration, as well as in other fields connected to migration in political rhetoric. Hence, they often have strong incentives to politicize this issue in its broader sense. By exploiting the symbolic power of immigration politics, in fact, local politicians debate issues in areas well beyond their concrete administrative competences. Moreover, the dynamics of interethnic competition and threat often depend on patterns of concentration across local territories, on problems of cohabitation at the urban level, and on the distribution of locally-based resources and locally-managed welfare assets.

Local conditions, party configurations, media and focusing events are all factors that might contribute to the construction of diverging debates on immigration. Much as national institutional profiles and 'citizenship regimes' have traditionally been considered fundamental to explaining different policy-making activities and debates at the international level, I suggest that local factors and opportunities substantially shape the politicization of migration affairs in local debates. In this sense, the dynamics of politicization of the immigration issue at the local level can differ significantly not only from those at the national level, but can also vary substantially between local settings. On the one hand, this is because immigration provides opportunities to political entrepreneurs at all levels of public administration; on the other, because of the crucial role that local actors play in regulating specific dimensions of immigration and integration issues.

The decision to investigate local electoral campaigns in Italy also had to do with the main focus of this study, which looks at competitive strategies *within* multidimensional issues, rather than competition strategies *over* issues. Understanding how parties frame a certain issue and its constitutive dimensions requires an in-depth investigation of the discourse that parties produce, and a detailed analysis of how these frames and dimensions manage (or fail) to manipulate the electoral agenda in the news media. A similar endeavour is often hard to perform when the unit of analysis is national electoral campaigns, because party strategies may vary across settings and contexts, and the news agenda is often heterogeneous due to the marketing strategies of different outlets in different areas of the country. By focusing on the national level, in other words, there would have been the risk of summarizing strategies by averaging out local differences in dimensional choices.

My attention is not on the traditional question concerning the degree to which parties manipulate the salience of the immigration issue in the news media, which could be addressed by looking at national parties, news media, and electoral campaigns. Contrarily, this study's interest lies with investigating how the dynamics of agenda definition at the local level influence the way in which problems are framed and publicly discussed (Caponio and Borkert, 2010; Morales and Giugni, 2011; van der Brug *et al.*, 2015). Approaches based on national models of immigrant incorporation have often neglected the complexity of immigrant policies and debates, which are frequently shaped by regional dynamics and local factors (Caponio, 2006; Jesuit and Mahler, 2004). On the one hand, this is due to the spontaneous and unplanned nature of migration flows and immigrant settlement in countries like Italy. On the other, local-level politics on immigration differ structurally from national-level politics because of the different challenges that local administrators face, and the different policy competences that they have (Gilbert, 2009; Hepburn and Zapata-Barrero, 2014). This underlines the importance of looking at local dynamics in immigration politics, as these may provide additional information on the rationales of immigration conflicts (Alexander, 2004; Penninx *et al.,* 2004).

Focusing on the supply side of electoral competition, moreover, the research design of this book is built on the analysis of electoral campaigns rather than party behaviour in between elections. This is because it is during these times that the game played by parties and electoral actors becomes most evident and explicit, exposing the influence that they exert on, and receive from, the political, social and media environment in which their competition takes place. A research design measuring party strategies of agenda construction during electoral campaigns must account for the socioeconomic, cultural and institutional characteristics of the place where competition takes place, the set of policies and arguments that political parties develop for a given electoral campaign, and the resonance of these propositions within the campaign period. For each election campaign, therefore, I looked at the degree to which one of the migration dimensions is central in the campaign and media agenda, and I uncover the campaigning activities of all involved political actors. As will be discussed later, the bulk of the analysis is based upon the media coverage of the immigration issue during the period of the electoral campaigns. Yet, in order to disentangle the strategies of the various actors involved in agenda setting, I not only look at differences across settings and time, but also differentiate news media reports from the electoral material, pledges and manifestos of the main actors running in the election campaigns.

To address these, I selected the three case studies of Prato, Milan and Rome based on a set of characteristics relating to the nature of immigrant settlement in each city, and studied the two most recent local electoral campaigns within each of these settings. In each setting, I considered the latest municipal electoral campaign at the time of the data collection, namely the elections 2008 in Rome, those of 2009 in Prato and those of 2011 in Milan. In order to have sufficient grounds for comparison, moreover, I also account for the three municipal elections that preceded the selected ones (Prato, 2004; Milan, 2006; Rome, 2006). In this way, the design allows both for within-case comparisons across electoral campaigns, and for between-case comparisons across local settings.[1]

I focus on three comparable cities within the same political system in order to keep constant the institutional framework of multi-level governance, investigating the systematic variation in specific characteristics of migration politics (Islamic migration in Milan, Roma immigrants in Rome and Chinese migrants in Prato). The case studies are most similar in terms of electoral system, media environment and institutional architecture, but differ with respect to the dimension of immigration that is crucial in electoral campaigns. This builds on the idea that local conditions can facilitate the mobilization of specific issue sub-dimensions, so that the variation in the characteristics of the migrant population across local settings influences the accessibility of local arenas to different types of debates on migration. The three cases should therefore help elucidating the process of campaigning on immigration issue dimensions.

The locations were identified carefully based on information on the distribution of foreign residents in Italy and in each of the three cities, and the corresponding problems and debates related to immigration at the city level. By 2010, Milan and Rome hosted the largest immigrant communities in the country,[2] whilst Prato, where the size of the immigrant community is considerably smaller, is one of the *chef-lieu* cities with the highest share of immigrant residents over the total population (ISTAT, 2010).[3] In addition, I considered the immigration debates that could be triggered given the composition of the immigrant population in the three cities. According to Gariglio *et al.* (2010), the main feature of public debates on immigration in Italy has been the tendency to build stereotypes and isolate 'groups of immigrants'. Hence, I anticipated that the composition of migrant communities offered opportunities for dimensional politicization of immigration, and considered cities where ethnic concentration might result in different issue dimensions dominating electoral debates.

Accordingly, Rome hosts the largest Romanian community in Italy, next to a number of illegal and nomadic camps mainly inhabited by Travellers of *Romani* and *Sinti* origin. These are the themes that have dominated crime stories and securitized immigration debates over the past decades in Italy and beyond (Legros and Vitale, 2011), and especially at the time of Romania's access to the EU (Bonetti *et al.*, 2011; Sigona, 2011). Muslim immigrants represents about 40% of the total number of foreign residents in the city of Milan (Bombardieri, 2011; Rebessi, 2011), and the presence of Muslims in the streets during the Friday prayer has been one of the main sources of conflict between neighbourhood organizations and migrant communities in Europe (Göle, 2013; Cousin and Vitale, 2012; Pogliano and Valetti, 2011). Finally, Prato offered a straightforward case where to test the nature of debates on socioeconomic aspects of immigration, due to its industrial economy and to the history of migration to the city, which was mainly driven by demand for a cheap labour force especially from China, and subsequently by the development of Chinese entrepreneurship.

Within each city setting, the comparative design focuses on coalitions of lists supporting mayoral candidates, looking at the changing importance of different actors, issue dimensions and events over time and across contexts. This choice to focus on coalitions is most appropriate given the electoral system in local Italian municipalities: a majoritarian system where voters express a preference vote for the mayor or his list/party; if no candidate receives at least 50% of the votes, the top two candidates are admitted to a second round after two weeks.[4] Concerning the local campaigns observed, three of the six elections considered (Rome, 2008, Prato, 2009 and Milan, 2011) required a second round of elections because none of the candidates managed to obtain an absolute majority at the first round.

Previous studies that tried to explain variation in the politicization of migration have primarily focused on specific party types, focusing on niche or populist radical right parties that mobilized around migration (Meguid, 2008). On the contrary, the empirical analysis of the present book distinguishes six main types of local political actors: mainstream left and right actors, radical left and right actors, centrist actors and interest groups. This choice was preferred to other possible categorizations because it allowed accounting for left–right differentiation in the politicization of migration, whilst simultaneously coming to terms with previous literature investigating the weakening of traditional cleavages in Western societies (Kriesi *et al.*, 2008). As argued by Peter Mair (2008, 2009), in fact, the main divergence between parties in contemporary democracies is between mainstream parties who are accustomed to being in office, and fringe or peripheral parties at either end of the left–right spectrum that have no government experience.[5]

Accordingly, I first differentiate between the mainstream left (centre-left) and mainstream right (centre-right) coalitions that run in all six election campaigns, which alternate in power and tend to address a broad set of issues in their electoral programmes. These correspond to the general cleavage between left- and right-wing politics existing at the national level, reproduced in scale in local arenas. In addition to these, I focus on those parties that are generally considered radical rather than mainstream, since the extent to which immigration plays a role in electoral campaigns is often strongly related to their strategies of competition.[6] At the extreme of the political spectrum, therefore, I make reference to unaffiliated radical left[7] and radical right lists and organizations,[8] when these run campaigns independently from the centre-left and centre-right. The same applies for the various centrist actors that do not affiliate with mainstream coalitions.[9] Finally, I also consider all those non-partisan actors intervening in public debates and representing societal or economic interests, ranging from trade unions, business organizations and institutional, religious and public figures such as journalists and experts.

The measurement of public debates was then based on the exploration and analysis of mass media reports and political advertisements and manifestos produced by the actors involved in the campaigns. This was done specifically by way of a systematic content analysis of electoral manifestos and news media coverage of the electoral campaigns (in local and national newspapers) over the two months preceding the six electoral events. I opted for the content analysis of newspapers rather than television, because the printed press is generally considered to report more extensively on political issues (Druckman and Parkin, 2005).

As illustrated in detail in Appendix 1, this strategy was composed of a number of successive steps: first, I selected the relevant newspapers to describe the local debates within electoral campaigns. Subsequently, I identified all newspaper articles (news stories) that referred to the electoral campaigns, to the politics at the municipal level in Prato, Milan and Rome (overall media coverage), or more specifically to migration. This also included the selection of the same time span across the six electoral campaigns. The third step, finally, involved the actual coding of the material, on a sentence-by-sentence basis, using the *core-sentence* method of analysis introduced by Kleinnijenhuis *et al.* (1997), and further developed by Kriesi *et al.* (2008). Given its focus on relational data, the main idea behind this approach is that the content of texts can be synthesized as a network of objects, allowing one to identify the relationship between political actors and political issues (in this case, sub-issues and frames as well).[10] Previous studies have confirmed that this approach and type of data is most appropriate for the analysis of how parties compete with one another (Helbling and Tresch, 2011).

This coding strategy allows for several types of comparisons, highlighting three different dimensions of politicization and competition over the migration issue. First, it permits one to evaluate the relative importance of immigration in the electoral campaign, relative to all alternative issue debates. Moreover, it allows for the calculation of the relative salience of a certain dimension in the total amount of immigration-related news stories. That is, it allows one to identify different types of debates across local electoral campaigns, and different types of discourse among competing coalitions. Similarly, it permits one to evaluate the degree to which each frame and argumentation is utilized within a debate on immigration. Finally, it enables one to investigate which frames and dimensions are mobilized to support, and which ones to oppose, immigration (again across cases and mayoral candidates).[11]

The structure of the book

The book is comprised of eight chapters. Chapter 2 presents the general theoretical framework of the study, a salience model of political competition integrated in order to account for spatial positioning with respect to issue dimensions and frames. Starting from previous research dealing with party and issue competition, electoral campaigning and immigration politics, I justify and contextualize the main conceptual contributions of this study. I then move to the discussion of multidimensional issues on the basis of their inherent characteristics, cognitive factors on the demand side, and strategic preferences on the supply side of electoral competition. Immigration is introduced as a prototypical example of a complex political issue, comprised of three alternative dimensions that cut across policy sectors: the socioeconomic, cultural and religious, and law and order dimensions. For each dimension, I present the framing categories identified empirically, and discuss their relevance in explaining electoral debates and understandings of immigration in local Italian elections. Finally, the chapter introduces the main argument of the book concerning party strategies and the politicization of issue dimensions, presenting the expectations for local electoral campaigns, partisan dimensional and framing strategies, and media resonance in constructing public agendas. Chapter 3 then introduces the case studies and offers a broader contextualization of migration in Italy, referring to existing literature on the local dimension of migration politics and to studies on other Western and Southern European contexts.

The second part of this book presents the empirical analysis of the supply side of the electoral competition on migration. Using the content analysis of newspaper media coverage in Prato, Rome and Milan, Chapter 4 compares electoral debates across six local campaigns. The analyses of the salience of the immigration issue across time and settings reveal the importance of context and dimensionality in determining variation in electoral debates. Chapter 5 builds on this to investigate debates from the point of view of the actors that engage in electoral campaigning. It focuses on whether specific political actors are associated with particular frames and dimensions which could explain the varying salience of the issue across local elections. In line with the main arguments of this book, I show that dimensional strategies vary depending on the salience of immigration, and on the composition of the party system. In particular I underline the role played by political actors in setting up dimensional strategies of competition, and analyze how they differ in terms of support and opposition to immigration. Chapter 6 deals with the question of how political actors frame immigration in electoral debates, and why they propose certain argumentations rather than others to articulate support or opposition to migration. The comparative design indicates that framing strategies depend not only on the position of actors on the left–right scale and the importance attributed to the issue, but also on the circumstances in which electoral competition takes place. Having assessed the dimensionality of the public electoral agenda, Chapter 7 advances the analysis of electoral campaigning by focusing on different channels of communication between political actors and the public. This chapter compares actors' pledges in their electoral platforms with the newspaper coverage of the campaigns, and differentiates political actors based on their left–right alignment, their role in election campaigns and their position towards immigration.

Chapter 8, in conclusion, combines the conceptual contributions of this volume with the empirical evidence of the electoral campaigns, drawing general conclusions concerning electoral debates on migration and integration at the local level. The final remarks synthesize the main findings of this research and their implications for the study of electoral competition and campaigning activities in political science, discussing the strategic options available to Italian and European political entrepreneurs once the immigration issue is integrated in the dominant political discourse.

Notes

1 See Chapter 3 for a case-by-case description of the three local settings, an overview of the migration patterns to Italy and Italian cities, and a discussion of the six electoral campaigns observed.

2 More than one-third of the immigrant residents in Italy live within the borders of metropolitan areas, in particular cities with a long history of international migration (Genoa, Rome, Turin and Milan; see: Testa, 2013). In addition, immigrant residents are concentrated in the so-called 'crown cities' of metropolitan areas of Central and Northern Italy (Venice, Florence, Bologna; see: Testa, 2013), where small and medium-sized cities tend to have high shares of foreign residents.

3 Further details and a discussion of the role of small and medium-sized municipalities for migrants' integration in Italy can be found in Chapter 3.

4 The electoral law in Italian municipalities is discussed in depth in Appendix 2. The results of the six elections under study are also available in the appendices.

5 Although the notion of mainstream parties is often used in opposition to that of niche parties (Meguid, 2008), the literature in this area is increasingly open to use the term in line with the choice of this volume (see: Kriesi *et al.*, 2008; Odmalm and Bale, 2014). Niche parties, moreover, usually are defined as parties that emphasize issues that existing mainstream parties ignore (Meguid, 2008), which is in contradiction with the main focus this book, as I address party behaviour at times in which neglected issues can no longer be ignored.

6 For these and other parties addressed in the book, I avoided using populism as a defining category, and I addressed it solely as a specific style characterizing defined traits of the electoral campaigning of an individual actor, in a specific point in time. From a conceptual perspective, in fact, I am generally more oriented towards viewing populism as a type of social and political mobilization, related to a specific way of understanding political action and discourse, rather than as a particular ideological content that enables categorizing actors as either populist or non-populist (Laclau, 2005; Taguieff, 2002; Tarchi, 2004). From a methodological perspective, moreover, adding populism to the theoretical model would imply measuring it as a dimension of discourse. Yet, my focus is on strategic framing as a second-level agenda setting process (cf. Chapter 2), and therefore addresses substantive and issue-specific framing rather than generic frames (Matthes, 2009).

7 Radical left parties are actors accepting democracy, although they combine this with aspirations towards direct democracy and/or local participatory democracy, including incorporating the rights of the excluded and marginalized (for example, the unemployed and migrant workers) in the political system. Their anti-capitalism no longer involves a planned economy but opposition to neo-liberal globalized capitalism. Extreme left parties, in contrast, have far greater hostility to liberal democracy. In Italy, radical left parties have been represented by *Rifondazione Comunista, Sinistra Ecologia e Libertà* and *Comunisti Italiani,* which have a tradition of dialogue with mainstream left and centre-left coalitions (Albertazzi *et al.,* 2011).

8 In this study, I use the definition 'radical right actors'. Despite the terminological and conceptual debate that is still open (Ignazi, 1992, 2003; Kitschelt, 1995; Mudde, 2000, 2007), previous literature has found no less than twenty-six different ways to identify this party family (Minkenberg, 2007). Generally, the groups pertaining to the 'radical right' or 'extreme right' are associated with values such as nationalism and exclusivism, xenophobia, welfare chauvinism, revisionism and conservatism. Although the two terms are often used interchangeably, the difference between extremism and radicalism is associated to the (degree of) hostility to the constitution and established order of political societies. By focusing on radicalism, I address not only the parties and movements of the neo-fascist scene in Italy (Albanese *et al.,* 2015; Castelli *et al.,* 2014; Castelli Gattinara *et al.,* 2013), but also those opposing only specific problems within the political system. With respect to the Italian Lega Nord (Northern League), I follow previous scholarship on this issue that has consistently excluded it from the radical right party family (Ignazi, 1992, 2003; McDonnell, 2006).

9 As well as the *Movimento 5 Stelle,* whose members reject identification with either of the two ends of the traditional left–right paradigm. This party, however, participated in local elections only sporadically in the years 2004–2011, and it emerged as a relevant political actor only in the years following the period observed here.

10 Accordingly, the number of core sentences in an article does not correspond to the number of grammatical sentences, since a core sentence may include one or more than one grammatical sentence, but it can also include none.

11 A detailed illustration of the coding procedures of subject, objects and relationships within actor-issue sentences can be found in Appendix 1 of this book.

References

Albanese, M., Bulli, G., Castelli Gattinara, P. and Froio, C. (2015) *Fascisti di un altro millennio? Crisi e partecipazione in CasaPound Italia.* Rome and Acireale: Bonanno Editore.

Albertazzi, D., McDonnell, D. and Newell, J. (2011) 'Di lotta e di governo: The Lega Nord and Rifondazione Comunista in Office', *Party Politics,* 17(4), pp. 471–487.

Alexander, M. (2004) 'Comparing Local Policies Toward Migrants: An Analytical Framework, a Typology and Preliminary Survey Results'. In: Penninx, R., Kraal, K., Martiniello, M. and Vertovec, S. eds. *Citizenship in European Cities. Immigrants, Local Politics and Integration Policies.* Ashgate: Aldershot, pp. 57–84.

Bombardieri, M. (2011) *Moschee d'Italia. Il diritto al luogo di culto, il dibattito sociale e politico.* Bologna: EMI.

Bonetti, P., Simoni, A. and Vitale, T. (2011) *La condizione giuridica di Rom e Sinti in Italia.* Milan: Giuffré.

Caponio, T. (2006) *Città italiane e immigrazione: discorso pubblico e politiche a Milano, Bologna e Napoli.* Bologna: Il Mulino.

Caponio, T. and Borkert, M. (eds.) (2010) *The Local Dimension of Migration Policymaking.* Amsterdam: Amsterdam University Press.

Castelli Gattinara, P. and Froio, C. (2014) 'Identity Building and Action Repertoires in CasaPound: Discourses, Symbols and Practices of Violence', *International Journal of Conflict and Violence*, 8(1), pp. 154–170.

Castelli Gattinara, P., Froio, C. and Albanese, M. (2013) 'The Appeal of Neo-Fascism in Times of Crisis: The Experience of CasaPound Italia', *Journal of Comparative Fascist Studies*, 2(2), pp. 234–258.

Cousin, B. and Vitale, T. (2012) 'Italian Intellectuals and the Promotion of Islamophobia after 9/11'. In: Morgan, G. and Poynting, S. eds. *Global Islamophobia: Muslims and Moral Panic in the West.* Aldershot: Ashgate, pp. 47–66.

Druckman, J.N. and Parkin, M. (2005) 'The Impact of Media Bias: How Editorial Slant Affects Voters', *Journal of Politics*, 67(4), pp. 1030–1049. doi: 10.1111/j.1468–2508.2005.00349.

Entman, R. (1993) 'Framing: Toward Clarification of a Fractured Paradigm', *Journal of Communication*, 43(4), pp. 51–58. doi: 10.1111/j.1460–2466.1993.tb01304.x.

Gamson, W.A. (2004) 'Bystanders, Public Opinion and the Media'. In: Snow, D.A., Soule, S.A. and Kriesi, H. eds. *The Blackwell Companion to Social Movements.* Oxford: Blackwell, pp. 242–261.

Gariglio, L., Pogliano, A. and Zanini, R. (2010) *Facce da straniero. 30 anni di fotografia e giornalismo sull'immigrazione in Italia.* Rome: Bruno Mondadori Editore.

Gilbert, L. (2009) 'Immigration as Local Politics: Re-Bordering Immigration and Multiculturalism through Deterrence and Incapacitation', *International Journal of Urban and Regional Research*, 33(1), pp. 26–42.

Göle, N. (ed.) (2013) *Islam and Public Controversy in Europe.* Burlington: Ashgate.

Hänggli, R. and Kriesi, H. (2010) 'Political Framing Strategies and Their Impact on Media Framing in a Swiss Direct-Democratic Campaign', *Political Communication*, 27(2), pp. 141–157.

Helbling, M. and Tresch, A. (2011) 'Measuring Party Positions and Issue Salience from Media Coverage: Discussing and Cross Validating New Indicators', *Electoral Studies*, 30, pp. 174–183.

Hepburn, E. and Zapata-Barrero, R. (eds.) (2014) *The Politics If Immigration in Multi-level States.* Basingstoke: Palgrave McMillian.

Ignazi, P. (1992) 'The Silent Counter-Revolution: Hypotheses on the Emergence of the Extreme Right-Wing Parties in Western Europe', *European Journal of Political Research*, 22, pp. 3–35.

Ignazi, P. (2003) *Extreme Right Parties in Western Europe.* Oxford: Oxford University Press.

ISTAT (2010) *La Popolazione Straniera Residente in Italia al 1° Gennaio 2010*. Rome: Istituto Nazionale di Statistica.

Jesuit, D. and Mahler, V. (2004) *Electoral Support for Extreme Right-Wing Parties: A Subnational Analysis of Western European Elections in the 1990s*. Working Paper #391, Luxembourg Income Study. Available at: www.econstor.eu/bitstream/10419/95478/1/472646389.pdf

Kitschelt, H. (1995) *The Radical Right in Western Europe*. Ann Arbor: University of Michigan Press.

Kleinnijenhuis, J., De Ridder, J. and Rietberg, E.M. (1997) 'Reasoning in Economic Discourse: An Application of the Network Approach to the Dutch Press'. In: Roberts, C.W. ed. *Text Analysis for the Social Sciences: Methods for Drawing Statistical Inferences from Texts and Transcript*. Mahawah: Erlbaum, pp. 191–207.

Kriesi, H., Grande, E., Lachat, R., Dolezal, M., Bornschier, S. and Frey, T. (2008) *West European Politics in the Age of Globalization*. Cambridge: Cambridge University Press.

Laclau, E. (2005) *On Populist Reason*. London: Verso.

Legros, O. and Vitale, T. (2011) 'Les migrants roms dans les villes françaises et italiennes: mobilités, régulations et marginalités', *Géocarrefour*, 86(1), pp. 3–14.

Mair, P. (2008) 'The Challenge to Party Government', *West European Politics*, 31, 1–2: 211–234.

Mair, P. (2009) 'Representative versus Responsible Government', *MPIfG Working Paper* 09/8.

Matthes, J. (2009) 'What's in a Frame? A Content Analysis of Media Framing Studies in the World's Leading Communication Journals 1990–2005', *Journalism & Mass Communication Quarterly*, 86(2), pp. 349–367.

McDonnell, D. (2006) 'A Weekend in Padania: Regionalist Populism and the Lega Nord', *Politics*, 26(2), pp. 126–132.

Meguid, B. (2008) *Party Competition between Unequals: Strategies and Electoral Fortunes in Western Europe*. Cambridge: Cambridge University Press.

Minkenberg, M. (2007) 'The Renewal of the Radical Right: Between Modernity and Anti-Modernity', *Government and Opposition*, 35, pp. 170–188.

Morales, L. and Giugni, M. (eds.) (2011) *Social Capital, Political Participation and Migration in Europe: Making Multicultural Democracy Work?* Basingstoke/NewYork: Palgrave McMillan.

Mudde, C. (2000) *The Ideology of the Extreme Right*. Manchester: Manchester University Press.

Mudde, C. (2007) *Populist Radical Right Parties in Europe*. Cambridge: Cambridge University Press.

Odmalm, P. and Bale, T. (2014) 'Immigration into the Mainstream: Conflicting Ideological Streams, Strategic Reasoning and Party Competition', *Acta Politica*, 50, pp. 365–37. doi:10.1057/ap.2014.28.

Penninx, R., Kraal, K., Martiniello, M. and Vertovec, S. (eds.) (2004) *Citizenship in European Cities. Immigrants, Local Politics and Integration Policies*. Ashgate: Aldershot, pp. 57–84.

Pogliano, A. and Valetti, R. (2011) 'Attitudes to Migrants, Communication and Local Leadership: Country Context Paper – Italy', *Fieri Research Reports,* Turin, June 2011.

Rebessi, E. (2011) 'Diffusione dei luoghi di culto islamici e gestione delle conflittualità. La moschea di via Urbino a Torino come studio di caso', *POLIS Working Papers N° 194*, December 2011. ISSN: 2038–7296.

Sigona, N. (2011) 'The Governance of Romani People in Italy: Discourse, Policy and Practice', *Journal of Modern Italian Studies*, 16(5), pp. 590–606.

Taguieff, P.A. (2002) *L'illusion populiste. De l'archaïque au médiatique*. Paris: Berg International.

Tarchi, M. (2004) 'Il Populismo e la Scienza Politica. Come Liberarsi del "Complesso di Cenerentola"', *Filosofia politica*, 18(3), pp. 411–429.

Testa, P. (ed.) (2013) *Le Città Metropolitane: Rapporto Cittalia 2013*. Rome: Cittalia.

Van der Brug, W., D'Amato, G., Berkhout, J. and Reudin, D. (2015) *The Politicisation of Migration*. Abingdon and New York: Routledge.

Part 1
Framework and context

2 Electoral debates on migration

A dimensional perspective

Introduction

This book analyzes electoral campaigning on the immigration issue in six local elections in Italy. The study of electoral campaigns by political scientists has focused on two aspects: the effects on voters and the strategies of political actors. The first stream of literature focuses on campaigns as a source for information processing by the citizens, suggesting that these provide voters with necessary information for making a choice in line with their pre-existing preferences (Arceneaux, 2005; Finkel, 1993; Gelman and King, 1993; Lazarsfeld et al., 1944; Stimson, 2004). In this sense, communication between political actors and voters is a multi-step process, which includes the media as the main transmission belt conveying political information and frames to the public (Hänggli, 2010). The second stream of research focuses more specifically on campaigning, looking at the way in which the political actors involved in electoral competition engage in public debates involving their competitors, the media and the public (Brandenburg, 2002; Hänggli, 2012; Kiousis et al., 2006; Kriesi et al., 2009; Matthes, 2012). In the course of electoral campaigns the conflict between political actors unfolds, as the actors involved form coalitions, compete and craft messages based on alternative arguments, frames and worldviews, with the goal of getting public and media attention and of mobilizing support.

I focus on the second aspect, and address the role of political actors, i.e. the actors who initiate campaign events and provide the main input into electoral debates. The key argument is that choices of politicization are driven by the attempt of political actors to control competitors and the media as to impose their preferred issues and messages in the campaign. Literature in this area is well established, as previous research has underlined that thematic emphasis is fundamental to understand electoral competition and to explain strategies and results (Budge and Farlie, 1983; Green-Pedersen and Blomqvist, 2004; Klingemann et al., 1994; Petrocik et al., 2003). At the core of 'saliency theory' approaches is the idea that parties do not engage in comprehensive debates addressing all policy issues, but rather privilege only those issues that they consider favourable to their side (Budge and Fairle, 1983).

This approach was applied predominantly to study the way in which parties introduce new issues on the agenda in order to manipulate the terms of the competition. The problem with this understanding is that we do not know much of what happens once the 'new' issues stabilize within party systems (Green-Pedersen, 2010; Rovny and Edwards, 2012; van der Brug and van Spanje, 2009). Moreover, by failing to differentiate between large policy themes, or bundles of issues, and their constitutive dimensions, this approach underestimates the complexity of policy issues in public debates. When complex bundles are publicly debated, instead, political actors generally focus on a limited, partial and often incomplete subset of their underlying dimensions (Baumgartner and Jones, 2002). In line with a growing amount of literature aiming at dissecting the elements that make up complex policy issues (De Sio, 2010; De Sio and Franklin, 2012; Froio, 2012, 2013; Guinaudeau and Persico, 2014; Helbling, 2013; Rovny, 2012), in this study I suggest looking at the different dimensions of the immigration issue upon which electoral competition takes place. I suggest that practices and efforts aimed at manipulating the electoral agenda may vary depending on the features of the issue at stake, since political decisions tend to encompass a multiplicity of dimensions of choice.

In this sense, political actors may strategically shift the point of reference of public debates from one aspect of a given political issue to another. When facing complex bundles of policy issues, political actors do not consider all features as equally important. On the contrary, they emphasize the dimensions on which they expect to enjoy a strategic advantage, which leaves them to adopt different approaches to each sub-category as well (Odmalm, 2012). Similarly, De Sio (2010) hypothesizes a 'second-stage' of selective emphasis: when confronted with complex issues, parties do not only choose whether to address the issue or not, but they can also decide which aspects of a given issue they want to highlight and which others they prefer to hide.

In order to test this idea, my choice is to focus on immigration, a policy issue that has often been recognized as being complex, multidimensional or at least cutting across traditional policy areas (i.e. Helbling *et al.,* 2010; Höglinger *et al.,* 2012, Odmalm, 2011; Odmalm and Super, 2014), yet it has predominantly been analyzed as a single issue in party competition. I shall compare three case studies that differ in terms of composition of the immigrant populations and of the corresponding key immigration problems. By looking at electoral campaigns in each city setting and by comparing campaigns across contexts, my aim is to assess the constraints and opportunities that determine discursive choices of actors in electoral campaigns on migration. The remainder of this chapter will first introduce the choice of focusing on the issue of immigration and present the rationale for the identification of its constitutive dimensions and frames. Then I shall outline the main argument of the book, and discuss a model for the understanding of electoral campaign strategies based on multiple issue dimensions and strategic framing of policy issues. Lastly, I present the main hypotheses and expectations concerning context conditions, campaign conditions and party conditions driving the electoral strategies of political actors with respect to the dimensions and frames of the immigration issue.

The immigration issue: culture, economy, security

To test the abovementioned model, this book looks at migration affairs as a proto-typical multidimensional issue field. Debates on this issue cut across several the-matic fields, and the politicization of the issue has been subject to a conspicuous degree of variation across parties, contexts and over time (Feldblum, 1999; Hel-bling, 2013; Lahav, 2004; Lakoff and Ferguson, 2006; Messina, 2007; Messina and Lahav, 2006; Perlmutter, 1996; Vliegenthart and Roggeband, 2007; van der Brug *et al.,* 2015). As I have illustrated earlier, although multiple issue attributes and problem definitions can coexist simultaneously within public agendas (Baum-gartner and Jones, 2002), debates will generally not address all of the aspects, top-ics or dimensions that could possibly be used to define immigration. In particular, political and media narratives often simplify drastically the complexity of the issue and its implication in terms of migrants' integration. The same applies for the justification of policy-making, since political actors have to rely on straight-forward stories which can be explained in terms of cause and effect. As a result, debates on immigration have a structural tendency to 'short-circuit' the complex-ity of the issue (Boswell, 2011, p. 13). Based on previous research in this area, I argue in this section that multidimensionality emerges from three interrelated domains pertaining to the politics of immigration and integration: policy-making, public opinion and public debates.

To begin with, policy analysts have insisted on the disaggregation of immigra-tion policy into distinct policy components (Lahav and Guiraudon, 2006). Baum-gartner and Jones (2002) suggest that, although primarily defined by the problem of controlling borders, immigration policies have implications on a number of policy areas. The migration policy arena is made of numerous issue dimensions, 'making immigration more similar to heath care policy (a complex policy arena with many ramifications) than to agricultural policy (a one-dimensional arena focusing primarily on the extent of subsidies offered to producers)' (p. 74). In this sense, immigration takes on distinct dimensional definitions, which the authors classify as policies on border control and for the preservation of the national iden-tity; policies addressing immigration as a labour resource for national industries; and policies looking at immigration through humanitarianism and oriented at the protection of the politically and religiously persecuted from other countries. Immigration policies therefore often overlap with policies on the consequences of migration in terms of civic integration, as border security and illegal migration is often associated with internal security and crime, whereas economic policies on migration directly affect labour market regulations and welfare state policies (see: Berkhout and Sudulich, 2011). Similarly, Guiraudon (2003) argues that due to its implications for labour, economics, foreign affairs, social affairs and internal affairs, migration as a policy issue can hardly be confined to a single ministry.

As a result, prior studies generally disaggregate the issue along two dimen-sions. On the one hand is the differentiation between issues pertaining to immi-gration and aspects concerning the integration of migrants. This is generally done in line with Tomas Hammar's (1985) distinction between immigration control policies and immigrant policy: the first refers to the framework regulating the entry and stay of foreigners, whereas the latter concerns their integration into host societies. On the other hand, authors differentiate among the various fields that are potentially affected (Messina, 2007; Messina and Lahav, 2006). Recent studies have also combined the two lines, assessing, for instance, whether security issues pertain to the access or the stay of migrants, and whether economic aspects have to do with labour market integration or economic migration (Berkhout and Sudulich, 2011).

For the present study, which focuses on local politics, issues of border control and immigration are generally of lesser importance.[1] My focus is therefore primarily on issues of integration of migrants, and distinguishes between three dimensions: the *socioeconomic dimension,* the *cultural and religious dimension* and the *law and order dimension.* The first two broadly correspond to the understanding of most previous studies, proposing a twofold differentiation where economic arguments are opposed to cultural and identity ones. Similarly, Kriesi *et al.* (2012) suggested that immigration and ethnic diversity have the potential of generating new political conflicts that have more to do with conceptions of national identity than they do with concerns about personal economic circumstances, labour competition and fiscal burdens (see also: Hainmueller and Hiscox, 2007). Economic challenges resulting from globalization interact with increasing cultural diversity at the societal level, which sets up processes of cultural competition for which ethnically different populations become symbols of potential threats to collective identity and to the standard of living of the natives (Kriesi *et al.,* 2012).

In addition, security arguments are increasingly crucial in driving migration debates. On the one hand, debates are securitized in terms of the illegal entry of migrants and the challenges of migration to international security. On the other, migrants are often perceived (and portrayed) as sources of criminality and even terrorism, so that ethnic stereotyping is often used in crime news to substantiate the nexus between immigration in general, minority communities and threats to the physical well-being of host populations (Bigo, 2014; Buonfino, 2004; Caviedes, 2015). Security, therefore, is considered here as a third independent category that refers specifically to securitized narratives on migration. Although similar discursive practices often trigger feelings of cultural insecurity, the cultural and security dimensions are based on different understandings of the relationship between migration and host societies. If cultural arguments opposing immigration consider migrants as the ones who disrupted a culturally homogeneous space, law and order ones accuse migrant communities of having brought physical insecurity and criminality to previously 'safe' societies. Securitization of migration refers to public concerns over immigration harming the quality of life and physical and societal security of native citizens (Buzan *et al.,* 1998; Huysmans, 2000; Weiner, 1993). More broadly, international migration is perceived as a potential source of conflicts, be that because of migrants' often imperfect economic and cultural integration, their marginalization in ethnic ghettoes and the related processes of blaming and stereotyping, or the emergence of negative sentiments or xenophobic movements and parties. Moreover, after 9/11 immigration came to be increasingly identified with invasion, terrorism, violence and physical insecurity (see: Bigo, 2002; Lahav and Courtemanche, 2011; Rudolph, 2007). In this way, specific groups (or migrants as a whole) tend to be targeted in public discourse as potential or actual sources of physical threats and insecurity, and come to be identified as 'problem' groups. Accordingly, the law and order dimension focuses on the explicit and implicit association of immigrants with insecurity, danger and emergency.

The three immigration dimensions provide the general framework for the classification of the arguments used by political parties to frame the immigration issue. As was discussed previously, my definition of framing processes involves both selection and diagnosis: once certain issue dimensions are emphasized, framing implies the active effort to provide meaning to the aspects in question. Hence, in line with previous research in this area, I opt to link a frame explicitly to an issue dimension and an evaluation (Chong and Druckman, 2007; Druckman, 2004; Hänggli, 2010; see also: Callaghan and Schnell, 2004; Entman, 2004).[2] Looking at substantive, issue-specific frames implies focusing on the aspect of the problem definition, and it entails that every issue can have different issue-specific frames. This is also in line with the choice of a vast array of studies on strategic framing, which focused on the proposition level as a unit of analysis and followed an inductive strategy for frame extraction diminishing the risk of overlooking types of arguments that were not anticipated *a priori* (Hänggli, 2010; Matthes, 2009; Matthes and Kohring, 2008).[3]

Table 2.1 below summarizes the threefold categorization of the immigration issue, specifying the seven alternative frames that I identified within each dimension,[4] and taking into account the crucial fact that parties may adopt different positions depending on the aspect of migration that is highlighted (Odmalm, 2011, 2012, 2014). These are the *multiculturalism* and *nationalism* frames (corresponding to the two alternative understandings of the cultural dimension), the *economic prosperity* and *labour and security* frames (consistent with arguments pushed forward to discuss the socioeconomic impact of migration), and the *urban issues, Roma issues* and *emergency issues* frames (corresponding to territorial, group-specific and emergency logics within the security dimension). Given that issue-specific frames are justifications of actor positions, each category can be interpreted in terms of Habermas' seminal typology of arguments: 'pragmatic', 'identity-related' and 'moral' types of argumentation in media and elite discourse (Habermas, 1993; see also: Helbling *et al.*, 2010; Lerch and Schwellnus, 2006; Sjursen, 2002).[5]

The socioeconomic dimension

Socioeconomic aspects are often at the core of technocratic and expert debates on migration (Citrin *et al.,* 1997). This is because economic factors are behind international labour migration, and because immigration is a factor that inevitably influences the receiving country's economy. Hence, this dimension is grounded on

Table 2.1 Categorization of immigration dimensions and frames

Dimension	Frames	Frame category	Examples
Socioeconomic	*Economic prosperity*	Pragmatic	Economic growth/ decay International competition
	Labour and security	Pragmatic	Welfare state Unemployment rates Unfair competition
Cultural and religious	*Multiculturalism*	Moral-universalistic	Tolerance Cultural diversity Failure of multiculturalism
	Nationalism	Identity-related	National identity Loss of tradition Citizenship
Law and order	*Urban issues*	Pragmatic	Suburbs issues Ethnic neighbourhoods Urban violence
	Emergency issues	Pragmatic	Refugee and asylum abuse Illegal migration/ amnesties Terrorism/civil liberties
	Roma issues	Pragmatic	EU citizenship Lifestyle incompatibility Nomadism

pragmatic reasoning: immigration is instrumentally connected to individual and collective interests, or to the achievement of specific outputs in terms of personal and group well-being (Helbling *et al.*, 2010). With respect to framing, immigration is discussed in terms of not only market logic and structural characteristics of the economy, but also economic wealth and growth *(economic prosperity frames)*. Alternatively, the logic may be that of stressing the relationship (and potential trade-off) between welfare and employment opportunities of national and immigrant workforce *(labour and security frame)*.

Concerning economic prosperity, this frame is primarily associated with pro-migration claims, but anti-immigration political entrepreneurs can also use it to contest the arguments of their adversaries or to deny the beneficial effects of migration. This frame connects migration to economic performance at the collective level (national or local), which in turn results in changing living conditions for the native population as well. Quotes from the data collected might help illustrate the main message that is associated with this type of frames.

> Due to immigration, since many years Milan has become a 'global city' [...].
> Without the support of its new citizens originating from around the world, the
> city would not stand economically.[6]

> According to Sandro Ciardi, the positive economic cycle is closed, and the
> conditions to welcome more foreigners no longer exist.[7]

In general, supporters and opponents of immigration may highlight different
aspects of how the issue of immigration is related to the national or local economy. Here, the focus is on the benefits that immigration brings to a country's
economic performance (also in fiscal terms) and to advantages that can arise from
admitting and integrating hard-working and highly motivated economic migrants.
Attention is given to the changes in the structure of the economy, which are held
to make it necessary and beneficial to have a steady supply of labour to fill the gap
in the sectors where native labour is increasingly scarce.[8]

In contrast, the labour and security frame is more easily mobilized to oppose
immigration than to promote it, as it makes reference to work opportunities for
natives and immigrants in terms of labour market and welfare resources. Compared to the prosperity frame, the focus is more directly on the consequences of
immigration for the native workers.

> In this period of economic hardship, conceding the right to participate in
> competitive exams to immigrants who hold a simple residence or visiting
> permit means taking jobs away from the Milanese people and the regular
> migrants who have resided here for long.[9]

> Their number [foreign residents and illegal migrants] has been growing
> steadily over the past years, and they currently take up 30% of the economic
> resources available in the social services.[10]

When used to oppose immigration, this frame often conceptually associates the
arrival of immigrants with decreasing opportunities for native workers, financial
burdens for taxpayers, and welfare reduction (although migrants can be depicted
as either net-receivers of social benefits or as net-contributors in the national welfare system). Similarly, this frame challenges the admission of asylum seekers
and refugees, when this is justified in terms of burdens to the economy, welfare
and housing. Immigrant workers are regarded as alien or even illegal competitors reducing the amount of resources and job opportunities available to native
ones. The logic is that immigrants tend to find jobs in the black market, corrupt-
ing labour relations by working at conditions unacceptable to native workers.
Pro-migration political entrepreneurs generally use this frame in a reactive way,
challenging the understanding that the economics of migrant and native labour
are a zero-sum game. Instead, they might approach the issue of labour, welfare
and migration in terms of general labour regulations, which apply to all workers
and employers, irrespective of whether they are of migrant origin.

They don't want to expel them [the immigrants]; they want to keep them here in order to put them in competition with precarious workers, in a contest between the last and the semi-last people in our society.[11]

A woman – says Cenni – wrote me that she failed to receive an apartment because there were fifty foreigners before her in the public housing list.[12]

The cultural and religious dimension

The cultural and religious dimension was built with Habermas' (1993) conceptualization of identity-related and moral-universalistic frames in mind. The main frames correspond to arguments stressing the core values of community belonging against perceived identity threats *(nationalism)*, or to moral-universal arguments calling for universal rights and peaceful coexistence of cultural and religious groups *(multiculturalism)*. Negative arguments involving the cultural and religious dimension therefore see (excessive) diversity and (uncontrolled) migration as inherently or practically dangerous for the integrity of national culture, and for peaceful coexistence within the nation state. National and local traditions are considered endangered because of increasing concentrations of immigrants in previously ethnic homogeneous areas, and city landscapes are described as corrupted by the increased presence of migrants' places, whether shops, houses or religious buildings. Fully nationalist arguments invoke local cultural and linguistic superiority. In this sense, the national community is defined in exclusive terms with respect to cultural and political rights. These arguments always juxtapose 'aliens' with 'natives', claiming the necessity to prioritize the latter over the former, and tend to reject the possibility of reformulating national identity and citizenship on multi-ethnic and multi-religious grounds.

Carla De Albertis [. . .] aims at strengthening the sense of identity of her fellow citizens. According to her, being 'Milanese' is a value needing preservation, protection and enhancement. This means zero tolerance towards illegal migrants residing in the city.[13]

Nobody likes immigrants [. . .] but we, the Italians, are a nation of emigrants. We must offer the same hospitality, rights and duties that our ancestors received. We must pretend that our constitution, laws, traditions and habits are respected. After all, the foreigners are guests.[14]

Multiculturalist arguments, by contrast, emphasize the opportunities provided by cultural and religious diversity, as well as the inevitability of ethnic differentiation. Diversity is described as beneficial for the quality of society, and hence the suggestion is made to promote tolerance and foster policies tackling inequalities in various domains, from education to political rights and access to citizenship. The main arguments have to do with acceptance and respect for difference of culture, traditions and religion. Political entrepreneurs aiming to capitalize on pro-immigration electorates claim that equality remains at insufficient levels, and promote integration-oriented policy-making and civil participation. Assimilation policies and practices, by contrast, lead to increased inequality, conflict and marginalization.

> The list claims to be 'secular' and 'multicultural', and it promises to engage in improving the political, social and religious opportunities for the city's migrants, in the name of 'hospitality, solidarity and multiculturalism'.[15]

> An effective integration policy can not be achieved by means of an absurd demand for assimilation against those that are considered different.[16]

In addition, the cultural and religious dimension emphasizes cultural compatibility between different ethno-religious communities, and promotes intergroup tolerance and integration. This can take the form of debates over multiculturalism and cultural integration. Multiculturalist frames foster respect for cultural difference of immigrant communities and expect enhanced integration to be a result of the increasing availability of instruments and infrastructures allowing the free expression of culture, religion and traditions of migrants. Although each frame can be easily associated with either the pro-immigration or the anti-immigration camp, contestation and trespassing are frequent among political actors in electoral debates. Supporters of immigration try to expose the nationalist nature of opponents' arguments, while anti-immigration actors criticize the intrinsic dangers and negative outcomes of multiculturalist policies and cultural tolerance. In this case, politicians aiming to capitalize on opposition to increased immigration stress the need for immigrants to adapt to the culture and traditions of the destination country, without necessarily mobilizing nationalist rhetoric. Migrants' predisposition to cultural assimilation is often regarded as a necessary condition for sustainable immigration and integration in the receiving country.

> The mayor claims that we are bound to become a multi-ethnic, multicultural and multi-religious city, but I pretend that we at least preserve our own history.[17]

> My experience among the Chinese in Prato taught me something: it is not possible to build a multicultural society when people are unwilling to communicate with one another.[18]

> Bringing the contest on the field of, so to speak, different 'ethnicities' is always a bad sign for the quality of electoral campaigns.[19]

The law and order dimension

The law and order dimension links the arrival and presence of migrants, or specific groups of migrants, to security and emergency issues like national defence, conflicts, legality and the safety of individuals. This applies to the security of borders, to international migration and to the perceived insecurity within the host country

(Caviedes, 2015; Lazaridis, 2011), since dangers might be associated with the entry or residence of migrants and also with migrants themselves, in case of international crises and criminal networks.[20] More precisely, I identify three 'logics' corresponding to three frames of the law and order dimension. First, the territorial logic of *urban issues* focuses on the context where migrants settle, linking the physical presence of migrants in a given territory with instability and threats to personal safety. Second, the group logic or *Roma issues* highlights stereotyped group characteristics in order to address one specific community as the source of social and security problems, defining a nexus between constructed lifestyles of ethnic minorities and illegality and criminality. Third, the emergency logic of *emergency issues* associates migration to unexpected happenings and traumatic events, ascribing the migration phenomenon itself to a category of exceptionality requiring action and resolution.

As far as *urban issues* are concerned, frames connect the presence of legal and illegal migrants to city-specific problems, claiming real or perceived insecurity for local communities due to the presence of migrants in city boroughs and neighbourhoods. The focus is often on decency and decorum in the areas of the city where migrants are settled (illegal settlements, housing and household conditions, street vending, etc.), or this frame more explicitly connects migrant residence to violence and crime in the city. Although most claims recognize that areas densely populated by migrants may be insecure or inaccessible to native citizens, pro-migration arguments do not blame deviance *per se,* but suggest the dismantling of ethnic 'ghettoes' to improve the quality of life of the residents, and the requalification of urban peripheries to reduce risks.

> The growth of immigration in specific sectors of the city has contributed to the exponential expansion of serious problems, such as security. Not being properly managed, immigration is likely to blow up the equilibrium of our city.[21]

> Concerning ghetto suburbs, the point is not how and when to use repressive instruments, but also to understand the emergence of youth problems that eventually cause these forms of violence.[22]

In addition, political actors frame law and order by targeting specific ethnic groups. In particular, local political entrepreneurs in Italy have been addressing the Romani community as a source of social problems, connecting perceived insecuirty to the 'nomadic lifestyle' of Roma people.[23] As suggested by McGarry and Drake (2013), the combination of lifestyle stereotyping and security concerns makes it that the Roma 'occupy a nexus of illegality, criminality, belonging and responsibility' in public discourse. The Roma are subject to pejorative stereotyping describing them as a collective threat for the host population, and individually as responsible for rapes, kidnappings and robberies, so that their very presence 'cause[s] troubles to their "decent neighbors"' (van Baar, 2011, p. 321). Security frames of this type create a favourable context for group-specific repressive measures, including the indiscriminate expulsion of Romani migrants. The law and order logic of this frame, therefore, addresses the Roma as a group rather than individuals within the community. Blatantly discriminatory claims are normally challenged by arguments stressing the need to integrate the Romani community, by arguments reconstructing the genocide of the European Roma during the twentieth century, and by pragmatic argumentations underlining that the vast majority of Roma residents in Italy are EU citizens.

> If Lega will get the position of vice-Mayor after the elections, 'nomadic settlements will disappear in a few days. With our representatives in the city council, similar situations of illegality will not be tolerated any longer.'[24]

> The Roma are EU citizens: security can not justify legal actions and discriminatory policies that are contrary to Community law.[25]

Finally, the law and order dimension is tackled by means of the *emergency frame,* which approaches security issues through an explicitly alarmistic logic stressing the urgency to take action. Political actors mobilize this frame pragmatically, to address the consequences of immigration in terms of deviance, crime, illegality and violence, or more broadly to define the whole phenomenon as an emergency. This happens when migration is not described as a long-lasting phenomenon of Western societies, but rather as a sudden, unexpected event which needs urgent and decisive tackling, such as in case of refugee crises, when the emergency discourse is articulated in humanitarian terms, expressed through concerns with cooperation and humanitarian intervention (Buonfino, 2004). Besides this, emergency frames connect migration to local, national and international crises leading to unforeseen outcomes and requiring exceptional interventions and decision-making, and focusing on security aspects related to the entrance, stay and repatriation of migrants. Pragmatic considerations generally tend to prevail, since the goal is that of pursuing national security in a way that does not jeopardize the life and basic rights of illegal immigrants, refugees or foreign residents, although moral arguments might also mobilize the urgent need for shelter and protection during migration crises.[26]

> Because of our geographic position, we represent the gateway to Europe. But I confirm, once again, that we do not have sufficient resources to be able to cope indefinitely with an humanitarian emergency of this magnitude.[27]

> Rejections are 'necessary though painful, as we face the arrival *en masse* of populations from the southern hemisphere and we have to react'.[28]

Agenda setting, framing and dimensional competition

The core theoretical assertion of agenda setting research is that the attention accorded to specific media objects or issues leads to increased public concern with those same issues (Kiousis and McCombs, 2004; Lopez-Escobar *et al.,* 1998). The related concept of agenda building was introduced by Cobb and Elder (1971, p. 905), who investigated 'how issues are created and why some controversies or incipient issues come to command the attention and concern of decision makers, while others fail'. In line with this approach, I investigate the ability of political actors to influence attention during electoral campaigns. Yet, whereas agenda building is concerned with the issue level, I look at the different dimensions and aspects of the same issue, following the approach that communication scholars generally call second-level agenda building (Kiousis *et al.*, 2006; see also: Riker, 1986). Lopez-Escobar *et al.* (1998, p. 337) contended that 'both the selection of *objects* for attention and the selection of *attributes* for describing these objects are powerful agenda-setting roles'. In a similar fashion, I suggest that in order to understand how complex political issues are politicized in electoral campaigns, one has to look at the salience of issues and issue dimensions. Accordingly, I use the salience of issue-specific attributes and frames in the media as a dependent variable and investigate the factors that influence the change in the relative salience of each dimension in the coverage of electoral campaigns.

A major advantage of this approach is that it offers a framework for examining issue and dimensional salience separately, and therefore for investigating how the shifts in dimensional attention can influence the overall salience of the issue (Ghanem, 1997; Kiousis *et al.*, 2006). Hooghe *et al.* (2002) have noted that certain issues (in particular EU integration) constitute a challenge for parties, as they are unable to assimilate them within either of the traditional dimensions of political conflict, namely the socio-cultural and the economic left–right dimension. The multiple dimensions of policy issues, in fact, structure the interplay between parties, resulting in a set of ideological 'pulls' on each issue dimension (Odmalm, 2011, 2012). More broadly, these tensions generate patterns of incentives and constraints for political actors, affecting their behaviour and competition *vis-à-vis* each issue aspects. Parties, therefore, are not only confronted with the question of when, why and how to emphasize the immigration issue in their election campaign. They must also engage in the much more delicate task of balancing their emphasis and positions on each issue dimension, using alternative frames and issue emphases in order to shift the focus over their key areas of strength.

As a result, campaigning strategies involve not only a struggle over what issues set the electoral and media agenda, but also how these issues are portrayed in public and electoral debates (Kiousis *et al.*, 2006). Previous studies used the concept of second-level agenda setting to describe the way in which the dimensions and frames pushed forward by political entrepreneurs are reproduced by the mass media (Huckins, 1999; Kiousis *et al.*, 2006; McCombs and Ghanem, 2001; Tan and Weaver, 2007; Wirth *et al.*, 2010). Hence, the concept of salience can be applied either to the degree of attention that is given to certain issues rather than others, or to the importance of issue-specific attributes relative to others (McCombs, 2004; McCombs and Reynolds, 2002). Similarly, literature on framing suggested that frames attract attention to certain aspects of an issue rather than others: by selectively emphasizing and evaluating certain issue features, frames provide coherence to political messages and convey an interpretation of a perceived reality (Ferree *et al.*, 2002; Gamson, 2004; Hänggli, 2010). Consequently, I focus on two ways in which messages are crafted, which represent two steps within the same communication process: selective emphasis on issue dimensions and framing (Riker, 1986; Odmalm, 2012).

Second-level agenda setting calls attention to the special status of certain attributes of policy issues in the content of political messages. The idea is that each 'object' (McCombs, 2004, p. 70) in the agenda is composed of numerous attributes, or dimensions, that define the scope, properties and traits that characterize the object. If first-level agenda setting is about transmission of issue salience, the second level involves the selective emphasis of certain attributes of a policy issue rather than others. Baumgartner and Jones (2002) proposed that 'every public policy of substance is inherently multidimensional, but official consideration (and public understanding) of the issue at any given time typically is only partial' (p. 47). Similarly, I contend that when political actors are confronted with complex issues such as immigration, they do not only choose whether to address the issue or not, but they will also try to highlight certain aspects whilst hiding others.

There are three main reasons supporting the idea that issue competition is about the selection of – and emphasis upon – particular issue attributes rather than policy themes as a whole. The first has to do with the substantial complexity of policy problems that may have multifaceted implications and cut across several policy sectors *(inherent complexity)*. In addition, complex policy problems are fragmented into distinct dimensions in order to facilitate information processing. Studies on framing and priming effects have demonstrated that human minds process information in a selective manner, focusing on the most relevant aspects, possibly producing partial and incomplete representations *(cognitive factors*; see: Iyengar, 1991; Iyengar and Kinder, 1987, 2010; Kiousis *et al.,* 2006; Sniderman and Theriault, 2004; Zaller, 1992). The third reason has to do with the fact that politicians have neither the resources nor the incentives to address political problems in all their dimensions. Rather, they will promote only the perspective on problems that they expect to favour them alone (Kriesi *et al.,* 2009; Swanson and Mancini, 1996). Struggles for attention to alternative dimensions of a general problem, hence, are essential to political competition *(strategic factors)*. Taken together, these three reasons support the idea that strategic political actors expecting an advantage from a certain dimension of the immigration issue will selectively emphasize the issue as to shift the terms of debate from one dimension to another. The implication is that each attribute of complex policy issues provides distinct opportunities for electoral campaign actors. Agendas are thus the result of the struggle between the preferences of political entrepreneurs regarding the main conflict dimensions of policy issues.

Framing, instead, involves not only selection and salience, but also diagnosis, evaluation and prescription (Gamson, 1992): frames define problems, detect their causes, make moral judgments and suggest remedies in function of costs and benefits. Numerous approaches to the concept of framing exist (Entman, 1993), yet the most widely accepted definition looks at frames as messages promoting 'a particular problem definition, causal interpretation, moral evaluation, and/or treatment recommendation for the item described' (Entman, 1993, p. 52). Although frames can be considered as 'spotlights' that drag attention to certain aspects of an issue, their main characteristic is that they provide coherence to a set of concepts and elements (Ferree *et al.*, 2002, p. 105). Hence, if attribute agenda setting focuses on salience, framing implies the active effort of an actor to construct a certain meaning for a given reality or phenomenon (Entman, 1993; Hänggli and Kriesi, 2010).[29]

Since political actors do not want their messages to be cancelled by those of their competitors, campaign strategies combine simultaneously the two communication processes. Competitive actors emphasize specific issue attributes and look for the appropriate framing of these, with the goal of influencing the public's interpretation of a problem in such a way that supports their own point of view. In other words, candidates make choices with respect to the various dimensions of an issue and then justify their positions in order to differentiate themselves from, or to challenge, their competitors hoping to shift the attention toward other dimensions of the issue. Although both strategies aim at dominance in the electoral agenda, their premises are markedly different. Based on selective attention, the first expects that the predispositions of individuals toward a specific aspect of a political issue are favourable, and therefore draws the public's attention to it. Based on rhetorical strategies of framing instead, the second one may lead to a change in the evaluative content of individual beliefs with respect to a specific issue dimension. Hence, the first one builds upon individual predispositions whilst the second can also imply an attempt to modify the beliefs and preferences of targeted parts of the electorate.

Starting from the case of the immigration issue, Figure 2.1 below depicts in graph form the multiple steps of issue politicization in a multidimensional framework. As can be seen, the more the strategy of Party A resembles the one of its competitor Party B at each step of competition (issue level, dimension level and framing level), the more the two parties engage in direct confrontation. To begin with, parties must decide whether to take up an issue (in this case immigration) or discard it altogether from their campaign. In line with Meguid's model (2005, 2008), mainstream parties can deliberately dismiss certain issues, thereby signalling their lack of importance. On the one hand, however, this approach seems to oversimplify the dilemmas and available choices for parties. On the other, dismissive strategies seem less and less rewarding as migration is incorporated into party-system agendas, which makes it increasingly difficult for mainstream parties to simply avoid discussing it.[30]

If parties take up the issue, multidimensional competition follows three basic strategic clusters, depending on party choices with respect to issue dimensions, support or opposition to migration, and framing. First, parties have to decide the dimensional focus of their campaign. Odmalm (2011) suggests that parties are required to perform a delicate balancing strategy in order to avoid criticism from their competitors and adverse electoral outcomes. Emphasizing the wrong stream *within* the immigration issue, in other words, may detract attention from the parties' core competences and provide an advantage to their competitors. In this sense, each party has to choose whether to take up the same issue dimension as their competitors or rather try to shift the debate toward alternative aspects. If they mobilize alternative dimensions, their strategy is oriented at raising attention on aspects that they deem electorally rewarding, and/or diverting attention away from aspects on which their opponents enjoy an advantage. The goal is therefore to attract swing voters whose interests and values are not captured by the dimensional politicization of other candidates. This strategy is likely to be followed by

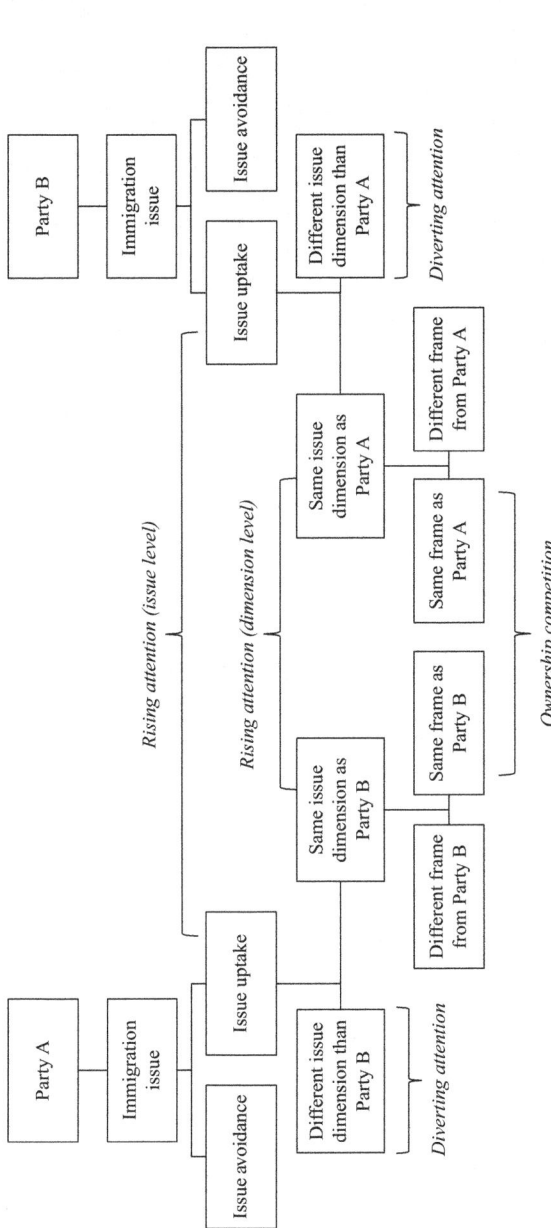

Figure 2.1 Dimensional and framing strategies of issue competition

parties belonging to different camps (pro- and anti-immigration), or by parties within the same camp that prefer not to compete directly.

Alternatively, parties can focus on the same issue dimensions as their competitors, which can be done by taking up the same position or the opposite position of their counterparts. In either case, parties also have to decide on the specific arguments that they intend to mobilize in order to explain *why* a given aspect of immigration is emphasized, and *why* a certain position is taken. Similar to the previous stage, parties can mobilize a single frame or multiple frames, and have to decide whether to apply the same framing as their competitors or not. If they focus on different explanations, parties try to divert voters away from each other, persuading them that their own interpretation of a given aspect of immigration is preferable to that of the opponent. If they mobilize the same frames and the same dimensions as their competitors, parties directly challenge one another, offering the same interpretation of one aspect of the issue. In line with literature on valence issues (Green, 2007; Stokes, 1963, 1992) and issue ownership (Green-Pedersen, 2007; Petrocik, 1996), this strategy implies that parties compete primarily in terms of their competence on the immigration issue. In the present case, parties will set up their strategies based on the competence that they display on each aspect of the issue.

Main hypotheses and expectations

As I hope to have shown, my main proposition is that speaking of immigration politics writ large provides only a superficial image of electoral campaigning, since political conflict unfolds over multiple dimensions of migration. In so doing, I seek to specify the factors that influence the emergence of issue attributes and frames in electoral campaigns. I address the dynamics of electoral campaigning within an actor-centred political process model, in which all actors are part of a contest for the control of the public agenda and its interpretation of specific political issues (Wolfsfeld, 1997, 2011). The argument is therefore that public understandings of the migration issue emerging from electoral debates are not restricted to one single meaning, but change depending on the actors involved in the debate, the relationship between them and the circumstances defining their involvement. More specifically, I look at three levels in the definition of electoral strategies on the immigration issue: the context level, the campaign level and the actor level. In this section, I discuss the main expectations of the study for each of the three levels (the full list of hypotheses is reported in Table 2.2 at the end of the section).

My focus is primarily on political actors, i.e. on the actors who engage in electoral campaign events, and who provide the key informational input to it. Campaigns, however, are embedded in specific political contexts with institutional, cultural, issue-specific and campaign-specific features, which are decisive for the choices of competing candidates. Context conditions may affect debates in election campaigns in two ways (Koopmans *et al.,* 2005). On the one hand, debates may differ across contexts according to the opportunities and constraints in each electoral environment. Because of changing political opportunities related to each dimension of the migration issue, the same type of strategy by political actors may have very different chances of gaining media attention and public legitimacy in election campaigns. On the other, the impact of contextual conditions may be indirect, via its effect on party predispositions, on the configuration of actors in the party system, and on other conditions pertaining to a specific campaign.

Odmalm and Bale (2014) suggest that party responses to immigration are not only driven by exogenous – environmental and societal – conditions, but also by intraparty constraints and by the dynamics of party competition, since endogenous and intermediate factors influence the way in which political actors respond to contextual circumstances (Morales *et al.,* 2014). Parties emphasize policy objects on which they expect to enjoy a strategic advantage, but debates may vary in terms of issue diversity (Hobolt *et al.,* 2008; Walgrave and Nuytemans, 2009), which is why dimensional priorities must be looked at in the light of the broader process of agenda setting competition. Accordingly, my model addresses factors at the contextual level, at the campaign level and at the party level, accounting for the composition of campaign agendas, the role of the different actors in an election campaign and each actor's stance on the immigration issue (Helbling *et al.,* 2010; Odmalm, 2012; Petrocik, 1996; Statham and Trenz, 2012).

First, I distinguish the context conditions that pre-structure electoral campaigns, such as the institutional setting, the media system, the discursive field (Steinberg, 1999) or discursive opportunity structure (Koopmans and Statham, 1999), and the more short-term circumstances that affect choices at the electoral campaign level. Other factors, such as the type of actors involved in a competition (Meguid, 2008), exogenous or unexpected events (Birkland, 1997), and changing public moods (Marcus *et al.,* 2000), might interact with the characteristics of the issue at stake and influence strategic choices. At this level, I argue that the three dimensions of the immigration issue identified in the previous section interact with local circumstances and issue-specific characteristics at the context level. Second, I look at how much leeway political actors have in attributing importance to immigration issue dimensions and in taking a position on these (Odmalm and Bale, 2014). While context conditions and campaign pressures are relevant in explaining their choices, one should also look at actors' ability to handle the multiple dimensions of the immigration issue. I therefore look at the electoral campaign level in order to identify the events and conditions that drive the selective emphasis and framing strategies of the competing parties. Thirdly, I consider each political actor taking part in the competition to assess the logics of their politicization strategies in terms of dimensional preferences and constraints. Figure 2.2 below summarizes the model.

At the first level, concerning context conditions, each setting is characterized by issue-specific conditions concerning the nature and socio-demographic features of local migration. Moreover, party actions can be explained by the institutional framework of competition, but also by the discursive opportunities and constraints determining which type of argument is likely to gain visibility in the media and achieve legitimacy in the public discourse (Koopmans and Statham, 1999). Of course, none of these factors is fully independent from the others, since the way in which the characteristics of the political context are translated into patterns of opportunity for political actors is inevitably related to the nature and features of the issue at stake.

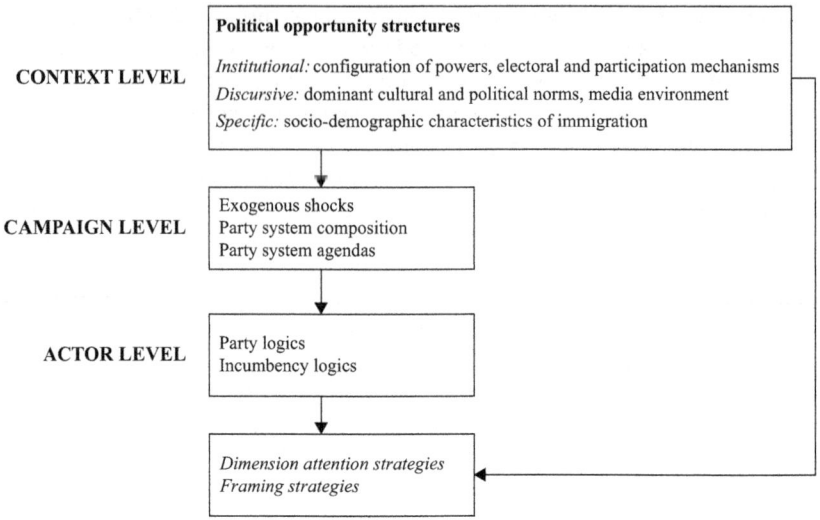

Figure 2.2 Framework for the analysis of electoral campaigning on immigration

At the second level, I account for temporal variation regarding issue attention and emphasis, looking at the impact of factors at the electoral campaign level on parties' electoral strategies and rationales. In particular, I consider the composition of the party system and the composition of party-system agendas. This is because in each election campaign political actors engage in continuous debates with each other, so that the content of party-system agendas also constrains the issue emphasis of individual parties (Green-Pedersen and Mortensen, 2010, 2014; Hobolt *et al.,* 2008). Moreover, previous literature underlined the relevance of immigration shocks in driving public debates (for example, as a consequence of refugee crises, migrant tragedies, sensationalistic news stories), looking at critical junctures and the way in which parties respond to these in terms of pledges and positions (Odmalm and Bale, 2014). I consider this aspect in terms of focusing events, which are 'sudden; relatively uncommon; can be reasonably defined as harmful or revealing the possibility of potentially greater future harms; [its consequences] are concentrated in a particular geographical area or community of interest; and [are] known to policy makers and the public simultaneously' (Birkland, 1998, p. 54).

At the lower level, I account for the agency of campaign actors in terms of their own politicization strategies, since 'the relative roles of parties and movements in taking leadership roles in framing issues in the media is an important and understudied aspect' (Ferree *et al.,* 2002, p. 296). My focus is on how mayoral coalitions and parties handle issue dimensions based on the different types of pressures that apply to each issue aspect. Electoral strategies are therefore likely to emerge from the tension between party positions on each issue dimension, candidates' ideological orientation and the degree to which they are constrained to respond to the pressures of their competitors. The next sections outline the hypotheses at the three different levels in detail.

Context conditions

Based on the assumption that the characteristics of national political landscapes affect the politicization of the migration issue, previous studies explained variation in immigration debates and attitudes according to variation in national contexts (Albertson and Gadarian, 2009; Green-Pedersen and Krogstrup, 2008; Ivarsflaten, 2008; Kitschelt, 1997; Rydgren, 2008; Thränhardt, 1995; van der Brug and van Spanje, 2009). By selecting three case studies that are most similar in terms of electoral system, media environment and institutional architecture, but that differ substantially in terms of regional or local conditions that can facilitate the mobilization of specific sub-dimensions of the immigration issue, I seek to do the same for the politicization of immigration in local arenas (Hopkins, 2007, 2010). The choice of the three local settings in Italy allows for minimizing the degree of variation in terms of institutional configuration while preserving substantial differences in specific local characteristics. The cities were carefully selected based on the composition of their migrant population and the corresponding key immigration problems. They differ systematically with respect to the dimension of migration that is expected to be crucial in electoral campaigns – economic in Prato (the local Chinese business community), cultural in Milan (the local Muslim community and the mosque issue) and law and order in Rome (the local Roma issue). This choice enables investigating the way in which different dimensions relate to electoral campaigning in each local setting.

The first expectation is that debates are shaped by the actual competences that local political actors possess in terms of migration affairs. As will be discussed more extensively in Chapter 3, Italian municipalities perform an important role in developing migration and integration legislation, in particular concerning the initial welcoming and sheltering of forced migrants. Moreover, local authorities hold important competences in the field of crime prevention and safeguarding public safety and urban security, with powers of injunction that apply to either extraordinary circumstances or routine regulations.[31] Given the importance of law and order among the responsibilities of local administrations, it is likely that similar aspects constitute the bulk of local debates on immigration. Accordingly, Chapter 4 investigates whether and why security aspects dominate local debates on migration more than any other aspect of migration (context hypothesis 1).[32]

Furthermore, I consider that political actors take into account – upon formulating their campaign strategies – the type of claims, pledges and demands that are most likely to be considered reasonable, realistic and legitimate in the context and at the time in which competition takes place. In particular, they will take into account the specific characteristics of migration at the local level, therefore focusing their attention on the aspects that have the most chances of achieving prominence in a given campaign. Accordingly, the mobilization of different dimensions of immigration can be the result of the available opportunities to mobilize on this issue, which differ across cities due to the characteristics and history of local migration. Social and economic aspects are crucial in an industrial city like Prato, where the demand for a cheap labour force has been the main drive of migration, and where the inflow and subsequent settlement of Chinese migrants represent a primary public concern. In Milan, debates are most likely to cluster around cultural and religious aspects of migration, since the Muslim population accounts for 40% of the total migrants in the city (Bombardieri, 2011; Rebessi, 2011). For years, the Islamic community demanded an official worship place but local authorities have been for a long time fully unresponsive to these calls. As for the case of Rome, securitized arguments are easy to mobilize, since urban security is often a salient aspect in large metropolitan areas. Discursive opportunities for law and order, moreover, have to do with the fact that Rome hosts one of the largest community of Romani people in Italy, which policy-makers almost exclusively tackle in terms of emergency and public order. In sum, I expect that the characteristics of the migrant population and the history of migration in each city influences the resonance of different types of argumentations across local settings, providing competing actors with varying sets of discursive opportunities (context hypothesis 2).

Campaign conditions

In terms of electoral campaign factors, variation is primarily interpreted as the result of migration shocks, in line with one of the main approaches in the study of party competition on the immigration issue (see: Mudde, 2004; Odmalm and Bale, 2014). First, changes have to do with the composition of party systems, such as in the case of emerging radical right parties.[33] Second, migration shocks refer to other factors such as increasing migration pressures, refugee and asylum seeker crises, changing levels of media attention and unexpected or focusing events, forcing political actors to increase attention to migration (Carvalho, 2013; Odmalm and Bale, 2014; Walgrave and Varone, 2006). Accordingly, campaign-level factors influence the composition of the party-system agenda, which has to be distinguished from the individual strategies of political actors aiming at influencing agenda contents. In agenda setting literature, the composition of agendas at the party-system level is crucial, since it constrains the issue emphasis of all actors involved in the campaign (Green-Pedersen and Mortensen, 2010). Being composed of a hierarchy of issues, party-system agendas force individual parties to allocate attention according to this hierarchy, even as parties compete on its future content (Green-Pedersen and Mortensen, 2014).

The first campaign-level hypothesis, therefore, has to do with the role of party-system agendas. In terms of issue dimensions, migration agendas describe the relative importance of each aspect of the issue at any given time, at the party-system level. In line with the above mechanism, parties must address the issue dimensions that are prominent in the agenda, while they compete to influence the dimensional composition of the agenda in the future. Hence, if the pressure of party-system agendas prevails over each party's individual preferences, party choices should differ more for the same party between elections than across parties within a single election campaign (Green-Pedersen and Mortensen, 2010). In other words, dimensional choices of any party at any given point in time will be relatively more similar to the allocation of attention of any other party in that context at that time, than to its own in another context or at another point in time (H1).

The remaining hypotheses at the campaign level anticipate that electoral debates focus on migration, and display high anti-immigration tones, when at least one independent radical right actor runs for office, and when a migration-related focusing event lends itself to be exploited by strategic-minded actors. Concerning the first aspect, previous research suggested that the increased salience of an issue pushes the position of mainstream parties in the direction of the position of the party owning the issue (Green-Pedersen *et al.*, 2013). In other words, parties adjust their policy positions on immigration to substantial changes in the political context in which they are operating, so that the presence of radical right actors leads to right-wing, anti-immigration shifts in debates (Van Spanje, 2010). Accordingly, the more important the immigration issue writ large is, the more the other actors in the competition will adapt their positions to the ones of the issue owner. I therefore anticipate that campaigns involving independent radical right challengers will be characterized by more emphasis on, and more negative tones about, the migration issue (H2a). In addition, I will test whether this rationale applies to dimensional competition on migration. In view of the considerations mentioned above, I expect that issue owners influence the choices of selective emphasis of the other parties in the system. If the presence of radical right actors shifts the general debate towards the position preferred by the radical right, than it is reasonable to anticipate that electoral debates might also shift towards the aspects of the immigration issue most preferred by the radical right (H2b).

The third campaign-level factor has to do with the presence of migration-related focusing events, which influence the behaviour of political actors by opening windows of opportunity to politicize aspects that – otherwise – could not gain public visibility. Similar junctures, in other words, have the potential to transform low-salience matters into concrete problems (Birkland, 2001). This mechanism takes into account that the definition of public problems can change over time because of changing media coverage of the issues connected to the focusing event's subject matter (Birkland, 2001; Kingdon, 1995). In line with Birkland's classification of focusing event types (Birkland, 1997, p. 147), I focus on crime-related events since these are often very powerful in driving media attention and policy change. In particular, I expect to find a link between the relative importance of security considerations and the occurrence of crime stories which fit in the category of 'common events under uncommon circumstances',[34] as these enjoy great newsworthiness due to their unusual features and sensationalistic tones (H3).

Party conditions

I look at party strategies from the point of view of issue and dimensional preferences and the constraints that they face when deciding whether to focus on specific issue aspects rather than others. Party choices are analyzed in terms of attention to the immigration issue as a whole, dimensional emphasis, positions and framing. In addition, I also address electoral debates by comparing parties' 'ideal agendas' – corresponding to the preferences emphasized at the beginning of the campaign within election manifestos – and 'tactical agendas' – emerging from media reports of the election campaign. First, I discuss the hypotheses that have to do with party logics and ideological preferences, and then the expectations on the potential constraints that parties face upon choosing their strategies of selective emphasis (structural and incumbency disadvantage logics).

In terms of party logics, the assumption is that the ultimate goal of any political actor is to convince the public of a specific interpretation of the social reality. Accordingly, it is reasonable to expect that the argumentations parties mobilize, whether for or against immigration, must somehow resonate with the broader ideological understanding of the party (Statham and Trenz, 2012). Similar ideological commitments are generally plotted along left–right scales, in which cosmopolitan and social security aspects characterize the left while nationalism and free-market liberalism characterize the right (Helbling, 2013; Knutsen, 1995, 2006). This is because although the immigration issue can be rightfully considered as a valence question when mainstream parties tend to agree on the general policy direction (Odmalm and Bale, 2014), it remains very ideologically loaded when it comes to its multiple issue dimensions. The mobilization of different issue aspects of the broad migration phenomenon may trigger tensions not only along the left–right axis but also within each party family. On the one hand, in fact, immigration puts in question the dilemma between cultural conservatism and market liberalism within mainstream right-wing parties; on the other, it contraposes left-wing parties concerned with the risk of splitting the working classes, with reformed left parties that address migration primarily as a fundamental human right (Bale, 2008; Odmalm and Bale, 2014). As a result, the choice of mainstream and radical parties to approach the immigration issue in terms of, for example, market economy rather than cultural and labour market protectionism, yields important implications for party behaviour and electoral competition.

Looking at migration in its entirety, the main expectations therefore follow traditional comparative research on issue politicization on the left–right scale (Alonso and Claro da Fonseca, 2009). Right-wing parties are generally advantaged in immigration debates: on the one hand, radical right actors offer overtly xenophobic discourses and build their electoral appeal on unconditional opposition to immigration; on the other hand, mainstream right-wing actors[35] exploit the nationalistic tendencies of their electorates (Bale, 2003; Green-Pedersen and Krogstrup, 2008; Ivarsflaten, 2008). Although the 'logic of defence' (Garner, 2005, p. 133) characterized mainstream right positions long before anti-immigration parties appeared (Bale, 2008), centre-right parties often exploit the presence of radical right actors in order to address immigration in ways that traditionally were more closely associated with the extreme rather than the mainstream (Bale, 2003). This is particularly the case in those countries, like Italy, where the centre and more right-wing parties cooperate or have recently cooperated to form governments. In short, I expect the radical, but also the centre-right, to emphasize the immigration issue the most, accounting for its increased salience over time (H4).

According to this literature, the mainstream left can adopt two possible strategies in response: it can opt to ignore the issue altogether, minimizing the attention to this issue and signalling its lack of importance (a strategy which has been called 'dismissive' by Meguid, 2008), or it can decide to include the issue in its agenda. Previous studies have illustrated that the latter strategy was followed by the French left, as a result of the shift of their traditional electorate towards Le Pen in 1986 (Meguid, 2005). Moreover, it has been suggested that the adoption of the immigration issue by centre-left parties takes place when the challenge of a new issue or new actor becomes manifest, and in particular, when an anti-immigration actor contributes to centre-right governments taking office (Bale *et al.*, 2010; see also: Van Spanje, 2010). It is therefore reasonable to expect that the mainstream left engages in competition over immigration when the issue becomes salient in an electoral campaign (H5).

Concerning dimensional emphasis, left-wing parties are generally expected to adopt more liberal views than their right-wing counterparts do and to seek to improve the social conditions of migrants as well as to extend their cultural rights (Andall, 2007a; Lahav, 2004). Bale *et al.* (2010) suggest that although a 'principled' strategy would entail openly making the case for tolerance of migration and multiculturalism, the substance, form and pace of the response of left-wing parties has been far from uniform (Bale *et al.*, 2010, p. 423). In particular, the abandonment of progressive welfare policies by established parties of the left has led to their gradual shift towards restrictive immigration policies (Andall, 2007a, 2007b; Lahav, 2004; Messina, 1990, 2002). For the Italian case, scholars tend to agree that the mainstream left could – at least in theory – adopt open stances on cultural tolerance and the inclusion of migrants in the labour market without having to deal with strong fears of 'social dumping' among its constituencies (Chaloff, 2005; Massetti, 2014). As a result, left-wing parties are likely to address immigration primarily in terms of cultural and economic arguments (H6a). More specifically, in line with previous studies on framing choices, left-wing parties are expected to frame their arguments primarily in terms of multiculturalism and labour and security frames, which correspond to their cosmopolitan and labour protectionist ideas (Helbling, 2013).

Conversely, security discourse is likely to be the primary argument on the right side of the political spectrum. Over the past decades, centre-right parties have often helped to prime the radical right's law and order agenda, stressing the supposedly over-generous treatment of foreign immigrants (Bale, 2003), mobilizing the feelings of insecurity among their followers, and referring in particular to crime issues (Helbling, 2013; Mudde, 2007) (H6b). In the Italian context, right-wing parties often ground these arguments on emergency logics, which tend to depict immigration-related problems as unexpected and immigration in general as a temporary phenomenon (Chaloff, 2005).[36] Given that opposition to immigration is one of the primary political activities for radical right parties, these parties mobilize on multiple aspects that could be used to oppose immigration (Helbling, 2013), including crime and security, cultural diversity and the erosion of the welfare state (H6c). In this sense, next to law and order, radical right parties mobilize nationalistic frames when debating the cultural dimension, and labour and social security ones to stress the trade-off between national and immigrant welfare and employment (De Lange, 2007).

Party choices, however, do not depend exclusively on party ideological preferences, but also on the constraints that parties are subject to in any election campaign. In particular, I account for the competence of parties on immigration affairs and their role as incumbents or challengers in election campaigns. Concerning the first element, previous research underlined that selective emphasis is the tool by which parties try to activate valence decision frameworks on given policy issues, i.e. the tool by which parties select aspects that connect them with good government performance (Budge and Fairle, 1983; De Sio, 2010; Green, 2007). The degree to which they are able to divert attention to their most favourable issue attribute, however, depends on their degree of competence. Issue owners are able to focus on the issue dimension on which they are considered most competent, whereas their opponents will be forced to take a position on that issue dimension rather than divert attention to other – potentially more beneficial – aspects.

Accordingly, actors enjoying a reputation on migration affairs will be more able to focus on their own issue dimensions than on the ones mobilized by their competitors, whereas disadvantaged parties will be more subject to the pressure of their competitors' attention profiles (structural disadvantage logics). In general, mainstream right parties are advantaged in these types of debates, alongside radical right actors that managed to play the immigration card, while mainstream left parties are seen as the most vulnerable actors when it comes to immigration (Alonso and Claro da Fonseca, 2009; Arzheimer, 2009). This implies that right-wing parties should be more able to focus on their preferred dimensions, whilst left-wing actors will be more likely to change their distribution of attention in favour of the issue dimensions politicized by their opponents (H7). Similarly, structural disadvantage logics might explain the difference between parties' ideal agendas (corresponding to the preferences emphasized at the beginning of the campaign within election manifestos) and tactical agendas (which instead result from the interaction with the media, ongoing events and political competitors). Although ideal agendas cannot be considered fully isolated from anticipations of media reactions, it is reasonable to expect that actors enjoying a reputation on immigration affairs get easier access to the media than weaker actors. Chapter 7 addresses this dynamics in detail, testing whether and why the immigration issue is overrepresented in the media for mainstream right and radical right parties compared to all other actors (H8).

Moreover, one should account for whether an actor runs as incumbent or challenger (incumbency disadvantage logics). This is especially so in local electoral campaigns with high degrees of personalization, two main coalitions and enhanced electoral accountability. Previous studies suggested that the immigration issue as a whole is more attractive to parties in opposition than to those in office (Green-Pedersen and Mortensen, 2010), because while government parties are held responsible for all policy sectors, opposition parties can focus selectively on advantageous issues, and hold incumbents accountable over immigration affairs. More generally, research has noted that the agenda setting strategies of opposition parties are likely to put pressure on the allocation of attention by incumbent actors (Hobolt *et al.,* 2008). Challenger parties have incentives to introduce new elements in public debates and/or reframing existing ones, since changing the nature of the debates may jeopardize the campaign of the actors in government and enable them to win office. In order to stay in power, governing parties, in turn, are compelled to respond to the elements brought in by the opposition parties through their manipulative strategies (Klingemann *et al.,* 1994; Riker, 1986; Walgrave and Nuytemans, 2009). As opposition actors are more able to exert an influence on the party-system agenda, they will be more able than governing ones to focus on favourable issue dimensions and frames. Conversely, as government parties are more responsive to party-system agendas, they will focus relatively more on the issue dimensions of their opponents (H9). Similarly, due to incumbency disadvantage logics, challenger parties may force incumbents to take up the issue and issue dimensions in the course of the election campaign. Hence, one may expect the difference between the salience of immigration in electoral manifestos and the media to be higher for incumbents than for challengers, since incumbents are more subject to campaign-specific constraints (H10).

Conclusive remarks

This chapter presented and discussed the main theoretical traits driving my analysis of the politicization of migration across multiple issue dimensions in local electoral campaigns in Italy. As I have illustrated, researchers in this field increasingly agree on the need to open the black box of policy issues, disaggregating the separate elements that make up complex political issues in order to improve the understanding of issue politicization. In this sense, rather than viewing issues and partisan strategies of mobilization as one-dimensional, I propose to take into account the complexity of political debates, analysing how the separate aspects of issues are taken up, contextualized and framed in partisan and media agendas.

I suggest that practices and efforts aimed at manipulating the electoral agenda may vary depending on the features of the issue at stake, since political decisions tend to encompass a multiplicity of dimensions of choice. This is because when parties are confronted with complex policy issues, they do not only choose whether they will address an issue in the electoral campaign, but they can also decide which aspects of that issue they want to highlight, and how. Beyond competition over saliency of policy issues, electoral actors interact with one another on the basis of issue dimensions, positions and interpretations. In other words, they act strategically in order to shift the focus of debates to dimensions and understandings of immigration over which they presume to be more credible than their rivals are. Accordingly, I identify a number of conditions – at the context, campaign and party levels – that are likely to drive the choices of politicization by competing political actors (Table 2.2).

As I will illustrate in the next chapters, this approach provides valuable insights for the study of campaigning. Firstly, it suggests that the scholarly understanding of the construction of public agendas must be refined. A comprehensive account of political conflict in electoral campaigns requires analysing not only partisan strategies *across* issues, but also strategies of politicization *within* issues, i.e. the strategies that parties adopt toward issues that they cannot avoid or cannot afford to dismiss. Secondly, this framework offers an innovative interpretation of the study of electoral campaigning, combining issue competition explanations and framing approaches to the construction of public debates. Third, this model suggests that variation in the composition, framing and tone of local electoral debates depends on a combination of conditions, opportunities and factors at three levels of analysis. Accordingly, the next chapters shall address the interrelated roles of the individual strategies of the actors involved, the characteristics of each electoral campaign and the socio-contextual features of the setting where competition takes place.

Table 2.2 Overview of the hypotheses

Context level

Electoral debates are influenced by the actual competences of local administrators
Electoral debates are influenced by the characteristics of local immigration
Campaign level

The party-system agenda
H1: *Dimensional choices are more similar across parties at a given time, than within parties across time*
The agenda setting role of the radical right
H2a: *Campaigns involving independent radical right actors will be characterized by more emphasis and more restrictive positions on immigration*
H2b: *Campaigns involving independent radical right actors will focus on the issues upon which the radical right mobilizes the most*
Focusing events
H3: *The salience of immigration and the relative salience of immigration dimensions are influenced by the presence of focusing events*
Party level

Party logics
H4: *The radical right and the mainstream right emphasize the immigration issue the most*
H5: *The mainstream left engages in immigration debates when the issue is salient in the election campaign*
H6a: *Left-wing parties tend to address immigration in terms of cultural and religious aspects and economic arguments*
H6b: *Right-wing parties tend to prioritize the security over the cultural and the economic dimensions*
H6c: *Radical right parties mobilize on all three issue dimensions*
Structural disadvantage logics
H7: *Right-wing actors are more able to focus on their preferred issue dimensions; left-wing actors are more likely to change their distribution of attention*
H8: *The immigration issue is overrepresented in the media for mainstream right and radical right parties compared to all other actors*
Incumbency disadvantage logics
H9: *Opposition parties are more able than governing parties to focus on their preferred issue dimensions and frames*
H10: *The difference in attention profiles in electoral manifestos and the media is higher for incumbents than for challengers*

Notes

1 In fact, distinguishing between immigration and immigrant politics often implies overlooking other aspects of public discourse. Previous research illustrated that this distinction is particularly difficult to 'unpack' in empirical terms, since incorporation arguments are often used by governments to deter new migrant entries (Lahav and Guiraudon, 2006, p. 208), whilst the distinction between international security and social fear has become increasingly thin (Buonfino, 2004). In this sense, I am interested in disentangling the various kinds of problems and opportunities that political actors address upon debating migration, rather than focusing on the differentiation between stages of policy implicit in the integration/immigration distinction.

2 This choice is the most appropriate for a study on strategic framing in electoral campaigns, but it is different from the one of comparative studies focusing simultaneously on multiple issues, or studying relatively long time periods (Boomgaarden and Vliegenthart, 2009; Helbling, 2013; Roggeband and Vliegenthart, 2007). These studies generally make use of what de Vreese *et al.* (2001, pp. 108–110) and de Vreese (2005) call 'generic frames' (as opposed to 'issue-specific' ones), which correspond to more general descriptions of a reality (or news), and are broadly applicable to a range of news topics, over time, and potentially in different cultural contexts. This is not to say that generic frames are unable to yield useful insights. However, they are more useful to advance theories of framing and framing effects in the field of communication than they are for a study on competition strategies in electoral campaigning.

3 The terms 'inductive' and 'deductive' are used to refer to frame extraction only and not to refer to the general epistemological orientation of the study. Inductive strategies imply that frames are generated as a result of the analysis rather than being (theoretically) derived beforehand. A deductive strategy would have implied that pre-defined frames are coded and that no new frames are generated (Matthes and Kohring, 2008).

4 For each claim, moreover, I further specify the directional nature, which allows accounting for the direction of the relationship between each dimension and frame and the immigration issue.

5 Pragmatic frames are present when positions are supported by arguments stressing the ability of proposals to reach a certain goal or interest. Identity frames focus on community-specific features, ideas and values as justifications. Finally, moral-universal frames have to do with universal standards of justice that are supposedly shared by everyone across and beyond community-based and individual interests.

6 'I nuovi cittadini dimenticati', in *La Repubblica,* 17/04/2011

7 'Immigrati, due visioni a confronto', in *Il Tirreno,* 10/06/2004

8 Some authors claim that pro-migration utilitarian reasoning may even rely upon unequal treatment of immigrants, suggesting that 'economic utility and humanitarian need are alternative and competing models' in the definition of the immigration discourse (Bauder, 2007, p. 109).

9 'L'ultima leggenda finti rom in metrò', in *Il Giorno,* 17/04/2011.

10 'Milone e Bini rilanciano: "Ci sono quarantamila clandestini"', in *Il Tirreno,* 31/05/2009.

11 'Comunali, lista in rosa nella "Sinistra per Pisapia"', in *Il Giorno,* 05/04/2011.

12 'Sedute di giunta pubbliche', in *Il Tirreno,* 14/05/2009.

13 'La Vanoni si candida per la Moratti', in *Il Giorno,* 04/04/2011.

14 'Taiti e Bernocchi: la città è satura' in *Il Tirreno,* 10/06/2004.

15 'Magdi Allam e Shaari sfida sull'immigrazione', in *La Repubblica,* 10/04/2011.

16 'Sull'immigrazione un'ondata di follia', in *Il Tirreno,* 11/06/2009.

17 'Un parco intorno alle mura', in *Il Tirreno,* 09/06/2004.

18 'Sull'immigrazione un'ondata di follia', in *Il Tirreno,* 11/06/2009.

19 'Caro Cenni, ma cosa è successo?', in *Il Tirreno,* 19/06/2009.

20 In fact, the protection of individuals' safety is not intended exclusively in terms of the host population, but it can also address a larger category including migrants themselves. As suggested by Caviedes (2015), security in immigration discourse is also mobilized to depict migrants as victims of dangerous and instable social environments.

21 'I romani si sentono insicuri', in *Il Messaggero*, 10/04/2008.

22 'Concerto per l' immigrazione', in *La Repubblica*, 30/04/2006.

23 Yet, the media and political actors involved in electoral campaigning often use the category 'Roma people' to refer to numerous non-Romani groups, including stateless persons of presumably Balkan origin, as well as Romanian citizens in general (Sigona, 2008).

24 'Lega: Mandiamo via I nomadi dalla città', in *Il Giorno*, 18/05/2006.

25 'Una messinscena elettorale dopo il boicottaggio fallito', in *La Repubblica*, 03/05/2011.

26 The vast majority of claims mobilizing egalitarian understandings of immigration used moral-universalistic arguments and referred primarily to multiculturalist aspects (rather than security). Whenever appropriate, therefore, I categorized these frames in the cultural dimension.

27 'Il sindaco incassa il sostegno del Pid', *Il Giorno*, 19/05/2011.

28 'Bagno di folla e ovazioni per Silvio', in *Il Tirreno*, 03/06/2009.

29 In this sense, the distinction between 'priming' and 'framing' effects may help elucidate the difference between issue dimensions and issue framing. Unlike studies on priming, which deal with the outcomes of agenda setting processes (Scheufele, 2000, p. 306), framing studies do not focus exclusively on what people talk or think about, but also on how they think and talk about political issues (Pan and Kosicki, 1993, p. 70). Similarly, in their discussion on the construction of public opinion on Europe, Hooghe and Marks (2009) distinguish between strategies of political entrepreneurs oriented at priming (making a consideration salient) and framing (connecting a particular consideration to a political object).

30 Of course, the extent of this varies across context, campaigns and settings. Morales *et al.* (2014) show that, although mainstream Spanish parties had started to incorporate the issue in their pattern of electoral competition, migration virtually disappeared from debates in the 2011 elections in Spain, when issues related to the economic crisis absorbed most of the attention. On the contrary, the scenario in Greece is quite different, since the economic crisis did not seem to drive attention away from migration issues (Tampakoglou, 2014).

31 In 2010, the regional administrative tribunal of Veneto contested the constitutional legitimacy of the articles of the Italian law on local administration (D.Lgs 267/2000) granting extensive powers of mayors in terms of the management of public order.

32 In particular, previous accounts on the development of the concept of 'urban security' as a distinctive policy field underline its connection to processes of urbanization and internal and external migration (Calaresu, 2013; Italia, 2010; Regione Piemonte, 2012).

33 For a definition of the way in which I use the concept of 'radical right' and an overview of the terminological debate on this issue, see Chapter 1 in this volume, and Mudde (2000, 2007); Ignazi (1992, 2003); Kitschelt (1995); Minkenberg (2007). Chapter 1 also presents a detailed discussion of the categorization of mainstream and radical parties and the conceptual implications of this terminological choice.

34 This type of events stand out, in terms of newsworthiness, compared to other types included in Birklands' classification, most notably normal events such as natural occurrences, and new events that have never happened before (Birkland, 1997).

35 Following Meguid's definition, by 'mainstream parties' we mean the electorally dominant actors in the centre-left and in the centre-right blocs of the left–right political spectrum (2005, p. 348). Given the increasingly bipolar nature of Italian politics, especially at the local level, the empirical chapters use indifferently the terms 'centre-right'

('centre-left') and 'mainstream right' ('mainstream left'). The research design section in Chapter 1 offers a broader discussion of this and other terminological choices in the selection and definition of party families.

36 Yet, this strategy has also been pursued by left-wing parties; see: Massetti (2014).

References

Albertson, B. and Gadarian, S.K. (2009) 'Is Lou Dobbs Frightening? The Effect of Threatening Advertisements on Attitudes Toward Immigration', paper presented at the *Politics of Race, Immigration, and Ethnicity Colloquium*, Los Angeles. Available at: http://proec. org/wordpress/wpcontent/uploads/2009/01/loudobbspaper.pdf

Alonso, S. and Claro Da Fonseca, S. (2009) 'Immigration, Left and Right', paper prepared for presentation to the panel "Immigrants vs. National Identity? The Problem of Integration in Europe" at the *Annual Meeting of the American Political Science Association* Toronto, ON, 3–6 September 2009. Available at: www.wzb.eu/sites/default/ files/personen/alonso.sonia.312/apsa09_alonso-fonseca.pdf (Accessed 19 May 2014).

Andall, J. (2007a) 'Introduction: Immigration and Political Parties in Europe', *Patterns of Prejudice*, 41(2), pp. 105–108, DOI: 10.1080/00313220701265478.

Andall, J. (2007b) 'Immigration and the Italian Left Democrats in Government (1996–2001)', *Patterns of Prejudice*, 41(2), pp. 131–153, DOI: 10.1080/00313220701265502.

Arceneaux, K. (2005) 'Do Campaigns Help Voters Learn? A Cross-National Analysis', *British Journal of Political Science*, 36, pp. 159–173.

Arzheimer, K. (2009) 'Contextual Factors and the Extreme Right Vote in Western Europe, 1980–2002', *American Journal of Political Science*, 53(2), pp. 259–275. doi: 10.1111/j.1540–5907.2009.00369.

Bale, T. (2003) 'Cinderella and her Ugly Sisters: The Mainstream and Extreme Right in Europe's Bipolarising Party Systems', *West European Politics*, 26(3), pp. 67–90.

Bale, T. (2008) 'Turning Round the Telescope. Centre-right Parties and Immigration and Integration Policy in Europe', *Journal of European Public Policy*, 15(3), pp. 315–330.

Bale, T., Green-Pedersen, C., Krouwel, A., Luther, K.R. and Sitter, N. (2010) 'If You Can't Beat Them, Join Them? Explaining Social Democratic Responses to the Challenge from the Populist Radical Right in Western Europe', *Political Studies*, 58, pp.410–426.

Bauder, H. (2007) 'Media Discourse and the New German Immigration Law', *Journal of Ethnic and Migration Studies*, 34(1), pp. 95–112. doi: 10.1080/13691830701708783

Baumgartner, F.R. and Jones, B.D. (2002) *Policy Dynamics*. Chicago: University of Chicago Press.

Berkhout, J. and Sudulich, L. (2011) *Codebook for Political Claims Analysis*. SOM Working Papers, Nr. 2011–02

Bigo, D. (2002) 'Security and Immigration: Toward a Critique of the Governmentality of Unease', *Alternatives*, 27, pp. 63–92.

Bigo, D. (2014) 'Death in the Mediterranean Sea: The Results of the Three Fields of Action of Eu Border Controls'. In: Celikates, R., Jansen, Y. de Bloist, J. eds. *The Irregularization of Migration in Contemporary Europe: Detention, Deportation, Drowning*. Lanham, MN: Rowman International, pp. 55–70.

Birkland, T.A. (1997) *After Disaster: Agenda Setting, Public Policy, and Focusing Events*. Washington: Georgetown University Press.

Birkland, T.A. (1998) 'Focusing Events, Mobilization, and Agenda Setting', *Journal of Public Policy*, 18(1), pp. 53–74.

Birkland, T.A. (2001) *An Introduction to the Policy Process: Theories, Concepts, and Models of Public Policy Making*. New York: M.E. Sharpe, Inc.

Bombardieri, M. (2011) *Moschee d'Italia. Il diritto al luogo di culto, il dibattito sociale e politico*. Bologna: EMI.

Boomgaarden, H.G. and Vliegenthart, R. (2009) 'How News Content Influences Anti-Immigration Attitudes: Germany, 1993–2005', *European Journal of Political Research*, 48(4), pp. 516–542. doi: 10.1111/j.1475–6765.2009.01831.x

Boswell, C. (2011) 'Migration Control and Narraives of Steering', *British Journal of Politics and International Relations*, 13, pp.12–25.

Brandenburg, H. (2002) 'Who Follows Whom? The Impact of Parties on Media Agenda Formation in the 1997 British General Election Campaign', *International Journal of Press/Politics*, 7(34), pp. 34–54.

Budge, I. and Fairle, D. (1983) 'Party Competition: Selective Emphasis or Direct Confrontation? An Alternative View with Data'. In: Daalder, H. and Mair, P. eds. *West European Party Systems: Continuity and Change*. London: SAGE, pp. 267–305.

Buonfino, A. (2004) 'Between Unity and Plurality: The Politicization and Securitization of the Discourse of Immigration in Europe', *New Political Science*, 26(1), pp. 23–49. doi: 10.1080/0739314042000185111

Buzan, B., Wæver, O. and Wilde, J. (1998) *Security: A New Framework for Analysis*. Boulder: Lynne Rienner Publishers.

Calaresu, M. (2013) *La politica di sicurezza urbana. Il caso italiano (1994–2009)*. Milano: Franco Angeli.

Callaghan K and Schnell, F. (2004) *Framing American Politics*. Pittsburgh, PA: Univeristy of Pittsburgh Press.

Carvalho, J. (2013) *Impact of Extreme-right Parties on Immigration Policy. Comparing Britain, France and Italy*. Abingdon and New York: Routledge.

Caviedes, A. (2015) 'An Emerging "European" News Portrayal of Immigration?', *Journal of Ethnic and Migration Studies*, 41(6), pp. 897–917.

Chaloff, J. (2005) 'Italy'. In Niessen, J. and Schiebel, Y. eds. *Immigration as a Labour Market Strategy: European and North American Perspectives*. Brussels: Migration Policy Group, pp. 111–128.

Chong, D. and Druckman, J.N. (2007) 'A Theory of Framing and Opinion Formation in Competitive Elite Environments', *Journal of Communication*, 57, pp. 99–118.

Citrin, J., Green, D.P., Muste, C. and Wong, C. (1997) 'Public Opinion Toward Immigration Reform: The Role of Economic Motivations', *The Journal of Politics*, 59(3), pp. 858–881.

Cobb, R.W. and Elder, C.D. (1971) *Participation in American Politics. The Dynamics of Agenda-Building*. Baltimore: The Johns Hopkins University Press.

De Lange, S.L. (2007) 'A New Winning Formula? The Programmatic Appeal of the Radical Right', *Party Politics*, 13(4), pp.411–435.

De Sio, L. (2010) *Beyond "Position" and "Valence": A Unified Framework for the Analysis of Political Issues*. Working Paper of the Robert Schuman Center for Advanced Studies, EUI. cadmus.eui.eu/handle/1814/14814.

De Sio, L. and Franklin, M. (2012) 'Strategic Incentives, Issue Proximity and Party Support', *West European Politics*, 35(6), pp. 1363–1385.

de Vreese, C. (2005) 'News Framing: Theory and Typology', *Information Design Journal*, 13(1), 51–62.

de Vreese, C., Peter, J. and Semetko, H. (2001) 'Framing Politics at the Launch of the Euro: A Cross-national Comparative Study of Frames in the News', *Political Communication*, 18, pp. 107–22.

Druckman, J.N. (2004) 'Political Preference Formation: Competition, Deliberation, and the (ir)Relevance of Framing Effects', *American Political Science Review*, 98, pp. 671–686.

Entman, R. (1993) 'Framing: Toward Clarification of a Fractured Paradigm', *Journal of Communication*, 43(4), pp. 51–58. doi: 10.1111/j.1460–2466.1993.tb01304.x

Entman, R. (2004) *Projects of Power: Framing News, Public Opinion, and U.S. Foreign Policy*. Chicago: University of Chicago Press.

Feldblum, M. (1999) *Reconstructing Citizenship: The Politics of Nationality Reform and Immigration in Contemporary France*. New York: State University of New York Press.

Ferree, M.M., Gamson, W.A., Gerhards, J. and Rucht, D. (2002) *Shaping Abortion Discourse. Democracy and the Public Sphere in Germany and the United States*. Cambridge, UK: Cambridge University Press.

Finkel, S.E. (1993) 'Re-examining the "Minimal Effects" Model in Recent Presidential Campaigns', *Journal of Politics*, 55, pp. 1–21.

Froio, C. (2012) *Que reste-t-il des partis? Une étude de l'influence des partis de gouvernement sur les politiques publiques en France entre 1981 et 2009*. Sarrebruck: Presses Académiques Francophones.

Froio, C. (2013) 'What Is Left for Parties? An Overview of Party Mandate in France 1981–2009', *French Politics*, 11(1), 98–116.

Gamson, W.A. (1992) *Talking Politics*. Cambridge: University Press.

Gamson, W.A. (2004) 'Bystanders, Public Opinion and the Media'. In: Snow, D.A., Soule, S.A. and Kriesi, H. eds. *The Blackwell Companion to Social Movements*. Oxford: Blackwell, pp. 242–261.

Garner, S. (2005) 'The Racialisation of Mainstream Politics', *Ethical Perspectives*, 12(2): 123–40.

Gelman, A. and King, G. (1993) 'Why Are American Presidential Election Campaign Polls So Variable When Votes Are So predictable?', *British Journal of Political Science* 23, pp. 409–51.

Ghanem, S. (1997) 'Filling in the Tapestry: The Second Level of Agenda-setting'. In McCombs, M., Shaw, D.L. and Weaver, D. eds. *Communication and Democracy*. Mahwah, NJ: Lawrence Erlbaum Associates Inc., pp. 3–14.

Green, J. (2007) 'When Voters and Parties Agree: Valence Issues and Party Competition', *Political Studies*, 5, pp. 629–655.

Green-Pedersen, C. (2007) 'The Growing Importance of Issue Competition: The Changing Nature of Party Competition in Western Europe', *Political Studies* 55, pp. 607–628.

Green-Pedersen, C. (2010) *New Issues, New Cleavages, and New Parties: How to Understand Change in West European Party Competition*. Working Paper University of Aarhus, 26 August 2010. Available at SSRN: http://ssrn.com/abstract=1666096 or http://dx.doi.org/10.2139/ssrn.1666096

Green-Pedersen, C. and Blomqvist, P. (2004) 'Defeat at Home? Issue-ownership and Social Democratic Support in Scandinavia', *Government and Opposition*, 39, pp. 587–613.

Green-Pedersen, C. and Krogstrup, J. (2008) 'Immigration as a Political Issue in Denmark and Sweden', *European Journal of Political Research*, 47, pp. 610–634.

Green-Pedersen, C. and Mortensen, P.B. (2010) 'Who Sets the Agenda and Who Responds to it in the Danish Parliament? A New Model of Issue Competition and Agenda-setting', *European Journal of Political Research*, 49(2), pp. 257–281. doi: 10.1111/j.1475–6765.2009.01897.x

Green-Pedersen, C. and Mortensen, P. (2014) 'Avoidance and Engagement: Issue Competition in Multiparty System', *Political Studies*: doi: 10.1111/1467–9248.12121

Green-Pedersen, C., Mortensen, P. and So, F. (2013) 'How Issue Saliency Makes Parties Change their Positions', paper presented at the *7th Annual CAP Conference*, 12–14th June 2014, University of Konstanz.

Guinaudeau, I. and Persico, S. (2014) 'What is Issue Competition? Conflict, Consensus and Issue Ownership in Party Competition', *Journal of Elections, Public Opinion and Parties*, 24(3), pp. 312–333, DOI: 10.1080/17457289.2013.858344

Guiraudon, V. (2003) 'The Constitution of a European Immigration Policy Domain: A Political Sociology Approach', *Journal of European Public Policy*, 10(2), 263–282.

Habermas, J. (1993) *Justification and Application: Remarks on Discourse Ethics*. Cambridge: Polity Press.

Hainmueller, J. and Hiscox, M.J. (2007) 'Educated Preferences: Explaining Attitudes toward Immigration in Europe', *International Organization*, 61(2), pp. 399–442.

Hammar, T. (ed.) (1985) *European Immigration Policy: A Comparative Study*. Cambridge: Cambridge University Press.

Hänggli, R. (2010) *Frame Building and Framing Effects in Direct-Democratic Campaigns*. Unpublished PhD dissertation. Faculty of Political Science, University of Zurich, Switzerland.

Hänggli, R. (2012) 'Key Factors in Frame Building: How Strategic Political Actors Shape News Media Coverage', *American Behavioural Scientist,* 56(3), pp. 300–317.

Hänggli, R. and Kriesi, H. (2010) 'Political Framing Strategies and Their Impact on Media Framing in a Swiss Direct-Democratic Campaign', *Political Communication*, 27(2), pp. 141–157.Helbling, M. (2013) 'Framing Immigration in Western Europe', *Journal of Ethnic and Migration Studies*, 40(1), pp. 21–41.

Helbling, M., Höglinger, D. and Wüest, B. (2010) 'How Political Parties Frame European Integration', *European Journal of Political Research,* 49(4), pp. 495–521. doi: 10.1111/j.1475–6765.2009.01908.

Hobolt, S., Klemmemsen, R. and Pickup, M. (2008) *The Dynamics of Issue Diversity in Party Rhetoric*. OCSID Working Paper OCSID_03, Available at: http://ocsid.politics.ox.ac.uk/publications/index.asp (accessed 02/10/2014).

Höglinger, D., Wuest, B. and Helbling, M. (2012) 'Culture versus Economy: The Framing of Public Debates Over Issues Related to Globalization'. In: Kriesi, H., Grande, E., Dolezal, M., Helbling, M., Höglinger, D., Hutter, S. and Wuest, B. eds. *Political Conflict in Western Europe*. Cambridge/New York: Cambridge University Press, pp. 229–253.

Hooghe, L. and Marks, G. (2009) 'A Postfunctionalist Theory of European Integration: From Permissive Consensus to Constraining Dissensus', *British Journal of Political Science*, 39, pp. 1–23

Hooghe, L., Marks, G. and Wilson, C.J. (2002) 'Does Left/Right Structure Party Positions on European Integration?' *Comparative Political Studies*, 35(8), pp. 965–989.

Hopkins, D.J. (2007) *Threatening Changes: Explaining Where and When Immigrants Provoke Local Opposition*, Working Paper, Centre for the Study of American Politics, Yale University.

Hopkins, D.J. (2010) 'Politicized Places: Explaining Where and When Immigrants Provoke Local Opposition', *American Political Science Review,* 104(1), pp. 40–60.

Huckins, K. (1999) 'Interest-Group Influence in the Media Agenda: A Case Study', *Journalism and Mass Communication Quarterly,* 76(1), pp.76–86.

Huysmans, J. (2000) 'The EU and the Securitization of Migration', *Journal of Common Market Studies*, 38(5), pp. 751–78.

Ignazi, P. (1992) 'The Silent Counter-Revolution: Hypotheses on the Emergence of the Extreme Right-Wing Parties in Western Europe', *European Journal of Political Research,* 22, pp. 3–35.

Ignazi, P. (2003) *Extreme Right Parties in Western Europe*. Oxford: Oxford University Press.

Italia, V. (2010) *La sicurezza urbana, Le ordinanze dei Sindaci e gli osservatori volontari*. Giuffrè: Milano.

Ivarsflaten, E. (2008) 'What Unites Right-Wing Populists in Western Europe? Re-Eexamining Grievance Mobilization Models in Seven Successful Cases', *Comparative Political Studies* 41(1), pp. 3–23.

Iyengar, S. (1991). *Is Anyone Responsible? How Television Frames Political Issues*. Chicago: University of Chicago Press.

Iyengar, S. and Kinder, D.R. (1987) *News That Matters: Agenda-Setting and Priming in a Television Age*. Chicago: University of Chicago Press.

Iyengar, S. and Kinder, D.R. (2010) *News that Matters: Television and American Opinion*. Chicago: University of Chicago Press.

Kingdon, J.W. (1995) *Agenda, Alternatives and Public Policies*. New York: Harper Collins.

Kiousis, S. and McCombs, M. (2004) 'Agenda-setting Effects and Attitude Strength: Political Figures during the 1996 Presidential Election', *Communication Research*, 31, pp. 36–57.

Kiousis, S., Mitrook, M., Wu, X. and Seltzer, T. (2006) 'First and Second-Level Agenda-Building and Agenda-Setting Effects: Linkages Among Candidate News Releases, Media Coverage, and Public Opinion During the 2002 Florida Gubernatorial Election', *Journal of Public Relations Research*, 18, pp. 265–85.

Kitschelt, H. (1995) *The Radical Right in Western Europe*. Ann Arbor: University of Michigan Press.

Kitschelt, H. and McGann, A. (1997) *The Radical Right in Western Europe. A Comparative Analysis*. Ann Arbor: University of Michigan Press.

Klingemann, H-D., Hofferbert, R.I. and Budge, I. (1994) *Parties, Policies, and Democracy*. Boulder: Westview Press.

Knutsen, O. (1995) 'Party Choice'. In: van Deth, J.W. and Scarbrought, E. eds. *The Impact of Values*. Oxford: Oxford University Press, pp. 461–491.

Knutsen, O. (2006) *Social Structure and Party Choice in Western Europe. A Comparative Longitudinal Study*. London: Palgrave-Macmillan.

Koopmans, R. and Statham, P. (1999) 'Political Claims Analysis: Integrating Protest Event and Political Discourse Approaches', *Mobilization* 4(1), pp. 40–51.

Koopmans, R., Statham, P., Giugni, M. and Passy, F. (2005) *Contested Citizenship: Immigration and Cultural Diversity in Europe*. Minneaopolis, MN: University of Minnesota Press.

Kriesi, H., Bernhard, L. and Hänggli, R. (2009) 'The Politics of Campaigning – Dimensions of Strategic Action'. In: Marcinkowski, F. and Pfetsch, B. eds. *Politik in der Mediendemokratie*. VS Verlag für Sozialwissenschaften, pp. 345–365.

Kriesi, H., Grande, E., Dolezal, M., Helbling, M., Höglinger, D., Hutter, S. and Wuest, B. (2012) *Political Conflict in Western Europe*. Cambridge/New York: Cambridge University Press.

Lahav, G. (2004) *Immigration and Politics in the New Europe: Reinventing Borders*. Cambridge: Cambridge University Press.

Lahav, G. and Courtemanche, M. (2011) 'The Ideological Effects of Framing Threat on Immigration and Civil Liberties', *Political Behavior*, 34(3), pp. 1–29. doi: 10.1007/s11109-011-9171-z

Lakoff, G. and Ferguson, S. (2006) *The Framing of Immigration*. Available at: http://academic.evergreen.edu/curricular/ppandp/PDFs/Lakoff%20Framing%20of%20Immigration.doc.pdf (Accessed 28 May 2014).

Lahav, G. and Guiraudon, V. (2006) 'Actors and Venues in Immigration Control: Closing the Gap between Political Demands and Policy Outcomes', *West European Politics*, 29(2), pp. 201–223, DOI: 10.1080/01402380500512551Lazaridis, G. (2011) 'Introduction'. In Lazaridis, G. ed. *Security, Insecurity and Migration in Europe*. Burlington: Ashgate, pp. 1–12.

Lazarsfeld, P.F., Berelson, B. and Gaudet, H. (1944) *The People's Choice: How the Voter Makes up his Mind in a Presidential Campaign*. New York: Columbia University Press.

Lerch, M. and Schwellnus, G. (2006) 'Normative by Nature? The Role of Coherence in Justifying the EU's External Human Rights Policy', *Journal of European Public Policy*, 13(2), pp. 304–321.

Lopez-Escobar, E., Llamas, J.P. and McCombs, M.E. (1998) 'Agenda Setting and Community Consensus: First and Second Level Effects', *International Journal of Public Opinion Research*, 10, pp. 335–348.

Marcus, G.E., Neuman, W.R. and MacKuen, M. (2000) *Affective Intelligence and Political Judgments*. Chicago: University of Chicago Press.

Massetti, E. (2014) 'Mainstream Parties and the Politics of Immigration in Italy: A Structural Advantage for the Right or a Missed Opportunity for the Left?' *Acta Politica*, advance online publication 22 August 2014, doi: 10.1057/ap.2014.29

Matthes, J. (2009) 'What's in a Frame? A Content Analysis of Media Framing Studies in the World's Leading Communication Journals 1990–2005', *Journalism & Mass Communication Quarterly*, 86(2), pp. 349–367.

Matthes, J. (2012) 'Framing Politics: An Integrative Approach', *American Behavioral Scientist*, 56(3), pp. 247–259.

Matthes, J. and Kohring, M. (2008) 'The Content Analysis of Media Frames: Toward Improving Reliability and Validity', *Journal of Communication*, 58, pp. 258–279.

McCombs, M. (2004) *Setting the Agenda: The Mass Media and Public Opinion*. Cambridge: Polity Press.

McCombs, M. and Ghanem, S. (2001) 'The Convergence of Agenda Setting and Framing'. In: Reese, S., Gandy, O. and Grant, A. eds. *Framing Public Life: Perspectives and our Understanding*. Mahwah, NJ: Lawrence Erlbaum Associates, pp. 67–81.

McCombs, M. and Reynolds, A. (2002) 'News Influences on Our Pictures of the World'. In: Bryant, J. and Zillman, D. eds. *Media Effects. Advances in Theory and Research* (2 ed.). Mahwah, NJ: Lawrence Erlbaum, pp. 1–18.

McGarry, A. and Drake, H. (2013) 'The Politicization of Roma sas an Ethnic "Other": Security Discourse in France and the Politics of Belonging'. In Korkut, U., Bucken-Knapp, G., McGarry, A., Hinnfors, J. and Drake, H. eds. *The Discourses and Politics of Migration in Europe*. New York: Palgrave McMillian, pp. 73–91.

Meguid, B. (2005) 'The Role of Mainstream Party Strategy in Niche Party Success', *American Political Science Review*, 99(3), pp. 347–359.

Meguid, B. (2008) *Party Competition between Unequals: Strategies and Electoral Fortunes in Western Europe*. Cambridge: Cambridge University Press.

Messina, A. (1990) 'Political Impediments to the Resumption of Labour Migration to Western Europe', *West European Politics*, 13, pp. 31–46.

Messina, A. (ed.) (2002) *West European Immigration and Immigrant Policy in the New Century*. Westport, CT: Praeger Publishers.

Messina, A. (2007) *The Logics and Politics of Post-WWII Migration to Western Europe*. New York: Cambridge University Press.

Messina, A. and Lahav, G. (2006) *The Migration Reader. Exploring Politics and Policies*. Boulder: Lynne Rienner.Minkenberg, M. (2007) 'The Renewal of the Radical Right: Between Modernity and Anti-Modernity,' *Government and Opposition*, 35, pp. 170–188.

Morales, L., Pardos-Prado, S. and Ros, V. (2014) 'Issue Emergence and the Dynamics of Electoral Competition around Immigration in Spain', *Acta Politica*, advance online publication: doi:10.1057/ap.2014.33

Mudde, C. (2000) *The Ideology of the Extreme Right*. Manchester: Manchester University Press

Mudde, C. (2004) 'The Populist Zeitgeist', *Government and Opposition* 39(4), pp. 541–563.

Mudde, C. (2007) *Populist Radical Right Parties in Europe*. Cambridge: Cambridge University Press.

Odmalm, P. (2011) 'Political Parties and "the Immigration Issue": Issue Ownership in Swedish Parliamentary Elections 1991–2010', *West European Politics* 34(5), pp. 1070–1091.

Odmalm, P. (2012) 'Party Competition and Positions on Immigration: Strategic Advantages and Spatial Locations', *Comparative European Politics*, 10(1), pp. 1–22.

Odmalm, P. (2014) *The Party Politics of the EU and Immigration*. New York: Palgrave MacMillan.

Odmalm, P. and Bale, T. (2014) 'Immigration into the Mainstream: Conflicting Ideological Streams, Strategic Reasoning and Party Competition', *Acta Politica*, doi:10.1057/ap.2014.28.

Odmalm, P. and Super, B. (2014) 'If the Issue Fits, Stay Put: Cleavage Stability, Issue Compatibility and Drastic Changes on the Immigration "issue"', *Comparative European Politics*, 12(6), pp. 663–679.

Pan, Z. and Kosicki, G.M. (1993) 'Framing Analysis: An Approach to News Discourse', *Political Communication*, 10(1), pp. 55–75.

Perlmutter, T. (1996) 'Bringing Parties Back In: Comments on "Modes of Immigration Politics in Liberal Democratic Societies"', *International Migration Review*, 30(1), pp. 375–388.

Petrocik, J.R. (1996) 'Issue Ownership in Presidential Elections with a 1980 Case Study', *American Journal of Political Science*, 40(3), pp. 825–850.

Petrocik, J.R., Benoit, W.L. and Hansen, G. (2003) 'Issue Ownership and Presidential Campaigning, 1952–2000', *Political Science Quarterly*, 118 (4), pp. 599–626.

Rebessi, E. (2011) *Diffusione dei luoghi di culto islamici e gestione delle conflittualità. La moschea di via Urbino a Torino come studio di caso*. POLIS Working Papers N° 194, December 2011. ISSN: 2038-7296.

Regione Piemonte. (2012) 'Sicurezza Urbana: Le competenze degli Enti locali, quelle dello Stato e la cooperazione tra Enti', *Manuale a dispense sulla sicurezza urbana*, 1, pp. 1–38.

Riker, W.H. (1986) *The Art of Political Manipulation*. Yale: Yale University Press.

Roggeband, C. and Vliegenthart, R. (2007) 'Divergent Framing: The Public Debate on Migration in the Dutch Parliament and Media, 1995–2004', *West European Politics*, 30(3), pp. 524–548. doi:10.1080/01402380701276352.

Rovny, J. (2012) 'Who Emphasizes and Who Blurs? Party Strategies in Multidimensional Competition', *European Union Politics*, 13, pp. 269–292.

Rovny, J. and Edwards, E.E. (2012) ' Struggle over Dimensionality Party Competition in Western and Eastern Europe', *East European Politics & Societies*, 26(1), pp. 56–74.

Rudolph, C. (2007) 'National Security and Immigration in the United States after 9/11', paper presented at the *Penn Program on Democracy, Citizenship and Constitutionalism*, University of Pennsylvania, Philadelphia.

Rydgren, J. (2008) 'Immigration Sceptics, Xenophobes or Racists? radical right-Wing Voting in Six West European Countries', *European Journal of Political Research*, 47(6), pp. 737–765.

Scheufele, D.A. (2000) 'Agenda-Setting, Priming, and Framing Revisited: Another Look at Cognitive Effects of Political Communication', *Mass Communication and Society*, 23(3), pp. 297–316.

Sigona, N. (2008) *The Latest Public Enemy: The Case of the Romanian Roma in Italy.* OSCE/ODHIR Working Paper. Available at: www.osservazione.org (Accessed 15 April 2013).

Sjursen, H. (2002) 'Why Expand? The Question of Legitimacy and Justification in the EU's Enlargement Policy', *Journal of Common Market Studies,* 40(3), pp. 491–513.

Sniderman, P. and Theriault, M. (2004) 'The Structure of Political Argument and the Logic of Issue Framing'. In: Saris, W.E. and Sniderman, P. eds. *Studies in Public Opinion: Attitudes, Non-Attitudes, Measurement Error and Change.* Princeton: Princeton University Press, pp. 133–165.

Statham, P. and Trenz, H.J. (2012) *The Politicization of Europe: Contesting the Constitution in the Mass Media.* London and New York: Routledge.

Steinberg, M.W. (1999) 'The Talk and Back Talk of Collective Action: A Dialogic Analysis of Repertoires of Discourse among Nineteenth-Century English Cotton-Spinners', *American Journal of Sociology* 105, pp. 736–80.

Stimson, J.A. (2004) *Tides of Consent. How Public Opinion Shapes American Politics.* Cambridge: Cambridge University Press.

Stokes, D.E. (1963) 'Spatial Models of Party Competition', *The American Political Science Review,* 57(2), pp. 368–377.

Stokes, D.E. (1992) 'Valence Politics'. In: Kavanagh, D. ed. *Electoral Politics.* Oxford: Oxford University Press, pp. 141–164.

Swanson, D.L. and Mancini, P. (1996) 'Patterns of Modern Electoral Campaigning and their Consequences'. In: Swanson, D.L. and Mancini, P. eds. *Patterns of Modern Electoral Campaining and their Consequences.* Westport, CT: Praeger Publishers, pp. 246–276.

Tampakoglou, E. (2014) 'Mainstream Political Discourse and its Implications: The Case of Greece'. In: Peterson, B. and Bevelander, P. eds. *Crisis and Migration: Implications of the Eurozone Crisis for Perceptions, Politics, and Policies of Migration.* Lund: Nordic Academic Press, pp. 103–130.

Tan, Y. and Weaver, D.H. (2007) 'Agenda-Setting Effects among the Media, the Public, and Congress, 1946–2004', *Journalism and Mass Communication Quarterly,* 84, pp. 729–744.

Thränhardt, D. (1995) 'The Political Uses of Xenophobia in England, France and Germany', *Party Politics,* 1(3), pp. 323–345. doi: 10.1177/1354068895001003002.

van Baar, H.J.M. (2011) *The European Roma: Minority Representation, Memory, and the Limits of Transnational Governmentality.* Unpublished PhD dissertation. Amsterdam School for Cultural Analysis.

Van der Brug, W. and van Spanje, J. (2009) 'Immigration, Europe and the 'New' Cultural Dimension', *European Journal of Political Research,* 48, pp. 309–334.

Van Spanje, J. (2010) 'Contagious Parties: Anti-Immigration Parties and their Impact on Other Parties' Immigration Stances in Contemporary Western Europe', *Party Politics,* 16(5), pp. 583–586.

Vliegenthart, R. and Roggeband, C. (2007) 'Framing Immigration and Integration', *International Communication Gazette,* 69(3), pp. 295–319.

Walgrave, S. and Nuytemans, M. (2009) 'Friction and Party Manifesto Change in 25 Countries', *American Journal of Political Science,* 53(1), pp. 190–206.

Walgrave, S. and Varone, F. (2006) 'Agenda Setting and Focussing Events: Bringinig Parties Back In: Policy Change After the Dutroux Crisis in Beligium', paper presented at the *Séminaire du Staff*, Departement de Science Politique, Université de Genève. Available at: www.unige.ch/ses/spo/Accueil-1/Papiers/Walgrave-et-Varone.pdf (Accessed 22 February 2014).

Weiner, M. (1993) 'Security, Stability, and International Migration', *International Security*, 17(3), pp. 91–126.

Wirth, W., Matthes, J., Schemer, C. Wettstein, M. Friemel, T., Hänggli, R. and Siegert, G. (2010) 'Agenda Building and Setting in Referendum Campaign: Investigating the Flow of Arguments Among Campaigners, the Media and the Public', *Journalism and Mass Communication Quarterly*, 87(2), pp. 328–345.

Wolfsfeld, G. (1997) *Media and Political Conflict: News from the Middle East*. New York: Cambridge University Press.

Wolfsfeld, G. (2011) *Making Sense of Media & Politics. Five Principles of Political Communication*. New York: Routledge.

Zaller, J. (1992) *The Nature and Origins of Mass Opinion*. Cambridge: Cambridge University Press.

3   Local politics, migration and integration in Italy

Migration to Italy: an overview

From emigration to immigration

Research on the politics of migration in Europe has overwhelmingly devoted itself to traditional immigration destinations like Germany, the United Kingdom, the Netherlands and France, which have experienced large-scale migration since the 1950s and 1960s. Far less attention has been devoted to countries in Southern Europe, which have only more recently become host societies, but are increasingly concerned by international migration, as every year thousands of people drown in the waters between Africa and Italy. As the ongoing refugee crisis demonstrates, Italy today plays a crucial role in the migration route to Europe, and events taking place on the Mediterranean have played a fundamental role in shaping public debates on migration. Today, Italy is at the core of the military patrol operations launched by the EU in the Mediterranean with the claimed goal of preventing further migration tragedies and of detecting illegal immigrants, and the regular migrant 'crises' experienced in its southern regions are customarily and widely addressed by the news media and national political actors.

Colombo and Sciortino report that immigration to Italy is commonly described as a 'new' phenomenon (2004, p. 49). The novelty refers not only to the beginning of the influx, generally held to coincide with the oil crisis of the early 1970s (when Italy's balance of migration became positive), but also to the difference between *old* and *new* types of immigration. Previously, Italy was a prominent example of classical migration flows: first, massive emigration took place in the nineteenth and twentieth centuries, mainly towards the Americas, followed by a smaller but still significant wave in the aftermath of World War II, when hundreds of thousands of Italians moved to the industrialized countries of Northern Europe as labour migrants. Since then the in- and outflow of migration has reversed, transforming Italy from a net emigration country into a net immigration destination. The shift has been attributed to push factors in the sending countries, such as conflicts and poverty (Macioti and Pugliese, 1991), as well as the development of restrictions on immigration in the older immigration destinations, which had the unintended effect of transforming Southern European countries into second-best choices for international migrants (Pugliese, 2002).

Italian immigration is considered unplanned because it resulted from transnational economic forces and choices of neighbouring countries more than from an actual willingness of Italian governments to attract migrants. For this reason, migration to Italy is hardly comparable to the strategic, state-led recruitment of foreign labour in Northern Europe. Some scholars have contested the second-best destination hypothesis (Colombo and Sciortino, 2004; Massey, 2002), underlying the specificities of the Italian economic 'miracle' *(miracolo economico)* of the 1950s and 1960s, and stressing the growing demand for labour in specific sectors of production, including informal ones.[1]

In the 1980s the increased inflow of immigrants became more consistent and steady, and began receiving greater media and public attention (Bonifazi, 1998; Macioti and Pugliese, 1991; Sciortino and Colombo, 2004). In line with most other Western European countries, however, it is only in the 1990s that Italy started experiencing the steady arrival of labour migrants and refugees from countries outside of Europe and, after 1990, from Central and Eastern Europe. During the 2003–2010 period the total number of foreign residents in Italy had almost tripled, from 1.5 to 4.2 million persons (ISTAT, 2010). Their share of total population is currently above 7%, which is still below the level of traditional destination countries in Europe, such as the U.K., France or the Netherlands (11%), but also Germany (12%), Sweden (14%) and Austria (15%), and Southern European countries such as Spain (14%).[2]

Figure 3.1 below displays the evolution of regular migration to Italy between 1985 and 2010, showing that the total inflow of migrants coming from outside EU-15 has grown progressively over the last two decades, with major peaks in 2002–2003 and 2008 due to government-led regularization campaigns. Throughout the 1990s and 2000s the amount of foreign-born residents more than doubled, increasing from less than half a million to more than one million (Figure 3.2). If in 1991 the ratio of foreign residents over the total Italian population was only 0.6%, in 2001 it had increased four times (2.3%), and in 2011 it reached 7.2%. By 2013, Italy counted about 4.4 million foreign-born residents. The number and the share of immigrants are still on the rise (334,000 more than in 2012, with a growth of +8.2%).

All these figures, however, only refer to foreigners residing in Italy under a legal status. Although estimations on the magnitude and features of irregular immigration are by definition quite difficult to come by, the *Fondazione Iniziative e Studi Sulla Multietnicità* (ISMU) provides since 2005 an annual survey on illegal migration to Italy. According to these estimates, the total foreign population by 2010 was above five million. The number of irregular immigrants residing in the country is assumed to fluctuate between 541,000 in 2005 to 651,000 in 2008, with Eastern Europe as the principal area of origin (ISMU, 2010a, 2010b).

Besides the quantitative dimension, the Italian immigrant community has seen qualitative changes as well, most notably in terms of main countries of origin and type of migration. A distinctive characteristic of the Italian immigration experience has to do with the country's considerable socio-cultural and economic differences across regions. In this sense, regional economies and labour market structures explain varying patterns of migrant labour recruitment, and the settlement of migrants across the country (Bonifazi *et al.,* 2009). Figure 3.3 shows the

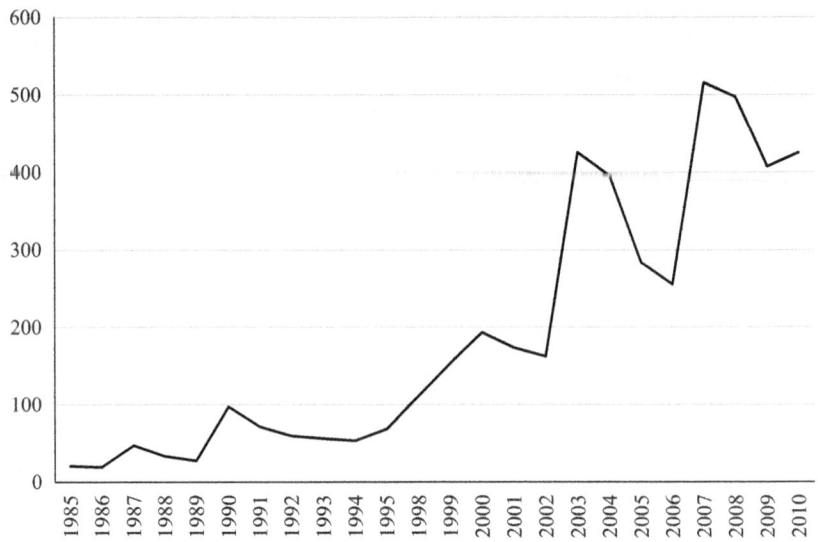

Figure 3.1 Total inflow of foreign population in Italy 1985–2010 (in thousands of people)
Source: OECD Statistics, 2010 (www.stats.oecd.org).

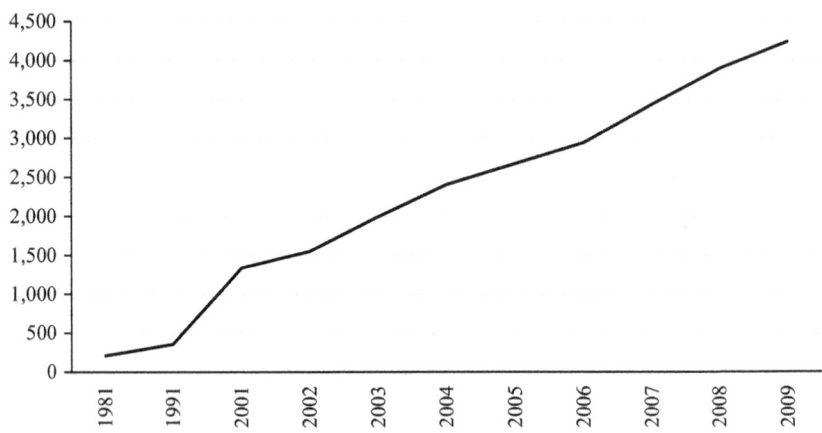

Figure 3.2 Foreign-born residents in Italy 1981–2009 (in thousands of people)
Source: Italian National Institute of Statistics (www.dati.istat.it).

distribution of immigrant residents across Italian municipalities, as a percentage of the total population. The figure illustrates the unequal distribution of immigrants across the country, as well as the varying proportions they make up of the total population at the municipal level. Central and Northern Italy offer employment in the industrial sector, whereas immigrant labour in the South is mainly concentrated in domestic and agricultural work.

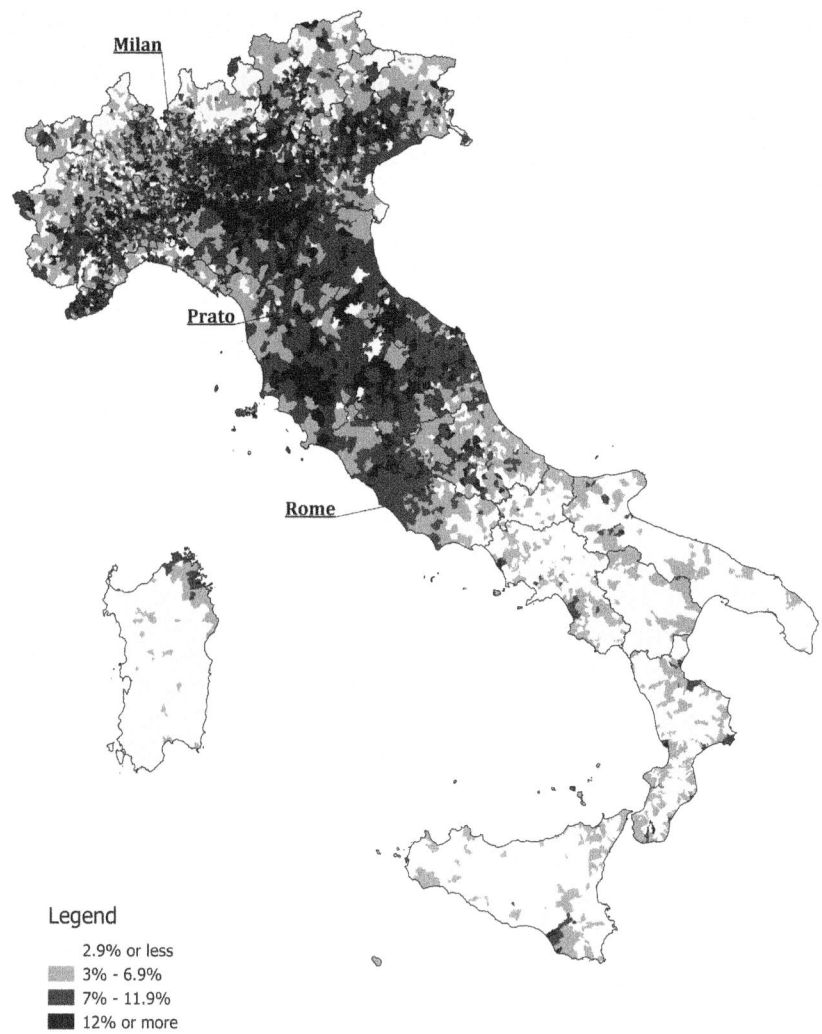

Figure 3.3 Share of immigrant residents in Italian municipalities, 2010

Source: Italian National Institute of Statistics (www.dati.istat.it).

Since pull factors in Italy vary geographically, migrants have progressively moved towards northern regions in search for stable and better-paid employment (King and Andall, 1999). As a result, the highest proportions of migrants are found in the regions of the Northeast (10.1% of total population) and Northwest (9.7%). Central regions have somewhat lower proportions (Lazio, Umbria, Toscana, Marche: 9.1%), while the South and the islands have substantially lower proportions of immigrants (3%). The regions hosting the largest numbers of immigrant residents are Emilia Romagna (11.3% of the total population), Umbria (11%), Lombardy (10.7%) and Veneto (10.2%).

Data from 1993 show an absolute predominance of large urban areas in terms of foreign residents, with particularly high concentrations in Rome and Milan. Already in the year 2000, however, migrant settlement had reached medium-sized towns such as Prato, Vicenza or Reggio Emilia. Recent statistics from 2007 show medium-sized cities (e.g. Prato, Brescia) overtaking the large urban areas of Milan, Rome and Turin in terms of immigrant concentration. As pointed out by Bonifazi *et al.* (2009, p. 44), however, 'immigrants no longer find work in large industrial estates in the suburbs but look for work in the service sector. They have the skills to carry out financial activities and advanced services, and still supply the labour force [. . .] needed even in the central sectors of the economy.' Today, migrants represent 12–13% of the population in northern cities such as Milan, Piacenza, Brescia, Mantova and Modena. In the centre, Prato's immigrant population makes up 14.7% of the total, which is higher than most other cities (Firenze, Perugia and Macerata, 11%). In the South, the concentration is generally lower: 7% in L'Aquila and Teramo.

In sum, there seem to be three territorial patterns of migrant settlement (Ambrosini, 2013). First, the industrial city of the centre-north, where male migrants find jobs as factory workers or in services related to industrial production, whereas female migrants find jobs in the domestic or care sectors. The second model is that of large metropolises, such as Rome and Milan, where migrant work is differentiated across the construction sector, restaurants, cleaning services and transportation. The third model is the temporary employment model of southern regions, which reproduces the 1980's model of initial 'gateway' employment for new migrants: jobs are mostly temporary and irregular, many workers do not have a regular status and are employed in the harvesting of Mediterranean agricultural products.

Migrant communities in Italy

The regionally-differentiated set of pull factors identified in the previous section played a key role in determining the ethnic composition of Italy's immigrant population. Already in the 1970s, communities of foreigners had settled in different areas of the country: 'Yugoslavs in the North, Tunisians in western Sicily, Ethiopians and Somalis in Rome and Filipino and Cape Verdean domestic servants recruited to work in wealthy households in the big cities' (King and Andall, 1999, p. 137).

Detailed information on the composition of the Italian immigrant population is shown in Figure 3.4 below. The largest communities of legal migrants during the 1980s were the French and the North Americans (data not in figure: 10.9% and 8.8%, respectively), and the total number of foreign residents was about 200,000. By the 1990s the largest group had become the Moroccans, and the total amount of foreigners had doubled. In the early 2000s, the total number of foreign residents increased to more than one million, mainly due to the inflow of Moroccans and Albanians. From the mid-2000s, moreover, Italy experienced a remarkable inflow of Romanian citizens. Romanian migrants were only a few thousands in the early 1990s,[3] but increased to 50,000 by the end of the decade. The state-sponsored regularization campaign of 2002 documented the presence of 240,000 Romanian temporary residents. The unofficial inflow of Romanian workers benefited from the country's negotiations with the EU: starting from January 2002, Romanian citizens became able to enter the Schengen Area without need of a visa for a three-month stay; following entry into the EU in 2007, Romanian residents in Italy have increased by about 100,000 per year. In 2013, one-fourth of the 4.5 million foreign residents in Italy were Romanian. The highest concentration of Romanian residents is in the regions of Lazio (36.2%) and Piedmont (34.4%). In Rome alone, there are more than 154,000 Romanian residents; 95,000 reside in Turin and 39,000 in Milan (Mara, 2012).[4]

The inflow of Romanian migrants in Italy has been accompanied by growing concerns from politicians and the media, which have often referred to EU enlargement as the source of an alarming 'tidal wave' of Romanian (and Bulgarian) migrants (Sigona, 2011), often incorrectly associated to Romanian Roma, or *Romani*. Despite most Romani settlements in Italy dating back more than fifty years, the arrival of Romani war refugees and economic migrants from the

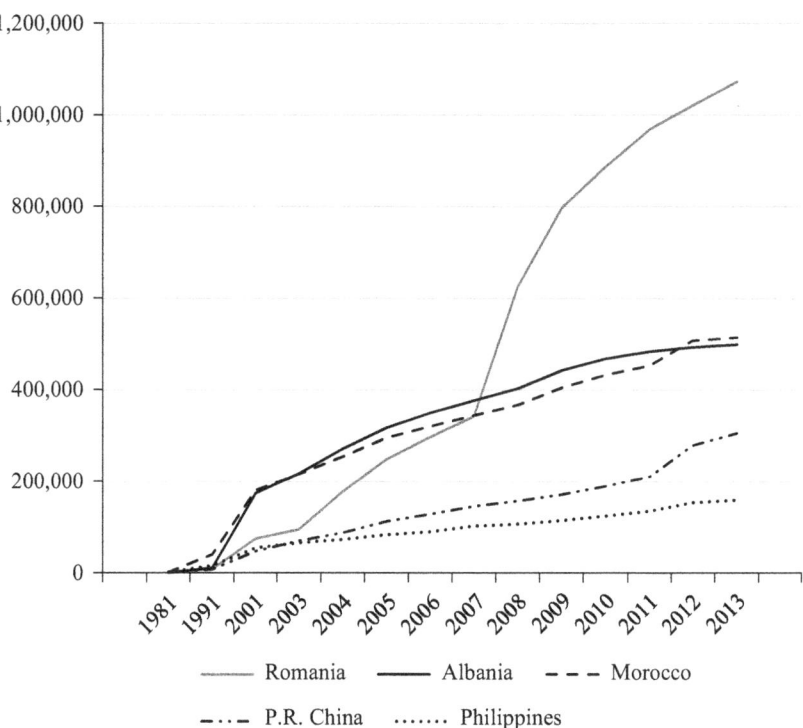

Figure 3.4 Nationality of foreign-born residents 1981–2013 (in thousands of people)

Source: Italian National Institute of Statistics (www.dati.istat.it).[5]

successor republics of Yugoslavia and more recently from Romania has changed the balance between Italian and foreign Roma (Sigona and Trehan, 2009).

Yet, the overall Romani population in Italy is considerably small, numbering 140,000–160,000 people (Clough Marinaro, 2010). The largest community is settled in Rome, with estimates ranging between 7,200 and 15,000. The hysterical tone of media reports resulted in collapsing several different groups into one single category. Although the Romanian Roma are commonly referred derogatorily as *zingari* and *nomadi,* which correspond to the English *gypsies,* these terms are used interchangeably as synonyms for Roma, and serve as shortcuts for all groups and subgroups of allegedly nomadic peoples. These terms, moreover, are incorrectly yet commonly used to define, and express negative attitudes towards, the Romanian (and to a lesser extent Bulgarian) immigrant population at large (Sigona, 2008).

In 2007 and 2008, the mass media gave much attention to criminal events involving Roma migrants (Sigona, 2008), and the government issued an emergency law facilitating the removal and expulsion of EU citizens from Italy in case of a threat to public and national security. The proclamation of the state of emergency resulted in waves of evictions: just in the municipality of Rome, local authorities evicted more than six thousand people from illegal camps in less than one year (Clough Marinaro and Daniele, 2011). Politicians and the media articulated security measures and repression of Roma people in terms of 'zero tolerance' towards illegality. The Berlusconi government undertook numerous policy initiatives, among which a decree appointing special commissioners in charge of implementing all necessary measures to deal with 'the state of emergency in relation to the settlements of nomad communities in Campania, Lombardy and Lazio' (Sigona, 2008). These measures – subsequently extended to Piedmont and Veneto – included the monitoring of the camps and the identification of all their residents, including minors.

The second largest group of foreign residents in Italy originates from Morocco. At least in the early stages, Moroccan immigration had to do with increasingly restrictive immigration policies in France and Northern Europe. Workers of Moroccan origin were generally reaching Italy with touristic visas, and then settling illegally in the industrial areas of Northern Italy. As a result, the government introduced processes of collective regularization of foreign workers,[6] by which Moroccan immigrants could legalize their status. Ever since, the number of Moroccan residents in Italy has grown steadily over time: 93,000 in 1996; 195,000 in 2000; and about 300,000 in 2005. According to the National Institute of Statistics (ISTAT), by 2013 there were over half a million Moroccan residents in Italy (71%).

Albanian migration in Italy is closely linked with Albania's transition to democracy in the 1990s. The first arrivals of Albanian refugees in the late 1990s (generally in small groups on boats or rafts) were followed by the decision of the Italian government to offer political asylum to the hundreds of Albanians who found refuge in the Italian embassy in Tirana. This triggered the first wave of mass migration, with about 25,000 Albanians reaching Southern Italy between March and August 1991. These events created channels of illegal migration in the years to come. The second wave of migration followed the Albanian economic crisis of

1997, when more than 9,000 people reached Italy in less than two months, mainly by means of self-made rafts or via smugglers. The third wave of migration followed the descent of Kosovo into war, when thousands of Albanian Kosovars left the country over a few months in 1999. From 1991 to 2001, the number of Albanians in Italy grew from 10,000 to more than 170,000, and the increase continued in the following years, reaching 460,000 in 2009. By 2013, the Albanians in Italy are 497,000, 60% of which are resident in the North, 27% in the centre, and 13% in the South and the islands.

The fourth largest foreign community in Italy is the Chinese. Pretty much like the rest of Western Europe, Chinese immigration to Italy can be traced back to the early years of the twentieth century, but it has significantly increased in terms of numbers and ratio only in the last 25 years. Figure 3.5 below shows the territorial distribution of Chinese residents across Italian provinces.

The first waves of Chinese migration took place in the early 1980s and were driven by job opportunities in the Italian textile and leather industries, where the first Chinese migrants had already been employed in the interwar years. In a relatively short time, however, chain-migrants developed self-entrepreneurial activities in the gastronomic and trade sectors, as well as in ethnic services. These were mainly oriented at importing 'Made in China' commodities and providing ethnic-specific services: groceries, hairdressers, video stores, call centres, translation services (Ceccagno, 2004a).

As shown in Figure 3.5, the largest communities reside in the large metropolitan areas of Rome and Milan, and in the so-called Chinese Industrial Triangle of the Tuscan cities of Florence, Prato and Empoli (Caritas, 2006). Overall, one-third of Chinese in Italy live in Central Italy, in particular in Tuscany (21%), especially in Prato (9.5%). The size of the Chinese community grew steadily over the past years, and the number of Chinese residents has doubled throughout the last decade. In addition, illegal migration and residence is common, as confirmed by the results of the regularization campaign of 2002, which confirmed the presence of more than 35,000 Chinese illegally residing in Italy.

The Filipinos – the fifth largest foreign community and one of the first migrant groups to reach the country in the late 1970s – found initial employment in Italy as temporary workers. By now, there are a significant number of permanent residents, reunited families and second-generation citizens. The community is mainly concentrated in the metropolitan areas of Northern and Central Italy (Milan hosts about one-third of the total Filipino population), where 80% to 90% of Filipino residents find employment as either domestic workers or caregivers (ERCOF-IOM, 2010).

Italian migration law and policy

The national context

As illustrated earlier, it was only in the 1980s that immigration emerged as a relevant policy issue and entered the Italian public debate. In its early stages, the

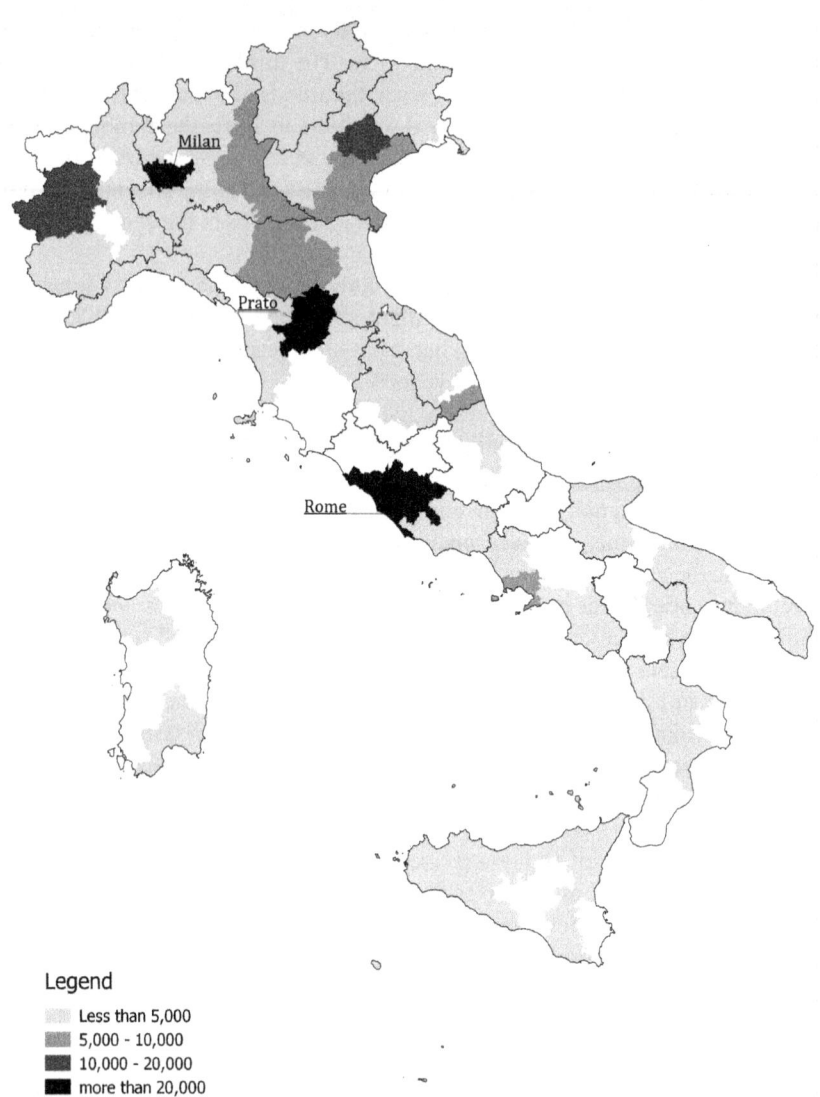

Figure 3.5 Distribution of residents of Chinese origin across Italian provinces
Source: Italian National Institute of Statistics (www.dati.istat.it).

debate was characterized by a high degree of consensus among political actors, most of whom saw immigration mainly from the point of view of labour relations. The discussion dwelled on the need to protect, on the one hand, native workers from unfair competition, and on the other, the rights of immigrants based on Christian ethics or international workers' solidarity. The first law on immigration was approved in 1986, and it provided a definition of the system of controls and employment of foreign workers to Italy, introducing the concept of family unification and providing measures to regularize migrants already resident in the Italian territory.

Consensus, however, resisted only as long as the issue was kept away from public and media attention (Statham, 1998). By the early 1990s, in fact, small government coalition parties *(Partito Repubblicano Italiano)* and radical right opposition parties *(Movimento Sociale Italiano)* started challenging the 'right to immigrate' (Magnani, 2012) and developed a renovated form of nationalism (Ignazi, 1992, 2002). Mainstream parties addressed problems of social inclusion and the need for measures enabling immigration control and expulsions. Both aspects were subsequently included in the new immigration law, which regularized more than 300,000 illegal residents. The late 1990s marked a change in Italy's immigration policy, with the passing of the so-called *Turco-Napolitano* law by the newly elected centre-left coalition government, which aimed at challenging opposition parties on illegal immigration. The Italian centre-right, in fact, asked for tougher controls on migration, and demanded the criminalization of illegal entry.[7] The new law introduced a quota system for employment-related immigration and new measures concerning expulsion, including detention centres for undocumented migrants.[8]

The right-wing coalition of Silvio Berlusconi, who entered into office in 2001, brought about a more securitized discourse on migration. As reported by Magnani (2012), the new government aimed to regulate immigration based on professional qualifications, knowledge of Italian culture and potential threat to societal security, and were facilitated by divisions among opposition parties, with the centre-left advocating a quantitative limitation of legal flows, and the radical left challenging the policy of expulsions. Polarization increased the salience of migration in the electoral programmes of both coalitions, before the approval of restrictive measures by the government in the *Bossi-Fini* law, which broadened considerably the area of irregularity for which expulsion applied. The new measures primarily concerned admission quotas and family reunification, next to a system of internal controls linking the right and duration of residence to the availability of a labour contract. This implied that a legal working immigrant who had lost her job would become illegal and thus eligible for forced repatriation. Policy-making on migration during Berlusconi's governments, moreover, contributed to the symbolic criminalization of migrants, by broadening the practice of fingerprinting and by extending the scope of externalized policies of control. The crime of illegal immigration and residence, however, was not introduced until the third Berlusconi government, within the 2009 Security Act, which culminated a growing debate over security in Italy. The law, which tripled the detention time for illegal migrants, faced profound criticism by opposition parties and interest groups, and the Italian Constitutional Court struck down some of its most restrictive measures.

The period covered in this study, therefore, corresponds to the peak of a *crescendo* of immigration policies in Italy, both in terms of the breadth of areas covered by legislation and in terms of the selectivity of admission criteria. Where the

1980s and early 1990s Italy were characterized by a high tolerance toward illegal residents (in terms of mass-regularization campaigns and openness towards intercultural dialogue), the decades since have been characterized by increasingly tight controls and securitization. Migration policy in Italy turned increasingly selective, discriminating between low-skilled workers and high-skilled professionals, and structuring the system of integration exclusively on employment, which facilitates the sudden transformation of legal residents into illegal, unemployed aliens. This implies that migrants' access to social rights and citizenship is subject to a level of uncertainty comparable to that of guest workers in post-war Europe (Caponio and Graziano, 2011), which in turns fostered criminalization campaigns against illegal residents and further securitization.

Local governments

The purpose of this section is to investigate the role of local authorities in developing and implementing immigration policy in Italy. Cities represent a fundamental catalyst for migration flows, as they provide job opportunities in the tertiary sector in large urban areas, and in the small and medium-sized enterprises of industrial areas and in their hinterlands. Hence, previous literature recognized the relevance of local governance of migration in Europe (Alexander, 2003, 2004; Caponio and Borkert, 2010; Lapeyrronie, 1992; Mahnig, 2004; Penninx *et al.,* 2004; Rogers *et al.,* 2001), as well as in Italy (Campomori, 2005; Caponio, 2006; Cinalli *et al.,* 2009; Crosta *et al.,* 2000; Fasano and Zucchini, 2001; Zincone and Caponio, 2006). Italian local governments in particular have become fundamental actors not only for the implementation of national policies, but also for developing new ones through the joint efforts of three levels of local governance: cities, provinces and regions (Caponio, 2006; Zincone and Caponio, 2006). Municipal administrations, in fact, coordinate the main aspects of multi-annual programmes with regional authorities, but preserve a certain degree of autonomy in managing and providing immigration-specific services.

Similar to other European countries, the first Italian legislation on immigration made exclusive reference to 'national interests', within a strongly centralized framework of policy-making and implementation. Since the early 1990s, however, national regulations have increasingly involved local authorities, identifying a number of domains and areas in which local administration could operate autonomously or in cooperation with national ones. These involved primarily the organization and provision of services for immigrant residents and communities, and less so the multi-level management of migration flows and the management of local labour market integration. Local administrations are responsible for the welcoming, hosting and accommodation of migrants upon their arrival and subsequent stay, but they officially have no voice in the development of specific plans and on the arrangement of funding. In addition, municipal governments are responsible for many aspects concerning the socio-cultural integration of migrants, their social and medical assistance, and issues such as housing, education in the Italian language and vocational training.

How actively municipalities can pursue the integration of migrant residents therefore largely depends upon the resources allocated by regional governments to welfare and social policies. Yet, through the 'System of protection of asylum seekers, refugees and foreigners holding humanitarian permits', the national government delegates the management of the most critical social problems related to immigrants, alongside urgent humanitarian matters, to its urban counterparts. Hence, municipalities have to develop projects dealing with issues of trafficking, management of unaccompanied minors and monitoring of refugees and asylum seekers in their territory. In terms of immigration policies, the national government consults its municipal and regional counterparts to define the three-year programmatic plans of immigration control and the yearly quotas regulating the inflow of foreign workers. In coordination with the national government, regions can also promote projects responding to the specific needs of local labour markets, and interact with sending countries in order to develop professional training programmes.

Local administrations in Italy also have substantial competences in the fields of crime prevention and urban security, which are often used to address immigration affairs. The delegation of powers of injunction to Italian mayors, in fact, was one of the answers to the interethnic conflicts and violence of the 1990s in a number of northern Italian cities (Regione Piemonte, 2012). The process of delegation of security competences to local administrations accelerated from 2006 onward, irrespective of the alternation in government between centre-left and centre-right cabinets. Although city administrations act as agents of the national governments, they have been appointed extensive injunction powers for the normative regulation of urban security *(competenze in materia di sicurezza urbana),* applying to both ordinary and extraordinary circumstances. City administrations develop Security Pacts[9] with the Ministry of Internal Affairs, consisting of working plans for the allocation of financial and human resources, as for the implementation of specific actions for 'tackling, for instance, Roma issues or counterfeiting crimes, as well as the exploitation of prostitution and illegal commercial activities' (Servizio Studi del Senato, 2010).

In sum, Italian municipalities indisputably perform a fundamental role in the development and implementation of legislation on immigration and integration, in particular with respect to involuntary migrants. In addition, they carry out key functions in educational, socio-cultural and welfare policies for legal residents, and they contribute to the development and promotion of plans based on the needs of local labour markets. The competences of municipal administrations, however, also depend on the availability of financial resources, meaning that city governments are not fully autonomous and can pursue their policy preferences only within the budgetary boundaries set up at the regional level. This notwithstanding, city-level authorities are responsible for policy-making on all three dimensions of the immigration issue that were discussed in the previous chapter: more or less autonomously, they operate on emergencies related to involuntary migration, on the distribution of welfare resources and management of labour issues, and on the socio-cultural integration of migrant residents.

Milan, Prato and Rome

This section discusses the context in which local politics takes place. For each city, it will describe how and why the immigration issue has entered public agendas, focusing on migratory patterns and discussing its implications in terms of cultural and economic integration, territorial development, security and welfare. I will show that the immigration profiles and models of integration of Rome, Milan and Prato are substantially different, which results in distinct opportunities for the politicization of migration.

Migration in Milan

As reported by Foot (1999), migration to Milan can be divided into two main periods, the first one involving Italians (1950s and 1960s) and the second one involving non-Italians (from the 1980s onwards), mainly dissidents from Latin America and Africa, international students and domestic workers from Ethiopia, Eritrea and the Philippines. In addition, the city hosted a number of Chinese enterprises and a relatively sizable Chinese community. In the 1980s, the two main communities of Egyptian and Eritreans moved to Milan to find employment in steelwork and in the domestic sector, and subsequently developed autonomous entrepreneurship activities. Until the end of the decade, however, these communities were scarcely visible because the municipal administration did not engage in integration and accommodation projects, so that most new residents (just like Italians in the 1950s) found housing in the suburbs and in the newly urbanized areas around the city of Milan. A second inflow of foreign workers took place in the early 1990s, when recently regularized North African workers left the informal sector in the South for Milan. Over these years, the migrant community diversified in terms country of origin,[10] thanks to the increase of female migrants from Central and South American countries. As the municipality did not plan to assign available or new houses to the growing non-Italian population of the city, religious and civil society organizations interceded in helping migrants obtaining access to the rented housing market in the city hinterland.[11]

Today, Milan hosts one of the largest migrant communities in Italy, counting 240,000 foreign residents over a total population of 1.35 million (17.6%). This is the result of the different waves of foreign immigration that have characterized the city over the last decades: Chinese migrants that have long worked in Lombardy's textile industry; political migrants and refugees from Latin America and the Balkans; North African workers attracted by opportunity in heavy industry; and Filipino workers employed in the tertiary and domestic sector. Table 3.1 below shows the principal nationalities of foreign residents in Milan in 2012, compared to previous population measurements in the 1980s and 1990s.

Peruvian, Ecuadorian and Filipino settlement in Milan followed similar paths, as female migrants employed in domestic care (in the late 1990s) were progressively joined by their families (throughout the 2000s). At the national level, more than 60% of Peruvian and Ecuadorian women residing in Italy work in the family

Table 3.1 Nationality of main groups of foreign residents in Milan 1979–2011[a]

Milan

Country of origin	2011	%	2005	%	2000	%	1995	%	1989	%	1979	%
Philippines	37,002	15.6%	26,645	16.4%	18,685	15.9%	6,505	10.1%	1,551	4.4%	16	0.1%
Egypt	31,999	13.5%	20,992	12.9%	13,309	11.3%	7,473	11.6%	3,829	10.8%	706	3.3%
P.R. China	20,852	8.8%	13,110	8.0%	8,675	7.4%	3,576	5.6%	1,595	4.5%	166	0.8%
Peru	19,655	8.3%	13,784	8.5%	7,965	6.8%	1,357	2.1%	176	0.5%	16	0.1%
Sri Lanka	14,512	6.1%	9,872	6.1%	6,118	5.2%	2,362	3.7%	455	1.3%	12	0.1%
Ecuador	14,232	6.0%	12,356	7.6%	2,006	1.7%	149	0.2%	34	0.1%	8	0.0%
Romania	12,701	5.4%	5,536	3.4%	1,752	1.5%	541	0.8%	193	0.5%	214	1.0%
Morocco	8,071	3.4%	6,067	3.7%	5,849	5.0%	3,294	5.1%	556	1.6%	116	0.5%
Ukraine	6,913	2.9%	2,995	1.8%	132	0.1%	2	0.0%	-	-	-	-
Bangladesh	4,738	2.0%	2,268	1.4%	1,120	1.0%	337	0.5%	18	0.1%	5	0.0%
Albania	5,441	2.3%	4,273	2.6%	2,205	1.9%	438	0.7%	19	0.1%	34	0.2%
El Salvador	3,720	1.6%	2,497	1.5%	1,751	1.5%	1,127	1.8%	507	1.4%	38	0.2%
Brazil	3,498	1.5%	2,580	1.6%	1,864	1.6%	1,173	1.8%	471	1.3%	83	0.4%
Moldova	2,971	1.3%	1,151	0.7%	41	0.0%	-	-	-	-	-	-
Ethiopia / Eritrea[b]	498	0.2%	2,603	1.6%	2,678	2.3%	2,351	3.7%	1,926	5.4%	567	2.7%
Senegal	2,124	0.9%	1,791	1.1%	2,002	1.7%	684	1.1%	94	0.3%	8	0.0%
Other origin	47,928	20.2%	34,359	21.1%	76,152	64.6%	31,369	48.7%	11,424	32.2%	1,989	9.3%
Tot.	236,855	100.0%	162,879	100.0%	117,816	100.0%	64,372	100.0%	35,495	100.0%	21,374	100.0%
Tot. Pop. (%)	1,341,830	(17.6%)	1,307,545	(12.4%)	1,303,279	(9.0%)	1,305,364	(4.9%)	1,432,184	(2.3%)	1,655,599	(1.3%)

[a] Data reported for the main nationalities of origin. 'Other origin' also refers to citizens of EU-15 and EFTA-countries, Andorra, San Marino, Monaco, North America, Australia and New Zealand.
[b] Cumulative data for Ethiopia and Eritrea since Eritrea obtained independence only in 1993.

Source: Comune di Milano, Settore Servizi Statistici (http://dati.comune.milano.it/).

services (Caritas, 2009). The Sri Lankan community of Milan is the largest such community in Italy, accounting for one-fifth of the 80,000 residents in the country. Sri Lankan migrants first settled in Milan in the 1990s, mainly temporarily prior to moving to Northern European countries. Today, instead, the city represents a first choice, as is shown by the growing rates of family reunification and of the inscription of Sri Lankan minors in Milan's schools (Ministero del Lavoro, 2012). Similarly, their traditional short-term employment in cleaning and surveillance companies has been more recently substituted by more long-term activities in food and ethnic services (Ministero del Lavoro, 2012).

Egyptians, Moroccans and other North African migrants are also central to Milan's immigrant panorama, as the city hosts one of the largest Muslim communities in Italy. This partly explains the visibility of migration affairs in the 2011 municipal elections, when the electoral campaign involved an open conflict over Muslim residents. In particular, the debate was triggered by the proposal by the centre-left candidate to construct an Islamic religious centre for the large Muslim population of Milan, before developing into a debate over diversity and cultural and religious identity (Allievi, 2010). Over the previous years, Islamic communities in Milan voiced their discontent with the lack of official Islamic worship places within the city. Since the only official Milanese mosque is located in Segrate, on the city's outskirts, Muslims gathered spontaneously in unofficial places such as abandoned buildings and big tents. Until the election campaign of 2011, however, the centre-right administration of the city had been strongly opposing the construction of a mosque, claiming the 'Christian roots' of Italian culture, and advancing potential dangers (mainly related to terrorism) associated with the recognition of Muslim communities by municipal authorities.

Moreover, numerous public controversies have dogged the Islamic community of Milan, including the Abu Omar case in 2003, concerning the disappearance of the Imam of Milan, Hassan Mustafa Osama Nasr.[12] National and international media reported this as one of the better-documented cases of extraordinary rendition. After being transferred to Egypt for interrogation, Hassan Nasr was released by an Egyptian court in 2007, which ruled that his detention was 'unfounded'. The subsequent court case raised public controversy in Italy on the behaviour of Italian and U.S. intelligence, before resulting in a ruling of the Court of Appeals of Milan (2013) sentencing the former deputy directors of Italy's military intelligence agency, and the CIA station chief in Italy, to up to 10 years of jail.[13] Before that, issues related to political Islam and radicalization have long characterized the Milanese Muslim community. Already in 1998, Milanese prosecutors claimed that Milan was the hub of a European terrorist network involving groups in France, Belgium and Switzerland.[14] In 2007 one Imam and 10 affiliates were arrested for criminal activities linked to terrorism and for attempting to recruit suicide bombers among illegal migrants in the city.[15] In the same year, a homemade bomb exploded in front of the religious centre of Via Quaranta, in Milan, producing no victims.[16] In 2008, the Ministry of Internal Affairs denounced the 'confirmed ideological intransigence' of one of the largest Muslim groups in the city (Via Quaranta).[17]

Chinese migration in Prato

The city of Prato is the prototypical medium-sized Italian municipality, the second most populous city in Tuscany, and the third in Central Italy. Since 2001, the city has been recognized as part of a vast metropolitan area (almost 5,000 km²) encompassing the territorial areas of Florence, Prato and Pistoia. Similar to other Tuscan cities, the textile industry dominates the economy of Prato, representing one of the main industrial centres in the textile and clothing sectors in Europe and employing more than 35,000 workers (Confindustria Prato, 2012). Prato's history of immigration is therefore strictly intertwined with the settlement and entrepreneurship of Chinese migrants in Italy.[18]

Established in medieval times, Prato's textile sector developed rapidly in the nineteenth century, when the city became popularly known as 'the Manchester of Tuscany'. The industry reached its peak in the years of Italy's industrial boom, when the inflow of workers from Southern Italy doubled the size of the resident population. Over the last two decades, moreover, Prato and its industrial district attracted migrants from outside of Italy. While in 1991 migrants in Prato were just 1,500 (0.8% of the local population), their number increased almost tenfold during the 1990s. In 2001, 5% of the population was foreign, slightly above national figures. In the following decade, the number of immigrant residents in Prato continued its rocket growth reaching above 30,000 legal migrants in 2013, 17% of Prato's total population of 180,000.

From the 1990s, Chinese migrants have revitalized Prato's fashion industry, first by increasing the competitiveness of Italian companies with Chinese imports, then by taking over Italian companies with Chinese-owned ones. By now, it is common to find former Italian entrepreneurs employed as sales managers in Chinese enterprises. Migrants found the economic network necessary for the construction of small-scale enterprises and individual ventures, and Chinese businesses currently make up 97% of the foreign-owned enterprises in the city. Between 1997 and 2010, Chinese businesses in Prato hugely increased in number (from 479 to almost 5,000; Barbu *et al.,* 2013) and area of entrepreneurship, including restoration, housing and services (Campomori, 2008, Marsden, 2002). In the early 1990s more than 50% of the foreign immigrants residing in Prato were Chinese. Today this ratio is lower, yet the city still hosts the second largest Chinese community in Italy with almost 12,000 residents. According to recent estimations accounting for undocumented Chinese residents, the number could reach 25,000 (Barbu *et al.,* 2013).

Table 3.2 below illustrates the main nationalities of migrants in Prato over time. In line with general immigration trends in Italy, Chinese migrants entered as unregistered migrants, and subsequently profited from amnesties extended by the Italian government (Ceccagno, 2004b). Starting from the late 1990s, the increasing demand for foreign labour by local industries led to the inflow of Albanian and Moroccan, and subsequently Romanian and Pakistani workers, which over time have come to constitute sizeable communities through family reunification processes.

Table 3.2 Nationality of main groups of foreign residents in Prato 1988–2011[a]

Prato

Country of origin	2011	%	2005	%	2001	%	1996	%	1991	%	1988	%
P.R. China	11,882	38.0%	8,636	43.6%	4,806	45.7%	1,761	46.7%	1,008	51.7%	39	5.2%
Albania	4,642	14.8%	3,560	18.0%	1,766	16.8%	332	8.8%	400	20.5%	-	-
Romania	2,806	9.0%	869	4.4%	172	1.6%	29	0.8%	21	1.1%	2	0.3%
Pakistan	1,957	6.3%	1,533	7.7%	622	5.9%	61	1.6%	3	0.2%	2	0.3%
Morocco	1,540	4.9%	1,177	5.9%	709	6.7%	265	7.0%	102	5.2%	34	4.5%
Other origin	8,450	27.0%	4,013	20.3%	2,452	23.3%	1,319	35.0%	415	21.3%	677	89.8%
Tot.	31,277	100.0%	19,788	100.0%	10,527	100.0%	3,767	100.0%	1,949	100.0%	754	100.0%
Tot. Pop. (%)	188,579	(16.6%)	183,823	(10.8%)	176,023	(6.0%)	168,892	(2.2%)	166,688	(1.2%)	163,287	(0.4%)

[a] Data reported for the main nationalities of origin. 'Other origin' also refers to citizens of EU-15 and EFTA-countries, Andorra, San Marino, Monaco, North America, Australia and New Zealand.

Source: Italian National Institute of Statistics (www.istat.it) and Ufficio Statistiche Comune di Prato (statistica.comune.prato.it/).

The settlement of the Chinese community in Prato went hand in hand with public controversy and tensions with locals, accompanied by growing negative attitudes towards the foreign population. First, native residents tend to perceive migrants as mainly unregistered or illegal, working outside any national regulations and administrative control. Second, they are perceived as part of a closed and homogeneous community, which lack interest in interacting with the Italian one. Third, China is considered a threat to the Italian industry at large, and to the textile and fashion sectors of the 'Made in Italy' in particular (Johanson *et al.,* 2009). In addition, Prato has its own Chinatown. Despite being located close to the city centre, the Chinatown of Via Pistoiese is generally regarded as peripheral due to low-quality infrastructure and urban degradation, lack of public spaces and insufficient public services. Encompassing the main industrial estates of Prato, the area forms a *de facto* factory-city, and is separated from the rest of the town not only by architectural barriers, but also by the 'white flight' from the area (Barbu *et al.,* 2013). Overall, there are signs of increasing xenophobia on the side of the Italian community. Johanson *et al.* (2009) have reported growing concerns over the social costs that the city has paid over the last years, transforming its industrial status from capital-intensive to labour-intensive and from high-quality to low-quality production systems.

Local politicians and the media have echoed similar sentiments, fuelling the perception that the Chinese community is expanding too rapidly. In 2006, the last centre-left mayor of Prato, Marco Romagnoli, said that Chinese migration to Prato is an 'economic blessing' but 'a catastrophe for the community' (Johanson *et al.,* 2009). Similarly, the president of Prato's Chamber of Commerce said that the community underestimated Chinese entrepreneurs and their unfair competition: 'We need a battalion, an operation like the one in Iraq, to keep them under control' (Di Castro and Vicziany, 2009, p. 14). Tensions arose in 2007, when municipal authorities banned the parade for the Chinese New Year, in order to persuade the Chinese community to collaborate with the Italian one and respect local regulations (Di Castro and Vicziany, 2009). Two years later, the centre-right coalition won the municipal elections for the first time in the history of Prato, which had been until then a stronghold of the Italian Communist Party and left-wing administrations (Poli, 2009a, 2009b).

Migration and security in Rome

Rome hosts the largest migrant community in the country, with more than 300,000 residents over a total population of 2.6 million (11%). Unlike the vast majority of European capitals, the immigrant population in Rome is highly diversified, due to the weak relationships between Italy and its former colonies. As a result, the urban panorama is characterized by a strong variety of ethnic and migrant groups, with only few concentrations in specific areas of Rome and rare ethnic neighbourhoods.

Modern migration to Rome broadly follows the national patterns, so that overseas labour migrants became a significant social presence only in the last decades. As

observed by Lucciarini (2010, p. 64), Rome is peculiar in the settlement and integration of its migrants because of the lack of an open industrial sector for employment of foreign labour, which was instead integrated in the service sector and in
entrepreneurial activities. Over the 1960s and 1970s, Rome witnessed a first inflow
of female migrants from Cape Verde, Eritrea, Somalia and the Philippines, who
settled in the city mainly as domestic workers. Egyptians and Filipinos residing
in Rome were generally moving to other cities in Italy once they acquired a legal
status via regularizations and amnesties. The mid-1980s mark a steep increase and
differentiation of Rome's immigration patterns, with the first arrivals of Northern
and Central Africans, as well as Southeast Asians. Different from previous arrivals,
these migrants were generally males reaching Italy from other European countries
looking for employment in food services and small craft businesses. By the late
1980s and throughout the 1990s, these communities were joined by a conspicuous
inflow of male migrants from Eastern Europe. Polish, and subsequently Romanian,
Ukrainian, Moldavian and Russian migrants joined the construction industry and
the low-qualified manual sector, whereas female migrants – which often reached
Italy without a work permit – found jobs in the domestic sector.

Bangladeshi and Pakistani communities settled in Rome over the 1990s, became
particularly active in food services, and set up numerous small businesses in the
city centre, whereas refugees from Turkey, Iraq and Sub-Saharan Africa reached
the city towards the end of the decade. In the early 2000s, the main countries of
origin in Rome were Morocco, Albania, Romania and the Philippines, though
there was also a significant amount of Chinese residents. Although the number of
foreign residents in Rome has grown steadily over the years – remaining above
the national average – in the last decade, the foreign population more than doubled, with an increase of 108%. At the same time, migrants have also left the city
in order to settle in the belt of Rome or in smaller cities in the region. Today, the
largest immigrant community is the Romanian (see Table 3.3 below), accounting
for one third of the foreign residents in the city, followed by the Filipinos, Bang-
ladeshis and Polish.

Romanian migration in Rome was the engine of the broader stream of Romanian
settlement in Italy. The presence of Romanian migrants has been fundamental –
although often undervalued – for the economic and social growth of the capital
in the last two decades (Sigona, 2008). The building industry of the city has benefited significantly from the availability of Romanian labour, and so did the capital's social services thanks to the involvement of Romanian migrants in domestic
services and care. Even if often employed irregularly, migrants have played a
relevant social role in Rome's contemporary history, and significantly increased
the wealth of the city. Despite this, political propaganda has repeatedly targeted
the presence and use of public spaces by Romanians and Roma citizens, describing these communities as a threat to local ones. Sigona (2008) underlines the
out-of-proportion attention provided by the press to fatalities and criminal events
involving migrants, and their systematic use to generate moral panics, indignation
and calls for repressive interventions by local authorities.

Above all, the presence of Roma people stirs up the hottest debates on urban
security. Estimates indicate that the Romani living in Rome are 15,000–18,000,

Table 3.3 Nationality of main groups of foreign residents in Rome 2001–2012 [a]

Rome

Country of origin	2012	%	2005	%	2001	%
Romania	89,636	25.4%	23,148	16.0%	9,080	9.2%
Philippines	36,150	10.3%	15,897	11.0%	13,105	13.3%
Bangladesh	19,025	5.4%	5,542	3.8%	3,124	3.2%
Poland	15,148	4.3%	7,611	5.2%	5,587	5.7%
P.R. China	13,742	3.9%	4,642	3.2%	2,903	2.9%
Perù	13,370	3.8%	6,503	4.5%	4,920	5.0%
Ukraine	11,782	3.3%	3,894	2.7%	-	-
Ecuador	9,844	2.8%	4,529	3.1%	-	-
Egypt	8,318	2.4%	4,240	2.9%	3,198	3.2%
Moldova	8,110	2.3%	2,384	1.6%	-	-
India	7,860	2.2%	2,945	2.0%	2,213	2.2%
Sri Lanka	7,466	2.1%	2,908	2.0%	2,296	2.3%
Albania	7,421	2.1%	3,504	2.4%	2,183	2.2%
Ex-Yugoslavia	6,651	1.9%	4,611	3.2%	2,334	2.4%
Other origin	97,741	27.7%	52,646	36.3%	47,484	48.2%
Tot.	352,264	100.0%	145,004	100.0%	98,427	100.0%
Tot. Pop. (%)	2,638,842	(13.3%)	2,547,677	(5.7%)	2,545,860	(3.9%)

[a] Data reported for the main nationalities of origin. 'Other origin' also refers to citizens of EU-15 and EFTA-countries, Andorra, San Marino, Monaco, North America, Australia and New Zealand.

Source: Italian National Institute of Statistics (www.istat.it) and *Ufficio Statistiche Comune di Roma* (www.comune.roma.it).

most of whom are illegal, and approximately half of whom are originally from Romania. The most significant inflow of Romanian Roma started after 2001, but many had already reached the capital in the 1980s and 1990s from Eastern Europe and the Balkans. When Romania joined the EU, Italian media and politicians raised concerns about a possible 'invasion' by Roma and Romanian people (Sigona, 2008). As previously mentioned, however, public opinion and local politicians tend to conflate the category of Romanian residents and that of the Roma, considering both issues as emergencies. The local administration of Rome reacted to the appearance of unauthorized settlements with the strategy of forced evictions, with few – if any – efforts to build up dialogue with Roma communities. The 2007 emergency decree by the national government that facilitated the removal of EU citizens from the Italian territory targeted more or less explicitly the Romani community. The then-mayor of Rome Walter Veltroni commented in fact that: 'Before Romania entered the EU, Rome was the safest capital in the world. We need to repatriate people again; otherwise cities like Rome, Milan and Turin can't cope with the situation.'[19] The Roma 'emergency' and the subsequent moral panic influenced strongly the April 2008 municipal elections. The political campaign saw unprecedented emphasis on security issues, both from the media and from political actors, with episodes of open speculation on crime stories. This created unprecedented feelings of opposition to migration, in particular towards Romanians and the Roma (Milella, 2008; Vitale, 2008).

Notes

1 Italy's economic growth, in fact, was not achieved by means of mass production in large industries, but on the basis of small and medium-sized businesses located mainly in the northeast of the country. This model allowed successful performances without fully discarding two important pillars of the country's traditional system of production: the informal economy, and the underground labour market

2 Cf. Eurostat (2012). Available at: http://epp.eurostat.ec.europa.eu (29 May 2014).

3 According to ISTAT data, Romanian migrants in 1990 were only 8,000.

4 Despite the relatively recent migration, Romanian naturalization is also on the rise. In 2011 Romanian is the third largest community for naturalization rates, following Albanians and Moroccans.

5 Main groups of foreign-born residents, not born in EU-15, EFTA-countries, Andorra, San Marino, Monaco, North America, Australia, or New Zealand.

6 22,000 in 1986; 51,000 in 1990; and 34,000 between 1995 and 1996.

7 The criminalization of illegal migrants implied, according to the proponents, that all undocumented migrants that are found in the country would be arrested and forcibly expelled.

8 The centres were officially intended for the identification of irregular migrants. Irregular migrants included all migrants that have eluded immigration controls, as well as asylum seekers with pending applications and legal migrants who did not obtain or renew a residence permit. Irregular migrants could be detained at specified facilities for a period strictly limited to the time necessary to determine the identity and qualification for remaining in Italy, and for determining whether or not they should be deported.

9 Among the most notables Security Pacts are the following: *Patto per Milano Sicura* (approved by the city council of Milan on 18 May 2007); the three Security Pacts in Rome: *Patto per Roma Sicura* (18 May 2007; 29 July 2010; 21 December 2011); and *Patto per Prato Sicura* (31 July 2007 and 26 January 2010).

10 This happened mainly thanks to the progressive increase weight of migration from Eastern European countries and the Balkans, as illustrated earlier in this chapter.

11 As a result, most immigrant workers had to travel daily as commuters to reach their work place.

12 'Arrestate l'ex imam rapito dalla Cia', in *Il Corriere della Sera,* 25/06/2005.

13 'Italy convicts Air Force O-6 in CIA kidnap case', in *Military Times,* 4/11/2009.

14 'Terrorismo islamico: decine di arresti in Italia', in *La Repubblica,* 10/06/1998.

15 'L'Imam di Viale Jenner condannato a 3 anni e 8 Mesi', in *La Repubblica Milano,* 20/12/2007.

16 'Milano, ordigno alla moschea', in *La Stampa,* 02/02/2007.

17 V. Polchi, 'Moschee d' Italia, la mappa del rischio', *La Repubblica,* 08/03/2008.

18 Without entering into a discussion that would be too extensive for this section, it is important to underline that – at the national level – Moroccan enterprises are the most widespread in Italy among immigrant-owned economic activities (16.9% of the total amount of immigrant enterprises), followed by Romanian (14.3%) and Chinese ones (13.6%). In particular, Tuscany and the Prato area represent one the most privileged locations for Chinese and immigrant entrepreneurship in Italy.

19 G. Vitale, 'Intervista a Veltroni "Basta orrori, è emergenza nazionale",' in *La Repubblica,* 01/11/2007.

References

Alexander, M. (2003) 'Local Policies Toward Migrants as an Expression of Host-Stranger Relations: A Proposed Typology', *Journal of Ethnic and Migration Studies,* 29(3), pp. 411–430.

Alexander, M. (2004) 'Comparing Local Policies Toward Migrants: An Analytical Framework, a Typology and Preliminary Survey Results'. In: Penninx, R., Kraal, K.,

Martiniello, M. and Vertovec, S. eds. *Citizenship in European Cities. Immigrants, Local Politics and Integration Policies.* Ashgate: Aldershot, pp. 57–84.

Allievi, S. (2010) *La Guerra delle moschee.* Venezia: Marsilio.

Ambrosini, M. (2013) 'Immigration in Italy: Between Economic Acceptance and Political Rejection', *Journal of International Migration and Integration,* 14(1), pp. 175–194.

Barbu, M., Dunford, M. and Weidong, L. (2013) 'Employment, Entrepreneurship, and Citizenship in a Globalized Economy: the Chinese in Prato', *Environment and Planning,* 45, pp. 2420–2441.

Bonifazi, C. (1998) *L'immigrazione straniera in Italia.* Bologna: Il Mulino.

Bonifazi, C., Heins, F., Strozza, S., Vitiello, M. (2009) *The Italian Transition from Emigration to Immigration Country.* IRPPS Working Papers, n. 24. Available at: www.irpps.cnr.it/e-pub/ojs/index.php/wp/article/view/24/73 (Accessed 2 June 2011).

Campomori, F. (2005) 'Integrare l'immigrato? Politiche di accoglienza a Vicenza, Prato e Caserta'. In Caponio, T. and Colombo, A. eds. *Stranieri in Italia. Migrazioni globali, integrazioni locali.* Bologna: Il Mulino, pp. 235–266.

Campomori, F. (2008) *Immigrazione e Cittadinanza Locale: La governance dell'integrazione in Italia.* Roma: Carocci Editore.

Caponio, T. (2006) *Città italiane e immigrazione: discorso pubblico e politiche a Milano, Bologna e Napoli.* Bologna: Il Mulino.

Caponio, T. and Borkert, M. (eds.) (2010) *The Local Dimension of Migration Policymaking.* Amsterdam: Amsterdam University Press.

Caponio, T. and Graziano, P.R. (2011) 'Towards a Security Oriented Migration Policy Model? Evidence from the Italian Case'. In: Carmel, E., Cerami, A. and Papadopoulos, T. eds. *Migration and Welfare in the New Europe: Social Protection and the Challenges of Integration.* Bristol: Policy Press, pp. 105–120.

Caritas Migrantes (2006) *Dossier immigrazione.* Rome: Antarem.

Caritas Migrantes (2009) *America Latina-Italia: vecchi e nuovi migranti.* Roma: Idos.

Ceccagno, A. (2004a) 'New Chinese Migrants in Italy', *International Migration,* 41(3), pp. 187–213.

Ceccagno, A. (2004b), *Giovani migranti cinesi – La seconda generazione a Prato.* Prato: Franco Angeli.

Cinalli, M., Morales, L., Bengtsson, B., Giugni, M., Kohut, T., Statham, P., Varadi, L., Wiener, N. (2009) 'Deliverable D5b: City Reports on Discurisve Indicators of the Local-multidem Porject', *LOCALMULTIDEM Project Report,* Available at: http://thedata.harvard.edu/dvn/dv/localmultidem/faces/study/StudyPage.xhtml;jsessionid=acd01a8 0aea9614ab78c7d4b7053?globalId=doi:10.7910/DVN/25658&studyListingIndex=0_ acd01a80aea9614ab78c7d4b7053 (Accessed 10 October 2014).

Clough Marinaro, I. (2010) 'Life on the Run: Biopolitics and the Roma in Italy', Paper presented at the *International Conference: Romani Mobilities in Europe,* 14–15 January 2010, University of Oxford.

Clough Marinaro, I. and Daniele, U. (2011) 'Roma and Humanitarism in the Eternal City', *Journal of Modern Italian Studies,* 16(5), pp. 621–636.

Colombo, A. and Sciortino, G. (2004) 'Italian Immigration: The Origin, Nature and Evolution of Italy's Migratory Systems', *Journal of Modern Italian Studies,* 9(1), pp. 49–70.

Confindustria Prato (2012) *Evolution of the Prato Textile District.* Prato: Unione Industriale Pratese.

Crosta, P., Mariotto, A. and Tosi, A. (2000) 'Immigrati, territorio e politiche urbane. Il caso Italiano'. In: Agenzia Romana per la Preparazione del Giubileo ed. *Migrazioni. Scenari per il XXI secolo.* Rome: ARPG, pp. 1215–1294.

Di Castro, A. and Vicziany, M. (2009) 'Chinese Dragons in Prato: Italian-Chinese Community Relations in a Small European Town', *Asian Business and Economics Research Unit Discussion Paper 47.* Prato: Monash University.

ERCOF-IOM (2010) 'The Italy-Philippines Migration and Remittance Corridor' *Economic Resource Center for Overseas Filipinos and International Organization for Migration,* Markaty City, Philippines.

Eurostat (2012). *Demographic Outlook: National Reports on the Demographic Developments in 2010.* Luxembourg: Publications Office of the European Union.

Fasano, L. and Zucchini, F. (2001) 'L'implementazione locale del testo unico sulla immigrazione'. In: Fondazione Cariplo ed. *Sesto rapporto sulle migrazioni 2000.* Milan: Franco Angeli, pp. 39–50.

Foot, J. (1999) 'Immigration and the City: Milan and Mass Immigration 1958–1998', *Modern Italy,* 4(2), pp. 159–172.

Ignazi, P. (1992) 'The Silent Counter-Revolution: Hypotheses on the Emergence of the Extreme Right-Wing Parties in Western Europe', *European Journal of Political Research,* 22, pp. 3–35.

Ignazi, P. (2002) *Il potere dei partiti. La politica in Italia dagli anni Sessanta a oggi.* Bari: Laterza.

ISMU (2010a) *Quindicesimo rapporto sulle Migrazioni 2009.* Milano: FrancoAngeli. ISBN 978–88–568–1622–8

ISMU (2010b) *Sedicesimo rapporto sulle Migrazioni 2010.* Milano: FrancoAngeli. ISBN 978–88–568–3500–7

ISTAT (2010) *La Popolazione Straniera Residente in Italia al 1° Gennaio 2010.* Rome: Istituto Nazionale di Statistica.

Johanson, G., Smyth, R. and French, R. (2009) *Living Outside the Walls: The Chinese in Prato.* Newcastle upon Tyne: Cambridge Scholars Publishing.

King, R. and Andall, J. (1999) 'The Geography and Economic Sociology of Recent Immigration to Italy', *Modern Italy,* 4(2), pp. 135–158.

Lapeyrronie, D. (ed.) (1992) *Immigrés en Europe: politiques locales d'intégration.* Paris: La Documentation Française.

Lucciarini, S. (2010) *Immigranti e città. Il caso di Roma.* Unpublished PhD Thesis, University of Rome, Roma Tre, Rome.

Macioti, M.I. and Pugliese, E. (1991) *Gli immigrati in Italia.* Bari–Rome: Laterza.

Magnani, N. (2012) *Framing Immigration Control in Italian Political Elite Debates: Changing Discourses about Territory, Identity and Migration.* Bologna: Emil.

Mahnig, H. (2004) 'The Politics of Minority-Majority Relations: How Immigrant Policies Developed in Paris, Berlin and Zurich'. In: Penninx, R., Kraal, K., Martiniello, M. and Vertovec, S. eds. *Citizenship in European Cities. Immigrants, Local Politics and Integration Policies.* Aldershot: Ashgate, pp. 17–37.

Mara, I. (2012) *Surveying Romanian Migrants in Italy Before and After the EU Accession: Migration Plans, Labour Market Features and Social Inclusion.* Research Report 378, July 2012, Vienna Institute for International Economic Studies

Marsden, A. (2002) 'Il ruolo della famiglia nello sviluppo dell'imprenditoria cinese a Prato'. In: Colombi, M. ed. *L'imprenditoria cinese nel distretto industriale di Prato.* Florence: Olschki, pp. 71–103.

Massey, D.S. (2002) 'La Ricerca Sulle Migrazioni Nel XXI Secolo'. In: Colombo, A. and Sciortino, G. eds. *Stranieri in Italia, Assimilati Ed Esclusi.* Bologna: Il Mulino, pp. 25–52.

Milella, L. (2008) 'Sicurezza, Berlusconi promette Subito le misure anti crimine', *La Repubblica,* 22 April 2008. Available at: http:/ricerca.repubblica.it/repubblica/

archivio/2008/04/22/sicurezza-berlusconi-promette-subito-le-misure-anti.html (Accessed 5 May 2013).

Ministero del Lavoro e delle Politiche Sociali (2012) *La Comunità Srilankese in Italia: Rapporto annuale sulla presenza degli immigrati, 2012.* Rome: Ministero del Lavoro.

Penninx, R., Kraal, K., Martiniello, M. and Vertovec, S. (eds.) (2004) *Citizenship in European Cities. Immigrants, Local Politics and Integration Policies.* Ashgate: Aldershot, pp. 57–84.

Poli, S. (2009a) 'Dopo 63 anni la sinistra perde la capitale del tessile Cenni passa per 1.600 voti ed esulta: Risultato storico', *La Repubblica*, 23 June 2009. Available at: http:// ricerca.repubblica.it/repubblica/archivio/repubblica/2009/06/23/dopo-63-anni-la-sinis tra-perde-la.html (Accessed 29 September 2012).

Poli, S. (2009b) 'Cardini: "Pratesi, non cedete alla destra l' ultima ridotta della democrazia"', *La Repubblica*, 21 June 2009. Available at: http://ricerca.repubblica.it/repub blica-archivio/repubblica/2009/06/21/cardini-pratesi-non-cedete.html (Accessed 29 September 2012).

Pugliese, E. (2002) *L'Italia tra migrazioni internazionali e migrazioni interne.* Bologna: Il Mulino.

Regione Piemonte (2012) 'Sicurezza Urbana: Le competenze degli Enti locali, quelle dello Stato e la cooperazione tra Enti'. *Manuale a dispense sulla sicurezza urbana,* 1, pp 1–38.

Rogers, A., Tillie, J. and Vertovec, S. (2001) 'Introduction: Multicultural Policies and Models of Citizenship in European Cities'. In: Rogers, A. and Tillie, J. eds. *Multicultural Policies and Model of Citizenship in European Cities.* Aldershot: Ashgate, pp. 1–14.

Sciortino, G. and Colombo, A. (2004) 'The Flows and the Flood: the Public Discourse on Immigration in Italy, 1969–2001', *Journal of Modern Italian Studies,* 9(1), pp. 94–113.

Servizio Studi del Senato (2010) 'L'evoluzione della normativa in materia di pubblica sicurezza fra Stato, Regioni ed enti locali', *Dossier Servizio Studi del Senato – XVI legislatura*, n.210/April

Sigona, N. (2008) *The Latest Public Enemy: The Case of the Romanian Roma in Italy.* OSCE/ODHIR Working Paper. Available at: www.osservazione.org (Accessed 15 April 2013).

Sigona, N. (2011) 'The Governance of Romani people in Italy: Discourse, Policy and Practice', *Journal of Modern Italian Studies*, 16(5), pp. 590–606.

Sigona, N. and Trehan, N. (2009) 'Introduction: Romani Politics in Neoliberal Europe'. In: Sigona, N. and Trehan, N. eds. *Romani Politics in Contemporary Europe Poverty, Ethnic Mobilization, and the Neoliberal Order.* Basingstoke: Palgrave McMillian, pp. 1–20.

Statham, P. (1998) 'The Political Construction of Immigration in Italy: Opportunities, Mobilisation and Outcomes', *Discussion Papers FS III,* Berlin: Wissenschaftszentrum, pp. 98–102.

Vitale, G. (2008) 'Alemanno-Rutelli, sfida su rom e Alitalia: Roma in pericolo. Il nemico è la Lega', *La Repubblica*, 23 April 2008, Available at: http://ricerca.repubblica.it/repub blica/archivio/repubblica/2008/04/23/alemanno-rutelli-sfida-su-rom-alitalia-roma-in. html (Accessed 11 September 2013).

Zincone, G. and Caponio, T. (2006) 'The Multilevel Governance of Migration'. In Penninx, R., Berger, M. and Kraal, K. eds. *The Dynamics of International Migration and Settlement in Europe: A State of the Art.* Amsterdam: Amsterdam University Press, pp. 269–304.

Part 2
Empirical analysis

4 Migration debates in context

Introduction

This study claims that looking at the salience of immigration as a whole provides only a very superficial image of electoral campaigning. Instead, it seeks to show that there are multiple ways in which political entrepreneurs can approach complex issues, and that these multiple choices account for the variation in debates across local settings. To this end, this chapter looks at the way in which immigration was mobilized in the six electoral campaigns under study, investigating the immigration issue's salience as a whole, the relative importance of its constitutive dimensions across city contexts, and the degree to which each dimension is used in order to express support or opposition to immigration. In doing so, it provides a first overview of the nature and characteristics of the immigration debate in Italian local elections, addressing the context hypotheses developed in Chapter 2.

As I illustrated in the previous chapter, the development of political conflict over migration in Italy was influenced by the considerable differences in terms of the timing and geographic distribution of immigration *within* Italy. This chapter follows on this by analysing whether these contextual differences can account for the politicization of migration at the local level. The logics explaining variation in local debates is derived from cross-national models prevalent in immigration studies, which illustrated the relationship between migration debates and national citizenship and migration regimes (Green-Pedersen and Krogstrup, 2008; Ivarsflaten, 2008; Kitschelt and McGann, 1997; Rydgren, 2008; Thränhardt, 1995; van der Brug and van Spanje, 2009). Similarly, at the local level it is likely that migration is discussed primarily in reference to the actual competences that local politicians and authorities possess in handling migration and integration affairs (Bommes and Thranhardt, 2010; Freeman, 1995).

Although the distinction between the symbolic and actual responsibilities of local authorities in the enforcement of law and order is often blurred (Biorcio and Vitale, 2011; Vitale, 2012), local administrations have gained in the past years extended competences in 'urban security' affairs, which have been used to reframe immigration in terms of law and order. Local governments frequently use emergency mayoral orders, to deny to 'nomads' the right to mobility and parking, allegedly for reasons of public health and safety, and have developed in the mid-2000s specific plans to tackle the so-called Roma emergency (Sigona, 2011).

According to Vitale (2012), the majoritarian, highly personalized logics of local politics in Italy led to a further emphasis on the symbolic role of local authorities as agents of law and order, especially the mayors. In this sense, the security pacts that local administrations agreed with regional and national authorities throughout the last decade marked a turning point in redefining the governance of security in Italian municipalities in terms of immigration.

In Rome, the 2007 pact referred the need for multi-level coordination to strengthen the activities of identification and expulsion of illegal foreigners and communitarian citizens who commit crimes or represent a danger for the city.[1] Even more explicitly, the Security Pact of Milan (2007) reports that the city 'suffers from the presence of numerous illegal extra-communitarian citizens and nomads, who have settled permanently in its territory making use of abusive structures and abandoned buildings'.[2] Finally, the security pacts in Prato for 2008 were 'made necessary since the city of Prato is one of the Italian territories with the higher ratio of foreign citizens over Italian residents, and is characterized by the high concentration of companies operated by extra-communitarians, especially Chinese'.[3] These documents offer just an example of the importance of law and order among the actual responsibilities and the symbolic competences of local administrations. Accordingly, it is likely that similar aspects constitute the bulk of local debates on immigration in mayoral electoral campaigns. Hence, local debates on immigration should be generally oriented towards security more than any of the two other issue dimensions, and I expect migration and integration to be primarily approached in terms of public order, emergency and security.

In addition, previous studies have underlined that the dynamics of interethnic competition and threat have to do with a mix of national and local factors, because contextual effects are not always as ubiquitous as they were once thought to be (Hopkins, 2007). Substantial resources and welfare-related assets are now directly managed by local administrations, which are in charge of distributing them among local constituencies, including immigrants. Local politicians must therefore develop political discourses to justify their choices and challenge their opponents' proposals. If institutional factors at the national level may explain differences in policy-making and discourse, the same is likely for the politicization of immigration in local electoral competitions, on the basis of local-level opportunity structures. Hence, as suggested in the theory section, local conditions and characteristics should influence substantially migration debates at the city level, so that different local settings are characterized by specific profiles. The cities were identified due to the characteristics of their immigrant populations, which is associated with a specific dimension of the immigration issue, and therefore likely to come to dominate electoral campaigns. Milan's foreign population paves the way to developing debates on the cultural and religious integration of migrants in the public sphere; campaigns in Prato are likely to discuss migration primarily in terms of the economic dimension due to the weight of the Chinese economy in the territory; and Rome – hosting the largest Romanian and Roma community in Italy – provides fertile grounds for securitized immigration debates.

Finally, concerning the difference across election campaigns, the theoretical chapter introduced the hypothesis of an effect of focusing events on the dimensional politicization of immigration. As outlined earlier, the growing alarm over the risks of a 'tidal wave' of migrants from Romania and Bulgaria in Italy grew exponentially in the period of the 2007 EU enlargement. Old and deeply-rooted prejudices and widespread *antiziganism* contributed to stirring a debate on an alleged invasion by Romanian Roma (Sigona, 2008, 2011; see also: ERRC, 2000; Sigona, 2006; Sigona and Monasta, 2006). The climax was reached in November 2007, few months before the mayoral elections in Rome, with the murder of an Italian woman by a Romanian Roma citizen in a peripheral neighbourhood in the capitol city. The national government responded to the incident by issuing, as a matter of 'necessity and urgency', an emergency law facilitating the removal of EU citizens from Italy in case of threat to public security (n. 181/2007). By officially recognizing the existence of a security emergency, these events are likely to have provided further incentives to politicize immigration in terms of law and order for the 2008 electoral campaign in Rome.

This chapter shall therefore look at electoral debates on migration across the three cities and six election campaigns. First, I look at the salience of the issue as a whole, measuring the fluctuation in the importance that is attributed to migration over time and across cities. Second comes an analysis of the relative importance of each dimension of immigration and an overview of the differences across cities and electoral campaigns. Finally, I investigate the articulation of support and opposition to migration in the three cities. By looking at the interrelations between the salience and the tone of the three political dimensions, a pattern of preferences between supporters and opponents of immigration in terms of issue dimensionality becomes apparent. I find that, although both sides of the debate make reference to law and order arguments, with symmetrical strategies between opponents and supporters of migration, the way in which dimensions are mobilized changes considerably across city contexts. The final part of the chapter therefore discusses the general implications of the empirical evidence for this study's framework, paving the way for the investigation of the electoral strategies of local political actors in migration debates.

Issue salience

To begin with, I look at the relative share of attention devoted to the immigration issue compared to all other issues debated in each city and electoral campaign. The total amount of core sentences coded in the national and local newspapers was 21,680, among which 2,408 sentences made reference to the immigration issue. Accordingly, the average salience of immigration across the whole period and the three city contexts was 11%. The rest of the attention was dedicated to a number of different local issues which are not relevant to the present study and which were not taken into consideration. Assessing the relevance of a political issue only based on its own share of attention (rather than looking at the distribution of attention across all the issues of an electoral campaign) is always a risky endeavour, as the best understanding of the importance of any issue is provided by complete figures. To cope with this limitation, I compare this assessment to benchmarks from previous studies based on similar data and designs. In this perspective, the importance given by the Italian media to the immigration issue in local campaigns is somewhat higher, yet generally comparable to the one reported in previous studies.

With respect to other European countries (namely Austria, the UK, France, Germany, the Netherlands and Switzerland), Kriesi *et al.* (2012) show that the immigration issue gained importance over time: its salience was very limited in the 1970s (1.6%), but it has increased greatly over the following decades, and in particular in the 1990s (7.4%) and the 2000s (8%). Similarly, Boomgaarden and Vliegenthart (2009), indicate that when immigration-related news account for more than 10% of the media attention, the issue can be considered salient. For the Italian case, previous research underlined that the 2006 elections marked a turning point in the politicization of migration, which never received as much attention in national election campaigns during the previous decades (Urso and Carammia, 2014). Although recent analysis of Italian TV and newspapers in 2008 (Morcellini *et al.,* 2009) shows a salience of the immigration issue of only 5%, previous research on immigration claims making in Milan over six months in 2006 shows quantitatively comparable results to the ones I retrieved for the two months preceding municipal elections (Cinalli *et al.*, 2009).

Concerning the observed period, therefore, I can conclude that the immigration issue is not only salient, but also somewhat more important than is normally the case at the national level in Italy. Nonetheless, the data suggest that this is not systematically the case. Table 4.1 reports the salience of immigration by electoral years in each of the municipal case studies under observation. The overall attention to the immigration issue increased between the first and the second electoral campaign in each city, both in absolute and in relative terms. The largest increases take place in Rome (+8.8% between 2006 and 2008) and Milan (+7.6%). In Prato the increase is relatively more limited (+5.8), but this case shows the highest salience for immigration both in the first and second electoral campaign.

Table 4.1 Overall salience of immigration across city and electoral years (%)

	Milan		Prato		Rome	
	2006	*2011*	*2004*	*2009*	*2006*	*2008*
%	5.5	13.1	11.1	16.9	3.7	12.5
N	120	827	239	452	116	654
Tot. N	**2.159**	**6.288**	**2.149**	**2.681**	**3.149**	**5.247**

Note: Share of core sentences dedicated to the immigration issue in newspapers.

Source: Author's data (see Appendix 1).

Issue dimensionality

This section investigates the relative weight of each dimension of the immigration issue in the electoral campaigns in Prato, Milan and Rome. Let's recall that my overarching expectation is that the characteristics of the immigrant population across local settings influence the openness and accessibility of local public debates and actors to different problems related to migration, providing them with varying sets of discursive opportunities, resulting in different types of debates. Table 4.2 below reports the distribution of attention across the three dimensions of immigration in each of the three cities during the two electoral campaigns. As the table shows, there are considerable differences in the relative salience of each aspect.

Nonetheless, the results are not fully in line with the overarching expectation that there will be clear-cut dimensional profiles in each of the three cities. Although there are local characteristics in the debates of each city, this seems to only apply to the share of attention that is not already dedicated to security matters. As envisaged, in fact, it appears that the law and order dimension dominates the debate on immigration in all city contexts. Securitized arguments are often at the core of symbolic immigration politics, but local administrators also share a number of responsibilities with national governments and law enforcement agencies on matters of law and order. Hence, concrete and symbolic security aspects are frequently mobilized in election campaigns, as the law and order dimension represents an aspect of migration on which candidates are expected to intervene if they are elected, and it represents a crucial valence dimension for the public evaluation of the activities of local administrators.

Besides this, however, the three cities also provide quite distinctive attention profiles in terms of migration debates. The law and order dimension is fully hegemonic in Rome, where cultural and socioeconomic aspects receive only marginal

Table 4.2 The three dimensions of the immigration debate (%)[1]

	Milan		Prato		Rome		Total	
	2006	*2011*	*2004*	*2009*	*2006*	*2008*	*Time 1*	*Time 2*
Socioeconomic dimension	14.5	10.0	26.6	32.8	10.1	5.8	17.0	16.3
Cultural and religious dimension	39.7	31.7	32.4	24.5	14.2	11.8	28.8	22.6
Law and order dimension	45.8	58.3	50.0	42.7	75.7	82.4	57.2	61.1
Total	100%	100%	100%	100%	100%	100%	100%	100%
N	131	999	320	543	148	791	599	2.333

[1] In order to further investigate dimensional variation by city, we performed Chi-Square tests of goodness of fit on the values reported in the above table. The results of the tests indicate that the dimensional issue attention across cities are statistically different at both time *t1*: X^2 *(4, N = 599) = 52.1, p < 0.01* (Cramér's V = 0.23); and time *t2*: X^2 *(4, N = 2,333) = 364.5, p < 0.01* (Cramér's V = 0.31).

Note: Share of core sentences dedicated to the immigration issue in newspapers.

Source: Author's data (see Appendix 1).

levels of attention. Moreover, as immigration grew in importance in 2008, so did the relative attention dedicated to security aspects, as more than 70% of attention to the immigration issue concentrated on this dimension in 2006 and more than 80% in 2008. Although this provides initial evidence on the specific role of the focusing event in this city context, the data show that security issues ranked high in the immigration agenda also prior to the event. Securitization, in other words, is crucial to understand how migration affairs are treated in local electoral campaigns.

However, the socioeconomic dimension receives substantial attention only in Prato, where it gathers about a third of the overall attention to immigration in 2009. Even if thus not fully predominant (law and order considerations are relatively more important here as well), this dimension is clearly overrepresented in Prato when compared to Rome or Milan (where it is systematically ranked third). In this sense, Prato stands out as an exceptional case not only compared to the other two cities under study, but also *vis-à-vis* national figures showing that socioeconomic aspects are progressively losing importance to cultural and security ones (Buonfino, 2004). The debate on immigration in Milan, instead, did not follow the hypothesized pattern, since the issue was tackled mainly in terms of law and order arguments, and increasingly so over time. Still, again here the cultural and religious dimension receives a substantial share of attention, generally higher than in Rome and in Prato. Moreover, given the increasing importance of the issue as a whole in the electoral campaign of 2011, the salience of the cultural dimension grew over time in absolute terms. Where in 2006 this dimension accounted for 2.3% of the overall electoral debate, in 2011 cultural aspects 'weighed' twice as much, accounting for 4.7% of the overall attention in the campaign.

To conclude, this section provided additional evidence on the main features of local electoral campaigns and the immigration issue in Italy. As expected, local debates are securitized and strongly suffused with law and order arguments. Individual and collective security stand out as the main aspect through which migration is understood and articulated in public debate, not only because this dimension responds to the need for local governments to confront public opinion moods, but also because it concerns aspects of municipal government which local administrations actually have the institutional power to affect. What is more, the analysis suggests that the way in which immigration is debated varies substantially across city settings. Although the city profiles are not as clear-cut as hypothesized, there is substantial empirical evidence suggesting that local characteristics matter in setting up immigration debates. If one therefore considers migration as a multidimensional policy object, it is safe to conclude that the multiple elements in this bundle of issues relate different across local contexts. If securitization stands out as the dominant character across city settings, it is also appropriate to speak of multiple 'immigration debates', since the constitutive dimensions of the issue are mobilized differently depending on contextual opportunities and dynamics of electoral campaigning.

Opposition and support to migration

This section analyzes the patterns of opposition and support to migration during local electoral campaigns in Italy. As illustrated in the theory section, the choice of the evaluative component that is associated with each issue dimension depends on the social, cultural and ideological resources available to the actors involved in the debate (Williams, 2004). Moreover, given the difference in immigration debates across cities, it is also likely that the tone in which issue dimensions are debated varies. By looking at whether and to what extent each immigration claim is used to oppose or to support immigration by a given actor, I account for the general tone of the migration debate across cities and electoral campaigns, and the degree to which each dimension is mobilized to support or oppose immigration. Based on these aggregate figures, it then becomes possible to investigate the extent to which electoral campaigns differ from one another in how pro-immigration and anti-immigration discourses are articulated. Previous research suggests that high issue salience is accompanied by predominantly anti-immigration discourses (Green-Pedersen *et al.*, 2013), generally because of the weight of actors exploiting the 'symbolic' politics of immigration (Faist, 1994; Thränhardt, 1995), or more broadly because of the influence of negative public opinion on immigration on campaigning strategies (Alonso and Claro da Fonseca, 2009; Hopkins, 2010). Our analysis of media coverage of electoral campaigns cannot disentangle whether increased issue conflict leads to increased attention or whether, *vice versa,* increased media attention polarizes issue positions. Yet, I look at the two processes simultaneously, since increased salience is likely to lead to polarization of positions, and polarization is, in turn, likely to further increase media attention.

Figure 4.1 below reports the degree of opposition to and support for migration in the three cities at each point in time, plotted along the anti-immigration pro-immigration continuum.[4] As can be observed, five out of the six election campaigns moderately lean towards the anti-immigration end of the continuum, and so does the average position across the six campaigns (−0.4). The sharpest anti-immigration tone is found in the 2008 election in Rome (−0.7), followed by Prato in 2004 and Rome in 2006 (−0.5). The only marginally positive score emerged from the 2006 elections in Milan (+0.1), whereas the position of the 2009 immigration debate in Prato is only somewhat negative (−0.1). Over time, the average positions across the three cities indicate that the balance between support and opposition to immigration did not change: the aggregate values of the two election campaigns are both negative and identical (−0.4). Yet, the change in support and opposition to migration across election campaigns is not homogeneous for the three cities. In Milan, the debate was characterized by a sharp turn from being basically 'neutral' in 2006, when the issue was not very salient (+0.1), to being markedly opposed to it as the importance of the issue grew in the 2011 electoral campaign (−0.4). The debate in Rome was dominated by opposition to migration already when the issue received very little attention (in 2006: −0.4), and this predominance of anti-immigration arguments further expanded in 2008 (−0.7). Prato, instead, followed the opposite pattern, as the tone of the debate was markedly negative on immigration in 2004 (−0.5) and it became substantially more positive as the overall importance of the issue increased in 2009 (−0.1).

Having reviewed the general tone of immigration debates, my analysis turns now to the evaluative content of the three constitutive dimensions. While some

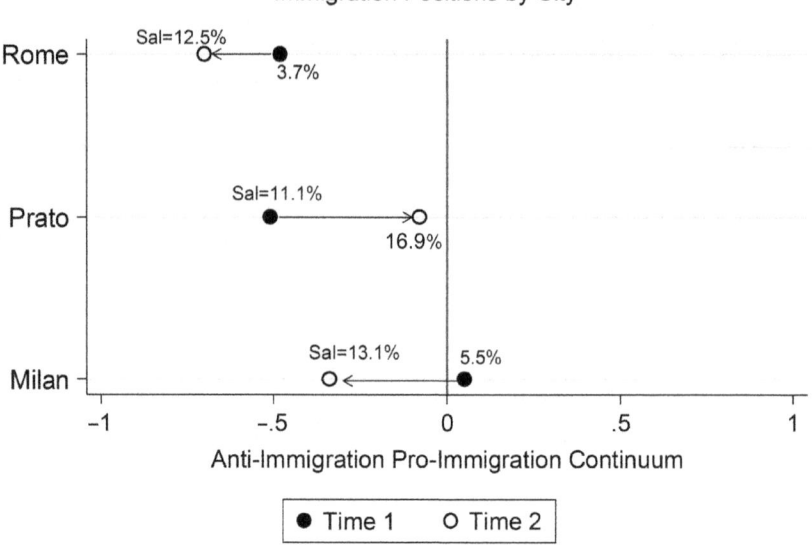

Figure 4.1 Average position towards immigration in Milan, Prato and Rome

Source: Author's data (see Appendix 1).

aspects of the immigration issue can be mobilized by either sides of the debate, in fact, others have a more clear-cut evaluative component, making them therefore less readily bipartisan. Although Chapter 6 offers a full discussion on the framing choices of parties engaged in electoral campaigning, I shall now focus on city differences, looking at whether the articulation of support and opposition to migration in terms of issue dimensions differs across the three cities. Table 4.3 below shows the relative composition of the competing discourses on migration in terms of issue dimension hierarchies. Vertically, the table shows the dimensional composition of the pro- and anti-immigration camps, whereas horizontally it shows the weight of pro- and anti-immigration arguments within debates on each of the three immigration dimensions.

At the most general level, the table confirms the previous findings that arguments in opposition to immigration largely outweigh supportive ones, and that the law and order dimension is the most recurring aspect that is debated in local electoral campaigns. Yet, two additional elements emerge from the analysis of the composition of the competing camps. On the one hand, the attention profile of the pro-immigration camp is more equally distributed (despite a tendency towards the cultural and religious dimension) than is the anti-immigration camp (which instead is skewed in favour of law and order arguments). On the other hand, the composition of dimensional debates show that negative arguments outweigh pro-immigration ones for both the socioeconomic dimension and, even more so, the law and order one, yet pro-immigration ones are somewhat more prominent when immigration debates focus on cultural and religious aspects. This provides

Table 4.3 Issue dimensions and competing discourses on immigration (%)[1]

Issue dimensions	Anti-immigration field	Pro-immigration field	Tot. %
Socioeconomic	14.2	20.9	-
N	234	144	378
% of dimension	61.9%	38.1%	100%
Cultural and religious	17.7	49.0	-
N	292	337	629
% of dimension	46.4%	53.6%	100%
Law and order	68.1	30.1	-
N	1.120	207	1.327
% of dimension	84.4%	15.6%	100%
Tot.	100%	100%	-
N	1.646	688	2.334

[1] The Chi-Square tests indicate that the association between dimensional preferences and the pro-immigration and anti-immigration camp is statistically significant: X^2 *(2, N = 2,334) = 312.2, p < 0.01* (Cramér's V = 0.37).

Note: Share of core sentences dedicated to the immigration issue in newspapers.

Source: Author's data (see Appendix 1).

initial evidence of the nexus existing between securitization of, and opposition to, migration.

In order to further investigate this, and based on these aggregate figures, I now look at which dimensions account for the change over time in the tone of the debates in the three cities. Figure 4.2 below reports the average positions on the anti-immigration pro-immigration continuum, in each city in each year, for the three dimensions of the immigration issue. In order to track changes over time in the tone of the debates and in the attention provided to the different aspects of immigration, the figure for each average position also specifies the absolute salience of the issue dimension during the electoral campaign.

The figure shows that the tone by which the three issue dimensions are debated in the three cities changes substantially over time. In particular, there is a high degree of conflict over cultural and religious aspects: arguments from this dimension were used to articulate support for immigration in three electoral campaigns (Milan and Rome, 2006; Prato, 2009), while they were used to express opposition in the remaining campaigns (Milan, 2011; Prato, 2004; Rome, 2008). Socioeconomic aspects are less subject to change in Prato and Rome than in Milan, whereas law and order values are negative in all cities and at all time points, meaning that this dimension is used mainly to express opposition to immigration. Again, this data confirms that securitization goes hand in hand with the progressive deterioration of debates on migration, as the general tone turns increasingly negative. A separate look at the three cities is useful to provide additional insights on the dynamics behind changes over time illustrated above. To this goal, I present in Tables 4.4a, 4.4b and 4.4c, the dimensional composition of the opposing camps for the two election campaigns in each city.

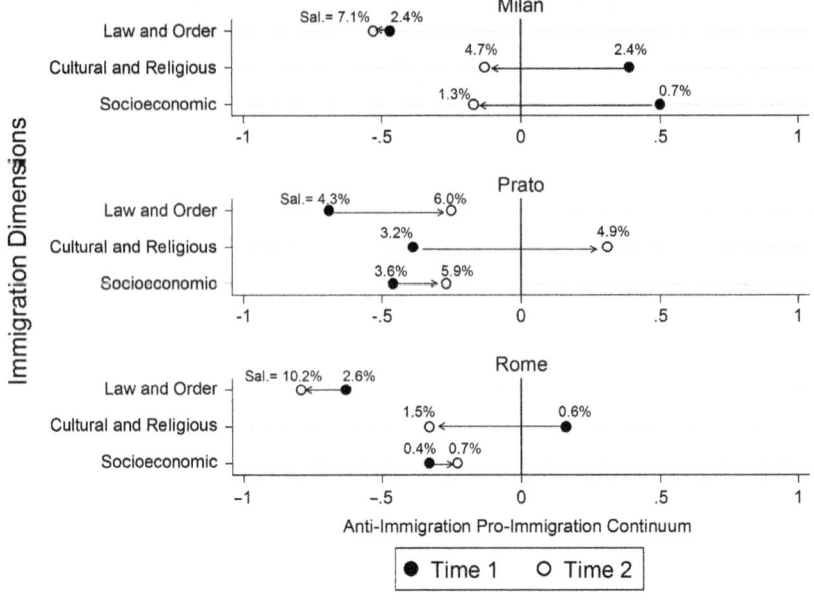

Figure 4.2 Average position of immigration dimensions by city and electoral year

Source: Author's data (see Appendix 1).

In Milan, the cultural and religious and the socioeconomic dimensions were mainly used to support immigration in 2006 but became slightly anti-immigration in 2011, as their absolute salience increased. Indeed, Table 4.4a shows that the relative weight of these two dimensions within the anti-immigration camp increased in 2011.[5] Concerning cultural aspects, as we shall see in the next chapter, this was due to the politicization of the mosque issue by both anti- and pro-immigration actors in the 2011 campaign. In other words, the mobilization on the mosque provided actors in the anti-immigration camp with opportunities to articulate their arguments over cultural and religious aspects that were previously used exclusively by the pro-immigration field. Concerning the socioeconomic dimension, results should be discussed with caution given the overall low salience of this dimension: in 2006, these aspects were mobilized almost exclusively by the pro-immigration camp, namely through the proposal of increased popular housing for immigrant residents in Milan. On the contrary, in 2011 the anti-immigration camp focused on the trade-off between immigrant and native opportunities, most notably in terms of access to popular housing and open competitive exams. Finally, the direction of law and order arguments remained stable and negative across the two elections, although attention to these aspects increased conspicuously. Security is confirmed as the driving element for opposing migration, as these aspects were frequently mobilized in terms of opposition to Romani settlements. In particular, the 2011 campaign was characterized by alarmistic claims by political

Table 4.4a Competing discourses on immigration in Milan 2006–2011

Issue dimension	2006			2011		
Immigration field	Anti-	Pro-	Tot.	Anti-	Pro-	Tot.
Socioeconomic	2.3	23.7	-	10.6	8.9	-
% of dimension	6.7%	93.3%	100%	72.1%	27.8%	100%
Cultural and religious	18.2	62.7	-	27.4	56.3	-
% of dimension	17.8%	82.2%	100%	51.4%	48.6%	100%
Law and order	79.5	13.6	-	61.9	34.8	-
% of dimension	81.4%	18.6%	100%	79.4%	20.6%	100%
Tot.	100%	100%	-	100%	100%	-
N	44	59	103	536	247	783

Note: Share of core sentences dedicated to the immigration issue in newspapers.

Source: Author's data (see Appendix 1).

entrepreneurs arguing that the city would soon become a *Zingaropoli,* literally a 'gipsy-polis'.

Concerning Prato, the results show a general shift towards support to migration across issue dimensions, i.e. in the opposite direction as in the other cities under observation. Most notably, there is evidence of a shift in the discursive priorities of the pro-immigration camp, counterbalancing the ones of the anti-immigration camp. If in fact in 2004 the anti-immigration claims are almost four times more frequent than pro-immigration ones, the two camps become approximately equal in size by 2009. In other words, there is initial evidence that issue avoidance is not sustainable anymore for the pro-migration camp, which is dragged into the competition. Although arguments drawn from the socioeconomic dimension were used to oppose immigration both in 2004 and 2009, the average position of socio-economic arguments became less negative in the second election (from −0.5 to −0.3), indicating that this is the main area on which competition unfolded. This comes as no surprise, given that the core of the conflict had to do with the Chinese community of Prato, and in particular with its implications on local economic performance. As shown in Table 4.4b, the predominance of anti-immigration arguments also decreases in terms of salience. Similarly, pro-immigration claims increased their relative weight within the cultural and religious and the law and order dimensions. The cultural dimension shows the most radical change, as the tone by which these aspects were debated turned positive in 2009, and the pro-immigration camp became predominant.

Concerning the case of Rome, finally, the figures show that the absolute salience of law and order increased conspicuously from 2006 to 2008. This is in line with our expectation that sensationalistic and crime-related news stories would boost the relative importance of these considerations. The tone by which this dimension was used changed, becoming even more negative to immigration in 2008 (−0.8), hence confirming that mediatized crime stories related to the focusing event might have offered an opportunity to further mobilize on security. This is precisely what happened in the 2008 electoral campaign, when candidates from left- and right-wing

Table 4.4b Competing discourses on immigration in Prato 2004–2009

Issue dimension	2004			2009		
Immigration field	Anti-	Pro-	Tot.	Anti-	Pro-	Tot.
Socioeconomic	30.6	40.3	-	39.8	29.1	-
% of dimension	70.5%	29.5%	100%	61.0%	38.9%	100%
Cultural and religious	23.9	43.9	-	17.4	43.7	-
% of dimension	63.2%	36.8%	100%	31.3%	68.7%	100%
Law and order	45.5	15.8	-	42.8	27.2	-
% of dimension	90.1%	9.9%	100%	64.3%	35.7%	100%
Tot.	100%	100%	-	100%	100%	-
N	180	57	237	236	206	442

Note: Share of core sentences dedicated to the immigration issue in newspapers.

Source: Author's data (see Appendix 1).

coalitions, but also representatives of civil society, actively engaged in the debate on perceived insecurity in the city, and on the responsibilities of the outgoing administration *vis-à-vis* the management and integration of the Roma community. What is more, the case of Rome shows that in 2008 the pro-immigration camp virtually disappeared from the debate, as supportive arguments account for only 13% of the immigration debate (whereas in 2006 they accounted for almost one-third of the debate). As a result, anti-immigration arguments dominate debates across all three issue dimensions, including the cultural and religious one which used to be marginally supportive of immigration in 2006. In other words, this case shows that when the opportunities are favourable, securitization might not only overlap with the anti-immigration camp, but also trespass the area of support for migration.

The comparison of data from 2006 and 2008, in sum, suggests that the focusing event that occurred in Rome few weeks before the beginning of the election campaign influenced campaigning in three main ways, confirming my hypothesis on the role of focusing events in driving migration debates. First, the event seems to have contributed to increasing the overall salience of immigration, which became an important issue only in 2008. Yet, this is found to be in line with the two other settings. Second, it seems to have contributed to boosting the importance of law and order considerations. Although this is certainly the case, data from 2006 shows the relevance of this dimension already before the event took place. This indicates that unexpected events are not always focusing events, and that only those news stories that resonate with already established discursive patterns in a given setting are actually able to attract media and political attention and represent critical junctures. Third, the event certainly contributed to changing the tone of the immigration debates, which turned more negative not only – as expectable – in terms of law and order arguments, but also for the dimensions that were previously used to support immigration, such as the cultural one. As a result, the campaign of 2008 shows the marginalization of the pro-immigration camp, as opposition to migration came to overlap with the law and order dimension and *de facto* monopolized the whole immigration debate for this election campaign.

Table 4.4c Competing discourses on immigration in Rome 2006–2008

Issue dimension	2006			2008		
Immigration field	Anti-	Pro-	Tot.	Anti-	Pro-	Tot.
Socioeconomic	4.8	27.3	-	4.1	18.6	-
% of dimension	30.8%	69.2%	100%	58.9%	41.0%	100%
Cultural and religious	10.8	36.4	-	7.8	39.5	-
% of dimension	42.9%	57.1%	100%	56.4%	43.6%	100%
Law and order	84.4	36.3	-	88.2	41.9	-
% of dimension	85.4%	14.6%	100%	93.3%	6.7%	100%
Tot.	100%	100%	-	100%	100%	-
N	83	33	116	567	86	653

Note: Share of core sentences dedicated to the immigration issue in newspapers.

Source: Author's data (see Appendix 1).

Conclusive remarks

Looking at migration debates in local electoral campaigns in Italy, I suggested that the dynamics of mobilization on this issue should be regarded in more detail than previous research has done. The analyses demonstrated that the immigration issue (though the argument applies to many if not all multidimensional policy issues) should not be conceived of as homogeneous, but as a multifaceted bundle of different aspects that are mobilized independently from one another. For local Italian elections, my analysis shows the overwhelming predominance of security aspects in immigration politics, although there is variation in dimensional attention and tones of debates across local contexts and over time. In this sense, this chapter also suggested that local factors can lead to substantial differences in the way in which migration is politicized across electoral campaigns.

Next to asking the question 'does immigration matter?' in a given electoral campaign, therefore, this chapter has revealed the need to ask another question: 'what aspects of immigration make it matter?' Though not providing a systematic answer for all the factors contributing to this, the results indicate that one should look at the specific issue dimensions that are responsible for the salience of policy issues and the tone by which these are debated. In the six campaigns, electoral debates on migration were dominated by law and order, not only because security was used symbolically to respond to public concerns on issues of personal safety, but also because local administrations actually have substantial institutional competences on matters of law and order, and often use these to address immigration politics. Overall, local debates are highly securitized: they are oriented towards security more than towards any of the other two issue dimensions, and immigration and integration are primarily discussed in terms of public order, emergency and security. By confirming one of the overarching expectations of this study, this also indicates that the broader process of securitization of migration politics, which takes place at the national and international level, permeates to the local level as well. Here, debates are composed of a mix between symbolic politics and actual competences of local administrators, so that local stories and crime events can boost the salience of security arguments that politicians and local actors are already inclined to mobilize. Hence, especially when unexpected events are highly mediatized, a law and order, restrictive approach to immigration and integration affairs monopolizes local electoral debates.

At the same time, there is considerable variation in the way in which the issue is debated across local settings. Although the high focus on security issues makes city profiles less clear-cut than originally hypothesized, there is substantial empirical evidence suggesting that local characteristics matter in setting up immigration debates. In other words, it appears that the characteristics of the context in which electoral competition takes place, that is of the interaction between native and immigrant populations, explains – at least to a certain extent – the variation in local immigration debates. The constitutive dimensions of migration are mobilized differently depending on contextual opportunities: while security arguments are particularly predominant in Rome, socioeconomic ones have relatively more resonance in Prato, and cultural and religious arguments are more important in Milan than in the other two cities.

Beyond dimensional issue salience, the analyses suggest that the evaluative content of the different dimensions is of major importance in structuring public debates. The general tone of debates changed greatly across cases, showing that increasing attention is not necessarily associated with increasing opposition to immigration. This suggests that the way in which debates unfold also depends on the strategic choices of the actors involved, as will be discussed in the next chapters. At the same time, the results indicate that the effects of focusing events had major impacts on the way in which immigration debates unfolded in Rome. Sensationalistic news stories affected not only the salience of the issue as a whole, but also the patterns of dimensional attention and, in particular, the tone by which the issue was debated and the relative strength of pro- and anti-immigration arguments.

In conclusion, the results of this chapter suggest that migration debates are not only fragmented, but also strongly related to the characteristics of local settings, local events and local competition. Although I find that local debates are, in general, highly securitized, their nature, composition and tone of appears to be also related to the way in which the issue interacts with local characteristics, the responsibilities and competences of local political actors, and the occurrence of focusing events. A thematic understanding of policy issues therefore yields promising insights for the study of the politicization of the immigration issue, as it helps accounting for the multiple aspects of complex policy issues and for the factors that contribute to shaping electoral debates.

Notes

1 *Patto per Roma Sicura,* Rome 2007. URL: www.issirfa.cnr.it/download/File/Patto_Roma_sicura (accessed 21 October 2015).
2 *Patto per Milano Sicura,* Milan 2007. URL: www.errc.org/cms/upload/media/02/4E/m0000024E.pdf (21 October 2015).

3 *Patto per Prato Sicura,* Prato 2009. URL: www.regione.toscana.it/documents/10180/
23718/Patto%20Prato%20Sicura%202008/d879227e-1f76–410f-bb7b-cb8d10257832
(accessed 21 October 2015).
4 The detailed description of the way in which the categories of the anti-immigration
pro-immigration continuum were created is available in Appendix 1.
5 The differences in the total values (when compared to previous tables and figures)
are due to the fact that neutral scores (= 0) are not reported in either the anti- or pro-
immigration camp.

References

Alonso, S. and Claro Da Fonseca, S. (2009) 'Immigration, Left and Right', paper prepared
for presentation to the panel "Immigrants vs. National Identity? The Problem of Integration in Europe" at the *Annual Meeting of the American Political Science Association,* Toronto, ON, 3–6 September 2009. Available at: www.wzb.eu/sites/default/files/
personen/alonso.sonia.312/apsa09_alonso-fonseca.pdf (Accessed 19 May 2014).
Biorcio, R. and Vitale, T. (2011) 'Culture, Values and Social Basis of Northern Italian Centrifugal Regionalism. A Contextual Political Analysis of the Lega Nord'. In Huysseune,
M. ed. *Contemporary Centrifugal Regionalism,* Brussels: The Royal Flemish Academy
of Belgium for Science and the Arts Press, pp. 171–179.
Bommes, M. and Thranhardt, D. (2010) 'Introduction: National Paradigms of Migration
Research'. In: Bommes, M. and Thranhard, D. eds. *National Paradigms of Migration
Research.* Osnabruck: IMIS, pp. 9–40.
Boomgaarden, H.G. and Vliegenthart, R. (2009) 'How News Content Influences Anti-
Immigration Attitudes: Germany, 1993–2005', *European Journal of Political Research,*
48(4), pp. 516–542. doi: 10.1111/j.1475–6765.2009.01831.x
Buonfino, A. (2004) 'Between Unity and Plurality: The Politicization and Securitization of
the Discourse of Immigration in Europe', *New Political Science,* 26(1), pp. 23–49. doi:
10.1080/0739314042000185111
Cinalli, M., Morales, L., Bengtsson, B., Giugni, M., Kohut, T., Statham, P., Varadi, L.,
Wiener, N. (2009) 'Deliverable D5b: City Reports on Discurisve Indicators of the Local-
multidem Porject', *LOCALMULTIDEM Project Report.* Available at: http://thedata.
harvard.edu/dvn/dv/localmultidem/faces/study/StudyPage.xhtml;jsessionid=acd01a8
0aea9614ab78c7d4b7053?globalId=doi:10.7910/DVN/25658&studyListingIndex=0_
acd01a80aea9614ab78c7d4b7053 (Accessed 10 October 2014).
ERRC (2000) *Campland. Racial segregation of Roma in Italy.* Budapest: ERRC
Faist, T. (1994) 'How to Define a Foreigner? The Symbolic Politics of Immigration in
German Partisan Discourse, 1978–1992', *West European Politics,* 17(2), pp. 50–71. doi:
10.1080/01402389408425014
Freeman, G.P. (1995) 'Modes of Immigration Politics in Liberal Democratic States', *Inter-
national Migration Review,* 29(4), pp. 881–902.
Green-Pedersen, C. and Krogstrup, J. (2008) 'Immigration as a Political Issue in Denmark
and Sweden', *European Journal of Political Research,* 47, pp. 610–634.
Green-Pedersen, C., Mortensen, P. and So, F. (2013) 'How Issue Saliency Makes Par-
ties Change their Positions', Paper presented at the *7th Annual CAP Conference,* 12–14
June 2014, University of Konstanz.
Hopkins, J. (2007) *Threatening Changes: Explaining Where and When Immigrants Pro-
voke Local Opposition.* Working Paper, Centre for the Study of American Politics, Yale
University.

Hopkins, D.J. (2010) 'Politicized Places: Explaining Where and When Immigrants Provoke Local Opposition', *American Political Science Review,* 104(1), pp. 40–60.

Ivarsflaten, E. (2008) 'What Unites Right-Wing Populists in Western Europe? Re-Examining Grievance Mobilization Models in Seven Successful Cases', *Comparative Political Studies* 41(1), pp. 3–23.

Kitschelt, H. and McGann, A. (1997) *The Radical Right in Western Europe. A Comparative Analysis.* Ann Arbor: University of Michigan Press.

Kriesi, H., Grande, E., Dolezal, M., Helbling, M., Höglinger, D., Hutter, S. and Wuest, B. (2012) *Political Conflict in Western Europe.* Cambridge/New York: Cambridge University Press.

Morcellini, M., Antinori, A., Cerase, A., Chiellino, L., Iannelli, L., Laurano, P., Meloni, M., Panarese, P., Rega, R., Ribaldo, C. and Tumolo, M. (2009) *Sintesi del rapporto di ricerca Ricerca nazionale su immigrazione e asilo nei media italiani.* Rome: Sapienza Università di Roma. Available at: www.cattivenotizie.wordpress.com (Accessed 11 April 2009).

Rydgren, J. (2008) 'Immigration Sceptics, Xenophobes or Racists? radical right-Wing Voting in Six West European Countries', *European Journal of Political Research,* 47(6), pp. 737–765.

Sigona, N. (ed.) (2006) *Political Participation and Media Representation of Roma and Sinti in Italy.* Rome: OsservAzione/OSCE.Sigona, N. (2008) *The Latest Public Enemy: The Case of the Romanian Roma in Italy.* OSCE/ODHIR Working Paper. Available at: www.osservazione.org (Accessed 15 April 2013).

Sigona, N. (2011) 'The Governance of Romani people in Italy: Discourse, Policy and Practice', *Journal of Modern Italian Studies,* 16(5), pp. 590–606.

Sigona, N. and Monasta, L. (2006) *Cittadinanze imperfette. Rapporto sulla discriminazione razziale di rom e sinti.* Rome: Edizioni Spartaco.

Thränhardt, D. (1995) 'The Political Uses of Xenophobia in England, France and Germany', *Party Politics,* 1(3), pp. 323–345. doi: 10.1177/1354068895001003002.

Urso, O. and Carammia, M. (2014) 'Political Parties and the Politicisation of Migration in Italy, 1994–2008', Paper presented at the *2014 ECPR General Conference,* Glasgow, 3–6 September 2014.

Van der Brug, W. and van Spanje, J. (2009) 'Immigration, Europe and the 'New' Cultural Dimension', *European Journal of Political Research,* 48, pp. 309–334.

Vitale, T. (2012) 'Conflitti urbani nei percorsi di cittadinanza degli immigrati: una introduzione', *Partecipazione e conflitto,* 3(2012), pp. 5–20.

Williams, R. (2004) 'The Cultural Context of Collective Action: Constraints, Opportunities and the Symbolic Life of Social Movements'. In: Snow, D.A., Soule, S.A. and Kriesi, H. eds. *The Blackwell Companion to Social Movements.* Malden: Blackwell Publishing, pp. 91–115.

5 Electoral campaign strategies

Introduction

Studies on the formation and development of cleavages have repeatedly pointed to the interrelations between the left–right divide and the emerging socio-cultural dimension of party competition and behaviour (Ignazi, 1992; Inglehart, 1977, 2008; Kriesi *et al.*, 2008, 2012). The growing salience of the migration issue in national arenas is interpreted as part of the broader process that led to the emergence of a new, socio-cultural dimension of party competition at the expense of topics from the traditional left–right spectrum. Hence, following the work of Kriesi *et al.* (2008, 2009, 2012), many have argued that party competition is structured along both the socio-cultural and the left–right dimension. Others, instead, have suggested that competition mainly takes place within the latter, claiming that cultural issues like immigration have not yet managed to cut across the traditional left–right divide (van der Brug and van Spanje, 2009). Moreover, research on party and electoral agendas has investigated the consequences of the appearance of new actors within West European party systems, focusing on the structural effects of emerging issues and on the reaction of mainstream parties to new challenges (Bale, 2003; Green-Pedersen and Krogstrup, 2008; Meguid, 2008).

Based on the results of Chapter 4 on local variation in immigration debates, the present chapter builds upon this literature to provide an empirical test of the multidimensional model of issue competition. As was argued earlier, in fact, research in this area has mainly focused on national arenas, looking at electoral issues as single, homogeneous topics. Most studies assume that immigration can have an impact either on the socio-cultural dimension or on the left–right dimension of party competition.[1] As a result, mainstream centre-right parties are considered to be the issue owners of immigration, together with radical right actors that managed to 'play the immigration card' (Arzheimer, 2009; Golder, 2003). On the left-wing of the immigration debate, meanwhile, small post-communist and green parties often benefited from their openly favourable positions on this issue. Instead, mainstream centre-left parties are considered the most vulnerable actors when it comes to immigration, as they tend to be challenged by both the mainstream right and the radical right (Alonso and Claro da Fonseca, 2009; Bale *et al.*, 2010).

By contrast, I suggest that political actors seeking to gain electoral support strategically mobilize separate aspects of the immigration issue, rather than opting for either fully endorsing or disregarding it. This model enables the overly simplified picture of parties as either pro- or anti-immigration to be overcome. I submit that much depends on the dimensions of the issue that are mobilized. Once immigration has become a stable object of electoral competition, in fact, electoral actors will not be able simply to neglect the issue, and will be forced to shift the focus of the debates to dimensions and understandings of the immigration issue in which they presume they are more credible than their rivals are. Moreover, the results provided in the previous chapter showed that the way in which the immigration issue is debated at the local level varies substantially depending on a locality's characteristics. That is, local conditions and opportunities shape the way in which migration is perceived and experienced, and thus the way in which electoral actors represent it.

In sum, this chapter builds upon the previous one by investigating when and whether actors are associated with certain dimensions of, and positions on, immigration. The focus is on actors' electoral strategies, which are interpreted in terms of the preferences of the coalitions running for office, contextual circumstances and party-system configuration.[2] The analysis focuses firstly on the salience of the immigration issue for each electoral actor across the three case studies and over time. This aggregated analysis paves the way for the investigation of the attention given by each type of actor to the different dimensions of the issue, over time and across the three electoral contexts. Thirdly, I provide an in-depth examination of partisan issue positions over the three dimensions of migration. The chapter closes by discussing the broader implications for the study of electoral campaigning and immigration politics.

Local electoral actors and migration

The first step is to look at the way in which the immigration issue is mobilized as a whole. Based on the data shown in the previous chapter, we already know that the overall importance of immigration has grown over time, and that the level of attention differs significantly across the electoral campaigns in Milan, Prato and Rome. Now, I shall illustrate which actors and coalitions account for the increased importance of migration in the different electoral campaigns. Looking at immigration in its entirety, the main expectations follow traditional comparative research on issue politicization. Right-wing parties are generally considered to be advantaged when electoral debates focus on migration, since radical right parties build ownership through overtly xenophobic discourses, whereas mainstream right-wing actors exploit the nationalistic tendencies of their electorates (Bale, 2003; Green-Pedersen and Krogstrup, 2008; Ivarsflaten, 2008). In short, the radical, but also the centre-right, should emphasize the immigration issue the most, accounting for most of its increased salience over time.

According to this literature, the mainstream left can adopt different strategies in response: it can opt to ignore the issue altogether, minimizing the attention to this issue in electoral campaigning and signalling its lack of importance (a strategy which has been called 'dismissive' by Meguid, 2005, 2008). Alternatively, it can decide to take up the issue in its electoral campaign. This may entail either holding their traditional pro-immigration positions, or adopt the more negative positions of its competitors. In either case, however, this means recognizing the importance of the immigration issue, which therefore increases its relative salience in the mainstream left's electoral offer. In general, centre-left actors tend to take up the issue when anti-immigration actors participate in electoral campaigns, and particularly so when they are crucial for the formation of right-wing governments (Bale *et al.*, 2010). In similar cases, in fact, the right-wing actors may use their reputation on immigration affairs to discredit centre-left competitors, questioning their credibility and reliability in handling sensitive policy issues, and capitalizing on the difficulty of the left in developing its own discourse on migration.

Moreover, in line with the framework of the book, I expect that political actors are more likely to engage on migration debates when they are in office. Government parties are in fact held responsible for all policy sectors, whereas opposition parties can focus selectively on advantageous issues, and hold incumbents accountable over immigration affairs. Hence, governing parties on the left may be pressed to address the issue even when they would prefer to dismiss it, once this has gained attention in the party-system agenda. In such cases, incumbent actors might be seen as responsible for the handling of immigration, so that they have to take up the issue to defend themselves (Green-Pedersen and Mortensen, 2010).

Based on this framework, the remainder of this section shall first describe the salience of immigration debates in Milan, then Prato and finally Rome, with the goal of identifying the politicization strategies followed by the involved political actors, and reconstructing why and when they choose to pursue the strategies they do. Accordingly, Table 5.1a describes the electoral campaigns in Milan, reporting the share of attention dedicated by the competing actors to the immigration issue (vertically) and the relative weight of each actor's discourse in migration-specific debates (horizontally).

Table 5.1a Overall salience of the immigration issue by party in Milan 2006 and 2011

Milan						
	Centre-right	*Centre-left*	*Centre*	*Minor lists*	*Public interest groups*	*Total*
	(Incumbent)	*(Challenger)*				
2006	6.1	3.3	-	0.0	9.6	5.5
N	49	31		0	40	120
%	41	26		0	33	100%
2011	15.0	9.9	2.7	17.8	20.9	13.1
N	531	163	11	13	108	826
%	64.3	19.7	1.3	1.5	13.1	100%

Note: Share of core sentences dedicated to immigration in newspaper articles.

Source: Author's data (see Appendix 1).

In the absence of autonomous radical right competitors, the centre-right coalition mobilized the immigration issue the most, playing the role of the issue's credible owner (about half of the immigration debate is driven by the centre-right, both in 2006 and in 2011). This comes as no surprise: in the region of Milan the mainstream right coalition is composed – and has been for more than 20 years – of an alliance between moderate right parties (Berlusconi's party and the Christian Democrats) and the populist anti-immigrants of the Lega Nord (Albertazzi *et al.*, 2011; McDonnell, 2006). In Milan therefore, the centre-right coalition can capitalize on the immigration issue without suffering the challenge of any relevant competitor on its right-wing side. Moreover, both electoral campaigns see the active involvement of non-partisan actors and public interest groups. Especially when the issue was high in the agenda, in fact, religious organizations and pro-migrant social movements actively engaged in the debates.

Yet, as long as the overall salience of the issue was low in the electoral agenda, the centre-left choose not to fully engage in the debate. As can be seen, the centre-right coalition mobilized the issue already in 2006, when the overall salience of immigration was very low at the party-system level, whereas the centre-left opted for a dismissive strategy, addressing the immigration issue only marginally. In 2011, instead, both coalitions engaged in campaigning on the issue. Importantly, although the centre-left tripled the attention it gave to immigration, the centre-right further consolidated its ownership over the issue, monopolizing about two-thirds of the whole debate.

As the composition of the two coalitions did not vary substantially, the change in the centre-left's strategy seems to have been primarily induced by the behaviour of the centre-right, whose campaign strategy was directly oriented at challenging the reputation of their adversaries. This is confirmed by the in-depth analysis of the campaign claims, which show that the right opted to 'trespass' over a specific policy proposal formulated by the left-wing candidate: the mosque issue. By addressing this issue, the centre-right picked up a distinctive element of the centre-left's discourse in order to discredit and neutralize it, highlighting the tension between the moderate and more left-wing components of the challenger coalition. The analysis of the debate shows that the incumbent coalition tried to take advantage of the lack of issue-specific credibility (in handling migration and integration affairs) of the coalition that had not been in power until then. The challengers were therefore accused of promoting a soft-touch approach to migration, one that would leave Milan in the hands of the 'gypsies' (Gabardi, 2012). The visual campaign by centre-right was very energetic, with posters on walls in the city explicitly intended to cue voters by referring to the potential security problems that would inevitably arise if the left had won the elections.

Counterattacks and rebuttals are a common practice in electoral campaigns. The centre-right opted for a 'trespassing' strategy (Sides, 2006), anticipating that their opponents may be disadvantaged in migration debates, and that the outgoing city administration would instead enjoy positive public opinion, reputation and credibility in the management of migration and integration. Hence, rather than voluntarily deciding to take up the issue, the centre-left was forced into a defensive strategy, having to deny the accusation of being prospectively unable to handle the immigration issue. The strategy therefore aimed at exposing the contradictions within the left-wing coalition, and was successful insofar as the centre-left had to respond, recognizing the importance of an issue over which the incumbent enjoyed a strategic advantage.

Table 5.1b shows the importance that each party attributed to migration in the two electoral campaigns in Prato. This case shows a high level of issue salience for immigration already in 2004 (11.1%), and a further increase in the subsequent elections (16.9%). As in Milan, the role of public interest groups was significant in Prato. This mostly had to do with the role played by employers' federations, business owner associations and trade unions, which actively participated in the debate and commented on the state of the affairs with respect to immigration and the economic crisis of the textile industry.

In 2004, right-wing challengers mobilized on the immigration issue, profiting from being in opposition to cue the debate in terms of the inefficient management of migration by the outgoing administration. As a result, the centre-left could not follow a fully dismissive strategy. Instead, the incumbents provided some attention to immigration, mainly in a reactive way and illustrating the achievements of the administration in terms of economic integration of migrants. In other words, the centre-left had to pick up the issue in response to the solicitations of its competitors, and did so trying to build upon the reputation it believed it acquired whilst in office. By 2009, however, the picture had changed substantially. To begin with, a radical right actor (the city-level association *Prato Libera e Sicura*) entered the competition demanding increased market liberalization and relentless opposition to irregular migration. The municipal list stressed problems of security in Prato, opposed the settlement of Chinese migrants, and questioned the legality of the local Chinese economy. This represented an innovation for the traditionally leftist area of Prato, where the radical right had never participated in elections

Table 5.1b Overall salience of the immigration issue by party in Prato 2004 and 2009

Prato								
	Centre-left	Centre-right	Radical left	Radical right	Socialists	Minor lists	Public interest groups	Total
	(Incumbent)	*(Challenger)*						
2004	7.5	14.5	4.6	-	15.9	20.3	7.1	11.1
N	54	81	14		57	28	5	239
%	22.6	33.9	5.8		23.8	11.7	2.1	100%
2009	17.5	12.4	-	30.4	-	9.9	32.3	16.9
N	183	101		72		42	55	453
%	40.4	22.3		15.9		9.3	12.1	100%

Note: Share of core sentences dedicated to immigration in newspaper articles.

Source: Author's data (see Appendix 1).

with its own lists, although there had been candidates of this persuasion within moderate centre-right coalitions. Faced with a new challenger, the left's strategy changed substantially, as the incumbents fully engaged in competition with the radical right, whereas the centre-right did not change considerably the attention provided to the issue.

The increased importance the centre-left gave to the issue has to do with incumbency, which forced the administration to take into account issues that are salient in the party-system agenda. Since the beginning of the electoral campaign, the incumbent coalition feared that the radical right could – at least potentially – contribute to the centre-right success by subscribing an electoral alliance during the second round of elections. Local party leaders supporting the outgoing administration accused their competitors of sharing the same securitized agenda on migration, and called for the vote of moderate electorates. By recognizing the importance of the migration issue, the incumbent tried to antagonize the centre-right and radical right challengers, increasing the competition between the two right-wing parties over similar electorates. The fact that the centre-right and the radical right allied for the second turn of the local elections further confirms this impression, and underlines the failure of the strategy of the incumbents.

The case of Rome is illustrated in Table 5.1c. If in 2006 only public interest groups accorded considerable attention to immigration, in 2008 the issue became highly salient, most notably in the discourse of the centre-right and radical right, but also in that of the centrist coalition of Catholics and moderates. Although right-wing actors almost completely monopolized the issue, the shift in attention to migration by the incumbent centre-left actor is also remarkable (from 2.6% to 8.7%). Public interest groups were overrepresented in the immigration debate in comparison to partisan actors, pretty much as in Milan and Prato. In particular, in 2008 the national visibility of the electoral campaign seems to have incentivized journalists, opinion-makers and no-profit and religious organizations to participate in the debate. The events occurring during the 2008 electoral campaign are crucial, since the already existing law and order rhetoric of right-wing parties intersected with a series of crime stories involving immigrants, one of which took place in the midst of the electoral campaign. This provided right-wing parties with new impetus in politicizing immigration affairs, while at the same time forcing the incumbent to change the distribution of its issue attention. Indeed, the analysis of the attention dedicated to migration in the last two weeks of the electoral campaign (i.e. the second round) shows an increase for both the centre-right (21.6%) and the centre-left (9.7%).

Similar to the case of Prato, as long as the issue was not salient in the party-system agenda, the incumbent centre-left coalition opted for a defusing strategy. Being aware that right-wing actors might be advantaged in immigration debates, and that the generally negative public opinion on migration would not be beneficial for the incumbent administration in electoral terms, the left preferred to focus the attention on issues on which it could demonstrate competence and trustworthiness. Yet, as the issue gained attention in the systemic agenda due to focusing events and to their exploitation by radical and moderate right actors, the parties

Table 5.1c Overall salience of the immigration issue by party in Rome 2006 and 2008

Rome							
	Centre-left	Centre-right	Centre	Radical right	Minor lists	Public interest groups	Total
	(Incumbent)	(Challenger)					
2006	2.6	3.8	-	-	3.3	13.3	3.7
N	43	49			1	29	122
%	35.2	40.2			0.8	23.8	100%
2008	8.7	17.2	9.9	13.8	2.4	23.1	12.5
N	179	320	45	51	3	53	651
%	27.5	49.2	6.9	7.8	0.4	8.1	100%

Note: Share of core sentences dedicated to immigration in newspaper articles.

Source: Author's data (see Appendix 1).

supporting the incumbent administration realized they could not pursue that strategy anymore. The strategy of the challengers was clear: since they could not demonstrate to voters their record in managing this policy area, they invested all of their efforts into discrediting the performance of their competitors. Since migration was framed primarily as blaming of the management by the administration, in terms of urban safety and individual security, the left had to 'respond' in order to defend its activity while in office.

In contrast to Prato, therefore, more than a strategy aimed at highlighting the contradiction within the right-wing camp, the picture for Rome hints more directly at the disadvantage that incumbent actors face in dealing with issues that address their bad performance in office. In fact, in a desperate attempt to acquire credibility on migration affairs, the outgoing administration implemented a number of security measures in the months prior to the elections, targeting especially Roma settlements. In other words, the centre-left administration was well aware that – due to the 'mood' created by the crime stories – law and order arguments would easily monopolize the electoral campaign, and tried to develop a last-minute credibility on an issue that was, until then, largely disregarded.

Overall, the above analysis of the strategies by which different electoral coalitions coped with the immigration issue confirms the findings of previous studies showing that centre-right and radical right parties tend to capitalize more on migration, especially but not exclusively when they run as challengers. Our cases show that centre-left actors focus on immigration less than right-wing ones, and that their response to increasing salience of the immigration issue, and the challenger of radical right actors, is far from uniform across local contexts. In the cases under study, the centre-left coalitions display different strategies of issue uptake. First, they campaign on migration because of incumbency constraints, i.e. because they are held accountable for their issue-specific performance while in office. Under these circumstances, left-wing actors tend to take advantage of the material results and reputation obtained during incumbency, since only the outgoing administration can 'demonstrate' its policy competence. Yet, if public opinion on immigration is particularly negative, such as with the anti-immigration public moods in Rome, this strategy by the incumbents ends up further legitimizing the credibility of their opponents.

Moreover, there is evidence that the choices of left-wing coalitions are not only influenced by the presence of the radical right itself, but also by the behaviour of the mainstream right. Even when the left finds itself in the position of challenger, in fact, it takes up the issue if their opponents preventively challenge their ability to handle migration and integration. Incumbency constraints are most evident in Rome, where the left was forced by its right-wing competitors to take up the issue defensively. Similar circumstances apply to Prato, although in this case the left also mobilized offensively, by antagonizing the two right-wing opponents. Instead, in Milan the left suffered its intrinsic lack reputation on immigration affairs in general.

These first results suggest that there are different circumstances and rationales explaining when and why left-wing parties opt to campaign on immigration. This provides additional leverage to the main goal of this study, focusing on the substance of immigration debates. In this sense, the next sections shall further clarify these dynamics by analysing the thematic nature of this complex policy issue from the point of view of issue dimensions and positions, investigating the role of incumbency constraints, the location of parties on the left–right scale, and local issue characteristics.

Issue salience and dimensionality

By looking at the three dimensions of the issue, it is now possible to open the 'black box' of the debates (Höglinger *et al.,* 2012), and illustrate and discuss the dynamics of competition over migration and integration in electoral campaigning. At the most general level, therefore, the interest of this section lies with establishing whether there is a relation between the types of actors involved in electoral competition, and their dimensional choices of issue selection and mobilization. As outlined in Chapter 2, the three dimensions of immigration should be mobilized differentially by parties depending on where they are located on the ideological spectrum. The law and order dimension is generally associated with the values of right-wing and anti-immigration parties, who draw arguments from it to demand tougher immigration controls and integration regulations. Previous studies suggested that centre-right parties often contribute to priming the radical right's security agenda by focusing on perceived insecurity and crime (Helbling, 2013; Mudde, 2007). Given their relentless opposition to immigration, I have suggested that radical right parties, next to law and order arguments, politicize also the cultural dimension in nationalistic terms, and socioeconomic affairs in terms of labour security (De Lange, 2007). In contrast, left-wing parties adopt more liberal views, seeking to improve the social conditions of migrants as well as to extend their cultural rights (Andall, 2007; Lahav, 2004), and therefore prefer to address immigration primarily in terms of cultural and economic arguments.

Table 5.2 addresses the above expectations, showing the attention given to the three dimensions of the immigration issue across the three cities and two electoral campaigns.[3] Vertically, the table shows the preferences of parties regarding the three dimensions, whereas horizontally it shows the weight of the discourse of the various parties within each dimensional debate on migration. The dimensional preferences of the centre-left and centre-right are very similar, with a slight preference for socioeconomic and cultural arguments on the left, in contrast to higher attention for law and order on the political right.

At the edges of the political spectrum, the results for the radical left show a clear preference for cultural arguments, although the number of observations is rather limited. The radical right mobilizes mainly the law and order dimension, yet it provides substantial attention to the socioeconomic one as well. Cultural aspects, however, play only a marginal role on the radical right in these three Italian cities, unlike what previous studies found (Kriesi *et al.*, 2012).[4] By looking at Table 5.2 horizontally, however, we can also see that the centre-right dominates debates across all the three issue dimensions. Its advantage over the mainstream left, as expected, is most evident in terms of law and order aspects, but it is also considerable within the cultural and socioeconomic dimensions. Overall, the centre-left appears unable to get a hold over any of the three dimensions of the issue.

I now turn to the analysis of the choices of mainstream parties when they are in office compared to when they are challengers. The main idea here is that challenger parties are freer to focus on advantageous issue dimensions. Hence, the centre-right – which derives the strongest advantage from mobilizing security issues – should focus more on this dimension when it is in opposition than when it is in office. Conversely, the centre-left should also focus more on relatively advantageous dimensions, e.g. cultural and religious affairs, when it is in opposition than when it is in office. The difference between the two actors is therefore a

Table 5.2 Overall distribution of attention by dimension and party

Dimension	Centre-left	Centre-right	Radical left	Radical right	Interest groups	Total
Socioeconomic	15.9	12.3	7.1	40.7	18.3	346
N	104	139	1	50	52	
%	30.0	40.2	0.3	14.5	15.0	100%
Cultural-religious	27.6	23.8	78.6	13.0	29.6	560
N	180	269	11	16	84	
%	32.1	48.0	1.9	2.8	15.0	100%
Law and order	56.5	63.9	14.3	46.3	52.1	1298
N	369	722	2	57	148	
%	28.4	55.6	0.1	4.4	11.4	100%
Tot.	100%	100%	100%	100%	100%	
N	653	1130	14	123	284	2204

Note: Share of core sentences dedicated to immigration in newspaper articles.

Source: Author's data (see Appendix 1).

result of the overall credibility that the centre-right and centre-left enjoy in immigration debates, so that the left should suffer the costs of being in office more than the right.

Results in Table 5.3 are generally supportive of this hypothesis. When waging a challenger's campaign, the centre-right focuses mostly on law and order and only marginally on socioeconomic and cultural aspects. When it is in office, however, the amount of attention provided to law and order shrinks, whereas the one provided to the cultural and religious dimension increases substantially. The opposite takes place on the centre-left: in opposition, it focuses mainly on cultural aspects and less so on law and order; yet, when in office, it is forced to concentrate its policy attention mainly on law and order affairs.[5] The magnitude of the difference between being incumbent or a challenger is more pronounced for the left than for the right, suggesting that the migration as a whole is more unfavourable to the centre-left, which is forced to change its distribution of attention more drastically. Put differently, left-wing coalitions seem to suffer relatively more disadvantages from incumbency than right-wing ones, which makes them less able to defend their performance while in government. The centre-right, instead, can provide a more stable and coherent discourse, taking advantage of their reputation on security issues and migration affairs both when in office and when in opposition.

Given the reciprocal nature of partisan strategies, especially when the focus is limited to mainstream coalitions, caution is in order when presenting these results. Moreover, the limited amount of cases upon which this study is based calls for additional attention, as the difference between incumbent and challenger actors might not be related exclusively to incumbency constraints but also to events and characteristics at the context and campaign level. Provisionally, however, Table 5.3 suggests that parties tend to focus more on the dimensions that they perceive as advantageous when they are challengers than when they are in office. This also means that governing parties are less able to avoid dimensions unfavourable to them when these emerge in migration debates, since they have to respond to the issues their competitors bring into the agenda.

To interpret these results, one has to take into account that city-level factors explain at least part of the dimensional preferences by mainstream parties. Nonetheless, the evidence reported here is generally supportive of the idea that

Table 5.3 Distribution of attention by incumbent and challenger parties

	Centre-right		Centre-left	
	Incumbent	*Challenger*	*Incumbent*	*Challenger*
Socioeconomic dimension	10.2	14.5	18.5	9.8
Cultural & Religious dimension	30.2	17.1	18.5	49.0
Law & Order dimension	59.6	68.4	62.9	41.2
Tot.	100%	100%	100%	100%
N	580	550	459	194

Note: Share of core sentences dedicated to immigration in newspaper articles.

Source: Author's data (see Appendix 1).

incumbency is constraining for political actors, as illustrated by the fact that both the centre-left and the centre-right, when incumbent, are forced to focus on disadvantageous dimensions more often. Moreover, the results further explain the general disadvantage of left-wing parties in migration debates, as the variation in the distribution of attention for the centre-left as an incumbent and as a challenger is higher than for the centre-right, indicating that the left suffers relatively more from being incumbent than the right. That is to say, when incumbent the left has to discuss law and order affairs more than right-wing incumbents have to focus on cultural and religious ones.

Overlap and continuity in dimensional politicization

So far, this study has shown that local contexts matter in structuring debates on migration, and that the dynamics of election campaigns drive parties to engage on specific dimensions of the issue. Two mechanisms are at stake when actors set up their dimensional strategies of mobilization. On the one hand, as was suggested in the theoretical chapter, parties follow what Helbling (2013) calls an 'actor-driven logic'. Accordingly, they are not fully free to select the way in which they politicize immigration, as they are constrained among other things by their own understanding of the social reality, as well as by their previous commitments. If this is the case, it is fair to expect that the dimensional choices with respect to the immigration issue of party x across contexts a, b and c, and over time $t1$ and $t2$ will be relatively steady, because they must reflect previous engagements and ideological profiles. Conversely, if an agenda logic prevails (Green-Pedersen and Mortensen, 2010), parties should focus on dimensions of immigration that resonate with the context in which the campaign takes place. This means that their choices should differ more *between* the different elections than *within* single election campaigns. Hence, the discourse of party x in context a, at time $t2$ will be relatively more similar (in terms of dimensions of immigration) to the discourse of party y in context a, at time $t2$, than to its own discourse in another context.

Table 5.4 describes the profiles in dimensional attention to immigration according to party and electoral campaign. These results cover the two mainstream coalitions and the radical right,[6] showing a noticeable degree of variation across both electoral contexts and different party families. The most straightforward case is that of the radical right: in Prato it devoted two-thirds of its attention to socioeconomic issues; in Rome it did so for security ones. In neither of the cases, moreover, did the cultural dimension seem to have played a significant role. With respect to mainstream parties, the results show a general tendency of according increased importance over time to the law and order dimension, across the three local settings and with only the centre-left of Prato as an exception. Prato also stands out for the degree of attention devoted to the socioeconomic dimension, which was almost absent from the debates of the two other settings. Similarly, law and order completely dominated the debates in Rome, at both points in time and for both mainstream parties. Dimensional profiles are less clear in Milan, where the high importance of security aspects went alongside a remarkable degree of attention to cultural and religious aspects.

Table 5.4 Dimensional attention by party and context

		Milan		Prato		Rome	
		2006	*2011*	*2004*	*2009*	*2006*	*2008*
Centre-left	*Socioeconomic*	16.1	8.6	35.2	32.8	2.3	2.8
	Cultural-religious	58.1	47.2	14.8	26.2	23.3	10.6
	Law and order	25.8	44.2	50.0	40.96	74.4	86.6
	Tot.	100%	100%	100%	100%	100%	100%
Centre-right	*Socioeconomic*	8.2	10.4	35.8	28.0	8.2	5.9
	Cultural-religious	38.8	29.4	24.7	31.0	16.3	10.9
	Law and order	53.0	60.2	39.5	41.0	75.5	83.2
	Tot.	100%	100%	100%	100%	100%	100%
Radical right	*Socioeconomic*	-	-	-	61.1	-	11.8
	Cultural-religious	-	-	-	6.9	-	21.6
	Law and order	-	-	-	31.9	-	66.6
	Tot.	100%	100%	100%	100%	100%	100%

Note: Share of core sentences dedicated to immigration in newspaper articles.

Source: Author's data (see Appendix 1).

In general, however, the results do not fully support the actor-driven logic. The increasing salience of the immigration issue over time is not associated with a clear pattern of party preferences in terms of dimensional attention. Instead, though the right shows a general preference for law and order arguments, while the left does the same for cultural aspects, mainstream and radical parties show a substantial level of variation in the way they approach the immigration issue. Despite the centre-right's overwhelming attention to law and order issues, in fact, its dimensional choices in Prato are considerably different from those in Rome and Milan. Similarly, the mainstream left also does not follow coherent strategies across different settings. The dimensional profile of the radical right is considerably different in the two electoral campaigns, and the difference is associated with the prevailing issue dimension in the election campaign. In other words, although this type of analysis can say little about causal mechanisms, it certainly show that radical right actors mobilize the issue dimensions that eventually come to dominate electoral campaigns.

Similarly, the table shows that the mainstream coalitions choose their respective strategies more consistently within city settings, suggesting that parties target those dimensions of the immigration issue that resonate the best in the context in which campaigns take place. In order to elaborate on this further, I constructed an index of dimensional consistency, measuring the degree to which one mainstream actor's dimensional choices overlap with the choices of the other. This measure of *interparty overlap* is then compared to one of *intraparty similarity* across subsequent election campaigns (Green-Pedersen and Mortensen, 2010). These measures enable one to see whether discourses on immigration are more similar across actors (which would underline the importance of the agenda logic) than they are to an actor's own discourse from previous elections (which would instead support the idea that the partisan component drives competition on immigration).[7]

As shown in Table 5.5, the results illustrate that both logics explain partisan competition. The issue overlap score is found to be above 80 on the 0–100 scale at time *t1* (first election campaign in each (city), and above 90 at time *t2* (second election campaign in each city). This suggests that the attention profiles of the competing actors grow increasingly similar as the overall salience of the immigration issue grows, confirming the appropriateness of the agenda logic interpretation for explaining dimensional preferences in local immigration debates.[8] There is also evidence supporting the logic of intraparty similarity across consecutive election campaigns, which is reported in the second and third column of the table for the mainstream left and right parties. The scores indicate that the centre-right keeps rather consistently to its previous dimensional profile, obtaining a score of 91.7 out of 100. The score of the centre-left is somewhat lower than for the right, but a continuity score of about 85% still means a considerable amount of continuity across elections.

Overall, the above analysis suggests that both party and agenda logics drive choices in the dimensional politicization of the immigration issue. My results suggest that the centre-right is more capable of providing a consistent discourse on immigration than the centre-left, but that the degree of overlap between profiles is high, indicating that similar dimensions tend to prevail in both actors' discourses. Moreover, this similarity grows with increasing levels of salience for the immigration issue. Combined, these findings suggest that (across local elections and beyond the contextual specifics of campaigning) higher salience for the immigration issue increases the degree to which right and left discourses are similar, yet it does so because the centre-left is forced towards the dimensional attention profile of the centre-right, rather than the other way around.

Determining the level of attention to migration

In order to provide a more exhaustive explanation of what determines the salience of the immigration issue and its dimensions, I ran OLS (ordinary least squares) regression analyses, using as dependent variable the share of attention (in percentage) given to each dimension of the immigration issue by each actor in a given election campaign.[9] The number of observations (93) refers to the salience given by each actor participating in the six electoral campaigns under study to each of the three dimensions of the immigration issue.[10] The salience provided

Table 5.5 Interparty overlap and intraparty similarity across election campaigns

	Interparty overlap	Intraparty similarity	
		Centre-left	*Centre-right*
Time *t1*	85.0%		
Time *t2*	91.3%	85.8%	91.7%

Note: Degree of dimensional similarity across parties and elections.

Source: Author's data (see Appendix 1).

to immigration issue dimensions is regressed across four subsequent models accounting for (1) the status of incumbent or challenger of the various actors involved, (2) the time of the election campaign, (3) the local setting of the election, and (4) the three issue-dimension dummies. In so doing, these models help clarifying the role of each actor in constructing electoral debates, from the point of view of salience. In particular, they will contribute to clarifying whether the radical right plays the role of immigration agenda-setter in local electoral campaigns.

Model A investigates the level of attention given by centre-right, centre-left and radical right actors, controlling for the role of mainstream parties as incumbents or main challengers. The model confirms that immigration dimensions are most salient for radical right parties, confirming the argument that they are the real owners of the issue. Although not statistically significant, the values of the coefficients suggest that the average attention provided by the centre-left to the three immigration issue dimensions is lower than that among the rest of the parties.

Table 5.6 Regression results for the salience of the immigration issue dimensions

Salience of immigration	Coef.			
	A	B	C	D
Intercept	4.33	3.55	4.50	3.48
	(0.917)	(0.728)	(0.695)	(0.797)
Centre-left	−0.56	−0.42	−0.94	−0.94
	(1.000)	(1.008)	(1.003)	(1.015)
Centre-right	0.49	0.64	0.83	0.83
	(1.107)	(1.065)	(1.186)	(1.200)
CL challenger	−1.56	−1.61	0.30	0.30
	(0.456)	(0.424)	(0.975)	(0.988)
CR challenger	−1.47	−1.57	−1.78	−1.78
	(0.911)	(0.848)	(0.899)	(0.836)
Radical right	3.77**	3.21**	2.46*	2.46
	(1.012)	(1.463)	(1.035)	(0.988)
Time (ref. t1)		1.38*	1.86**	1.85**
		(0.795)	(0.846)	(0.856)
Rome (ref. Prato)			−1.12***	−1.12***
			(0.484)	(0.489)
Milan (ref. Prato)			−2.58**	−2.58**
			(1.123)	(1.013)
Cult. & relig. dimension				0.32
				(0.653)
Law & order dimension				2.74***
				(0.741)
R-squared	0.09	0.11	0.16	0.24
No. observations	93	93	93	93

Note: Standard errors are reported in parentheses.

*, **, *** indicate significance at the 90%, 95% and 99% levels.

Source: Author's data (see Appendix 1).

Conversely, the centre-right slightly exceeds the mean. As opposed to what was previously observed, there is no statistically significant association between salience and whether either mainstream party participated in the elections as challenger or incumbent. Model B adds the effect of time, checking for the difference between the first and second election campaigns. The results indicate a positive and significant effect of time, confirming the time trend of increasing importance of migration in election debates in the three cities. The subsequent model accounts for the differences between local settings in terms of the salience of issue dimensions. Model C shows that the immigration issue is significantly less salient in Rome and Milan than in Prato. Finally, Model D accounts for the separate effects of the three dimensions.[11] The results indicate that the average attention provided to the law and order dimension is higher than that provided to the reference category – the socioeconomic dimension. In this model, moreover, the direct effect of the radical right on salience turns out to be non-significant, suggesting that the effect of the radical right on migration debates mainly lies in the attention it gives to security issues.[12]

To conclude, the results of the regression analyses explain about one-fourth of the variance in the salience of the immigration issue's dimensions. Although a large share of the variance remains unexplained, the results indicate that at least 23% of the salience given to immigration by parties across electoral campaigns has to do with the presence of radical right parties in the competition, and with the mobilization of security arguments. In line with the analysis here and in the previous chapter, moreover, salience also seems to be differentially associated with the three local contexts, and with the timing of the election campaigns, confirming the relevance of a party-system agenda interpretation of the dynamics of local electoral competition in Italy.

Opposition and support to migration

As illustrated in the previous chapter, the choice to mobilize a specific dimension of the immigration issue often has to do with the predominance of a given tone within the debate, and thus with the evaluative intentions of the actors involved in a campaign. In this section, I account for the actual positions of electoral actors, in order to see to what extent their discourse opposes or supports migration in general and in terms of each issue dimension in particular. In so doing, and building on the findings of the previous sections, the point is to investigate what factors and political actors account for the varying tone in which the immigration issue is dealt with across the different settings and electoral campaigns.

The first part of the analysis addresses the overall positioning of electoral actors along the pro- to anti-immigration continuum. The general positions *vis-à-vis* the immigration issue are reported in Figure 5.1 below, which shows a clear left–right pattern: the most anti-immigrant party is the radical right closely followed by the centre-right, whereas the most pro-immigrant is the radical left, followed by the centre-left. Minor lists and interest groups are generally neutral to immigration, as the diffuse composition of these categories is likely to contain both tendencies.

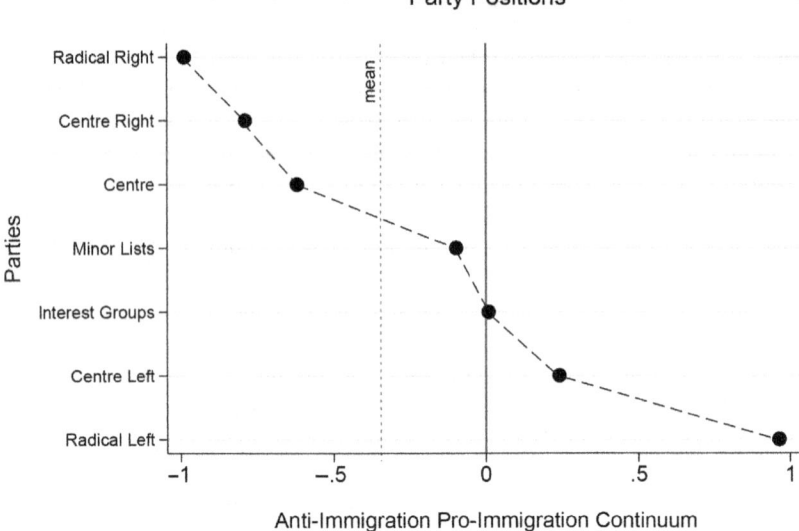

Figure 5.1 Party positions on the immigration issue (overall)

Source: Author's data (see Appendix 1).

Although this figure is largely in line with previous studies on left–right preferences for immigration, the graph also provides two additional pieces of information. First, the centrist actors are not located in the centre of the axis, but are clearly positioned within the anti-immigration camp (with a score of −0.67). Second, the positional distance between the radical right (−0.98) and the centre-right (−0.79) is remarkably smaller than the one between the radical left (0.96) and the centre-left (0.24).

What, however, if one breaks these results down according to the three municipal contexts? Chapter 4 showed that the tone of the debates on immigration varies substantially across contexts. Figure 5.2 below disaggregates the data of Figure 5.1, underlining city-specific differences in the way in which local electoral actors deal with the immigration issue. Overall, the figure shows that the positions of right-wing actors are much more stable across cities than the ones of the centre-left, centre, minor lists and interest groups.

Right-wing actors tend to have a very negative position towards migration regardless of the context. Still, the position of the centre-right in Milan – the only context where there is no independent radical right candidate involved in electoral competition – is slightly less opposed to immigration than in Prato or Rome, which may indicate that the presence of radical right competitors pulls the mainstream right towards sharper opposition to immigration. Conversely, the position of the centre-left is most supportive of immigration in Milan and in Prato (although less so than in Milan), while in Rome it is in fact part of the anti-immigration camp. Similarly, the discourse of the centrist coalitions and that of the interest groups is much more opposed to immigration in Rome than in the other cities.

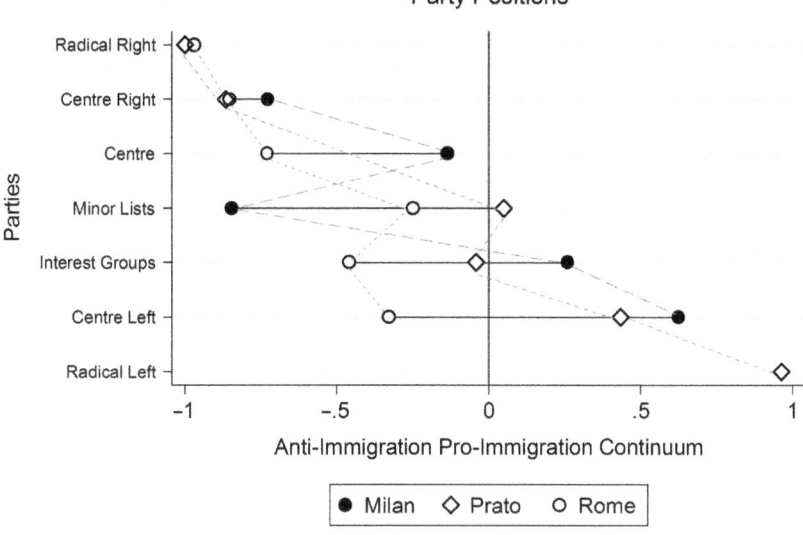

Figure 5.2 Party positions on the immigration issue by city

Source: Author's data (see Appendix 1).

These results highlight the relevance of studying the local level of immigration debates. Doing so revealed that the positional distance between mainstream and radical right actors is much lower than the distance between the mainstream left coalition and radical left parties. In addition, actors on the right of the political spectrum tend to be more consistently opposed to migration than parties on the left are supportive of it, since the positions of the latter change more substantially depending on the local context. Moreover, I find evidence that opposition to immigration for most actors is highest in Rome and lowest in Milan. The next section shall further develop this point by looking at the relationship between actor positions and the three dimensions of the immigration issue.

Actor positions and issue dimensionality

The framework of this book identified three basic ways in which immigration dimensions and actors' positions may interact. First, candidates may decide to set up their electoral discourses around full-fledged opposition to, or support for, immigration. If this is the case, all three dimensions will be used in favour of a single position towards immigration, as actors will use them interchangeably. In other words, they will use either the socioeconomic, cultural, or law and order dimensions to express wholesale support or opposition to immigration. Alternatively, local actors may set up their strategies around issue aspects, using certain dimensions to support immigration and others to oppose it. Such strategies may be oriented at electorates holding mixed preferences *vis-à-vis* the immigration issue, such as citizens who evaluate the economic consequences of migration positively according to, for example, national productivity and development, yet fear illegal immigration; or, conversely, individuals who do not discriminate against migrants on cultural grounds, yet fear the economic competition of foreign-born labour. Third, actors may take different positions on the three immigration dimensions across local campaigns. If this is the case, electoral strategies are likely to be affected strongly by local factors, since they are based upon expectations of local electorates' preferences at a given point in time and in a given context. The problem with this strategy is that the reputation of political actors is generally produced by the 'history' of their approach towards a problem; hence, variation in their positions *vis-à-vis* a certain issue dimension across local context may not be beneficial in electoral terms, as it risks loosening the connection between the actor and the handling of the policy problem.

Figure 5.3 has a first cut at these dynamics by showing the positions of various electoral actors on immigration according to issue dimension. On the law and order dimension, most parties are more inclined to oppose rather than support immigration. This is particularly the case for right-wing actors, yet it is also true for centrist ones, minor lists and interest groups. Most importantly, the centre-left is also negative on immigration when dealing with security and law and order aspects. In the socioeconomic dimension, instead, the immigration debate is more polarized: the location of these aspects on the anti-immigration pro-immigration scale parallels the left–right scale, with actors of the extreme and centre-right opposing migration on socioeconomic grounds and parties on the left supporting it based on the same dimension. Likewise, in the cultural and religious dimension electoral actors either fully support immigration (the left and public interest groups), or are quite critical of it (the centre, centre-right and radical right).

Figure 5.3 also provides information on the type of argument that each actor mobilizes. On the right of the political spectrum, actors tend to provide rather homogeneous discourses, as their positions across the three dimensions are coherently opposed to immigration. This is particularly the case for the radical right, for which the dimensional differentiation is almost non-existent, and somewhat less for the centre-right, which privileges law and order over the other two dimensions when expressing strong opposition to migration. Meanwhile, dimensional differentiation is most evident for the centre-left, as well as for public interest groups and minor lists. The discourse of the centre-left is highly differentiated between law and order arguments (with a slight tendency to oppose immigration: -0.13), cultural and religious arguments (overwhelmingly used to express support: 0.82), and socioeconomic ones (in the midway, although leaning towards support: 0.52).

In sum, the results outlined so far support only in part the expectation that parties use certain dimensions to oppose and others to support immigration. More precisely, the aggregate data shows that right-wing actors do not differentiate their positions across the three issue dimensions, whereas the centre-left and non-party actors involved in electoral competition do. In order to investigate this further, it is worth looking at partisan dimensional positions in each individual city. As

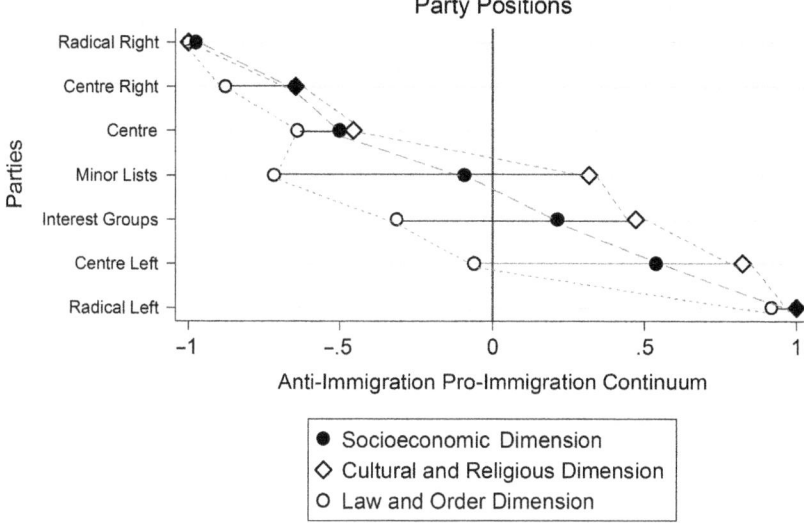

Figure 5.3 Party positions on the immigration issue by dimension

Source: Author's data (see Appendix 1).

shown in Chapter 4, in fact, city contexts shape substantially different immigration debates, and actor positions as a whole change across local settings too. Figure 5.4 below reports the dimensional party positions in each of the three cities under consideration. The figure confirms that the discourse of radical right actors is consistently anti-immigration, irrespective of the issue dimension under debate and the city context. Similarly, campaigning by centre-right parties is generally more consistent than by centre-left ones. The distance between the issue positions on socioeconomic, cultural and law and order dimensions for the centre-left is in fact higher than for the political right. The highest variation is in Rome: both the centre-right and the centre-left differentiate their positions across the three issue dimensions, and take polarized anti-immigration positions on security. For the centre-right, dimensionality is lowest in Prato, where the three issue dimensions display anti-immigration tones; for the centre-left, dimensionality is lowest in Milan, where the three issue dimensions are discussed in generally pro-immigration tones. More broadly, immigration discourses in Milan show the lowest variation also for non-party actors, such as interest groups and minor lists.

However, what happens if one differentiates dimensional discourse between cities rather than parties? Concerning the socioeconomic dimension, the discourse of right-wing actors is more negative in Prato than in any other setting. In particular, the score of Prato's centre-right (−0.86) is significantly higher than in Milan (−0.57) or Rome (−0.34). Moreover, even public interest groups and minor lists adopt a generally anti-immigration tone toward these aspects in Prato, though the centre-left's tone is more or less in line with that of its counterparts in

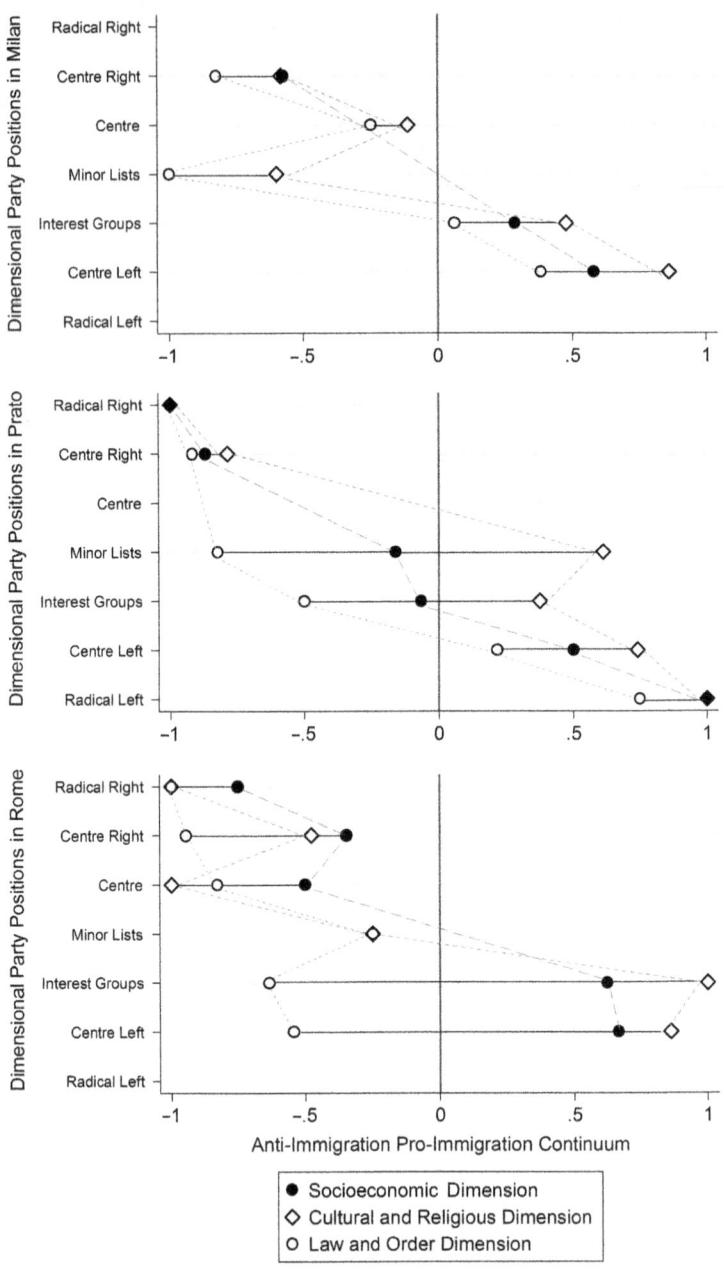

Figure 5.4 Dimensional party positions on the immigration issue by city context
Source: Author's data (see Appendix 1).

Rome and Milan. With only Rome as an exception (where the centre-left adopts an anti-immigration discourse that outdoes the centre-right's one), party positions on socioeconomic aspects again see the anti-immigration pro-immigration continuum parallel those on the left–right scale.

In all three case studies, virtually all actors involved adopt their most anti-immigration (or least pro-immigration) tone when the law and order dimension is concerned. Centre-right and radical right-wing actors mobilize this dimension in a similar way across the case studies, with marginal variations. The centre-left meanwhile mobilizes law and order to moderately support immigration in Milan (0.38) and Prato (0.21), while adopting a fully anti-immigration discourse in Rome (−0.54). Other actors, such as centrist parties and minor lists, but also interest groups, tend to adopt anti-immigration tones upon discussing law and order affairs in all cases. Finally, the cultural and religious dimension is marked by a considerable degree of polarization: right-wing actors mobilize it in negative terms consistently across the three cities (especially in Prato), whereas the left and interest groups do so in pro-immigration terms in all three cities. Hence, actors seem to follow a clear-cut differentiation along the left–right divide with respect to this issue dimension. The other actors seem to follow city-based strategies, as the positions of minor lists and centrist parties on this issue dimension vary from largely pro-immigration to fully anti-immigration depending on the context of the competition.

The results of this section provide evidence for a dimensional approach to partisan strategies of electoral competition on immigration. Upon selecting their respective strategies, in fact, parties clearly take into account the multidimensional nature of the issue, and strategically take a position based on the characteristics of the issue dimensions and city contexts. A left–right pattern prevails, yet this is articulated not only along opposition vs. support for migration, but also in terms of issue-dimensional differentiation. Right-wing actors tend to be more consistently anti-immigration, and use different aspects interchangeably to oppose immigration. Although they differentiate across issue dimensions considerably less than left-wing actors, the degree to which each dimension is used to oppose immigration varies across city contexts. By contrast, left-wing actors use certain dimensions (mainly the cultural one) to support immigration and others to oppose it (the law and order dimensions). Moreover, even if dimensional differentiation is noticeable in all three cities, showing a certain degree of change in politicization strategies across different local elections, the position of the centre-left on the law and order dimension in Rome stands out as remarkably more restrictive than any other observation.

If on the one hand these results corroborate my expectation of a structural disadvantage of left-wing parties, they also suggest that local political actors are driven by multiple logics upon setting up their election campaign strategies. First, centre-right actors are more consistent, as they change less their anti-immigration positions across all issue dimensions and cities than do the centre-left actors. Second, the positions of mainstream parties on the cultural and religious dimension are steady: restrictive for the right and supportive for the left. This implies that the position of the centre-left on the cultural dimension is less subject to change across city settings than their positions on other issue dimensions. Similarly, the positions of the centre-right are stable when it comes to security issues. Third, city-level characteristics play a role in structuring partisan positions on different issue dimensions, as is shown in the changing tone of socioeconomic affairs in Prato for the centre-right and, even more so, in that of the law and order dimension in Rome for the centre-left.

Determining the tone of migration debates

Table 5.7 reports the regression results for the mean partisan position on immigration dimensions, using as dependent variable the position of each party on each dimension of the immigration issue in the two election campaigns in the three cities.[13] Partisan positions are again based on a scale ranging from -1 (full opposition) to $+1$ (full support). As a result, the number of observations (79) refers to the position of each actor (31 actors) with respect to the three dimensions, in the six electoral campaigns under study.[14] All non-dummy variables were standardized to facilitate the interpretation of results. Mean positions were regressed across four models accounting for (1) the main electoral actors and their role as incumbents or challengers, (2) the time of the election campaign and the salience of the immigration issue (standardized), (3) local settings and (4) immigration dimensions.

Model A investigates the positions of centre-right, centre-left and radical right actors, controlling for incumbents and challengers. In line with the previous discussion, the left is found to have a significantly more positive position on the three migration dimensions than do the other actors on average. Conversely the centre-right and – even more so – the radical right are significantly more anti-immigration than any other actor. Moreover, controlling for incumbency effects, I find that when the centre-right runs as challenger, its positions on the three issue dimensions are significantly more anti-immigration than when it runs as an incumbent, whereas the same is not confirmed statistically for the centre-left.

Model B adds the effects of time and salience of issue dimensions. Although time *per se* does not seem to influence the tone in which the three aspects of the immigration issue are debated, the salience attributed to each of them is negatively associated with mean positions. This confirms the link between attention to specific issue dimensions and anti-immigration positions, indicating that increasing salience is associated with increased hostility to migration. The dummy specifications accounting for the differences between local settings (Model C) only show a small positive coefficient for Rome, suggesting that, having accounted for all other effects, there is a marginally statistically significant difference in the tones in which the three issue dimensions are debated in Rome and Prato. Finally, Model D describes the separate effects of the three constitutive dimensions of the issue.[15] The results indicate that the positions on the law and order dimension are significantly more negative than on the cultural and socioeconomic dimensions. Compared to debates over the other two, in fact, debates on security are characterized by a significantly higher hostility to migration. Even more importantly,

Table 5.7 Regression results for the mean position on the immigration issue dimensions

Position on immigration	Coef.			
	A	B	C	D
Intercept	0.01	0.27	0.22	0.27
	(1.887)	(0.248)	(0.263)	(0.262)
Centre-left	0.51**	0.43**	0.45**	0.48**
	(0.180)	(0.218)	(0.209)	(0.194)
Centre-right	−0.53***	−0.58***	−0.56***	−0.56***
	(0.182)	(0.227)	(0.236)	(0.211)
CL challenger	0.06	0.01	0.06	−0.07
	(0.067)	(0.064)	(0.117)	(0.133)
CR challenger	−0.23*	−0.26*	−0.32	−0.28
	(0.135)	(0.123)	(0.197)	(0.193)
Radical right	−0.86***	−0.74***	−0.73***	−0.76***
	(0.180)	(0.196)	(0.179)	(0.155)
Time (ref. t1)		−0.05	−0.06	−0.09
		(0.170)	(0.173)	(0.178)
Salience		−0.04***	−0.04***	−0.02
		(0.014)	(0.016)	(0.018)
Rome (ref. Prato)			0.12*	0.14*
			(0.059)	(0.061)
Milan (ref. Prato)			0.10	0.16
			(0.195)	(0.221)
Cult. & relig. dimension				−0.02
				(0.051)
Law & order dimension				−0.51***
				(0.127)
R-squared	0.44	0.50	0.50	0.61
No. observations	79	79	79	79

Note: Standard errors are reported in parentheses.

*, **, *** indicate significance at the 90%, 95% and 99% levels.

Source: Author's data (see Appendix 1).

once this specification is introduced, the coefficient of the salience of immigration dimensions turns non-significant, indicating that the focus on security explains most of the effect of salience.[16]

In sum, the results of the regression analyses explain about two-thirds of the variance in the positions on immigration. Centre-left parties tend to be less opposed to immigration than the rest of the actors, whereas radical right and centre-right are significantly more so, particularly when running as challengers. As previous results likewise demonstrated, the tone by which the multiple issue dimensions are debated across electoral campaigns has to do with salience and the mobilization of security arguments, especially by the radical right. Nevertheless, when controlling for the attention and positions of mainstream and radical right actors, one cannot confirm that city contexts differ in terms of mean positions on the three immigration dimensions.

Conclusive remarks

Analysing campaigning across local elections, I have showed earlier that issue dimensions are crucial to understanding debates on migration. In this chapter, I built upon this idea in order to assess the degree to which local contexts shape partisan strategies for the politicization of this issue. In line with previous research suggesting that parties of the radical right, and to a lesser extent the mainstream right, play the card of tough immigration regulations while left-wing parties occupy more moderate positions (Arzheimer, 2009; Ellinas, 2007; Golder, 2003; Ivarsflaten, 2008; Kitschelt, 1995), this chapter's results generally confirm that competition on immigration is structured along the left–right axis. However, the threefold typology of immigration dimensions allowed for a more detailed investigation of the dynamics of politicization across local contexts in Italy.

The analyses confirmed the idea that political debates on migration are better understood on the basis of multiple issue dimensions, since it is these that parties strategically mobilize in order to gain an advantage over (or reduce a disadvantage towards) their competitors. In line with the findings reported in Chapter 4, I showed that not all three dimensions are equally important in determining local competitors' electoral strategies. Although actors display specific dimensional preferences, their strategies are often based on the mobilization of dimensions with particular resonance in given local contexts. My results suggest that the centre-right is generally better at providing a consistent discourse on immigration, but that the degree of overlap between profiles is high, indicating that the same dimension tends to prevail across actors within a single election campaigns. In this respect, my findings illustrated not only that the increasing salience of immigration reduces the differentiation between the discourse of right- and left-wing actors, but also that this is mainly because the centre-left is forced towards focusing on the issue dimensions mobilized by the right. Hence, this chapter confirmed that parties tend to adjust their selective emphasis and policy positions on immigration depending on the political context in which they operate. Moreover, the campaigns involving independent radical right actors displayed higher emphasis on migration affairs, and more opposition to it, primarily because parties converged on the main dimension upon which the radical right mobilized: security.

These results illustrate the relation between parties' politicization strategies, political contexts at the local level, and the thematic structure of complex policy issues. A left–right pattern in immigration debates in fact does exist, yet this is structured not only in terms of support and opposition to migration, but also in terms of issue-dimensional differentiation. Right-wing actors tend to be more consistently anti-immigration, using different aspects interchangeably, whereas left-wing actors use certain dimensions (mainly the cultural one) to support migration and others to oppose it (the law and order dimensions). By showing that parties align with – and diverge from – one another based on issue dimensions, my results buttress the argument that the study of debates on migration should be refined. This is first because the immigration issue has been largely subsumed by the left–right division, in particular when it comes to the cultural and religious dimension;

and second because it has underlined that focusing events and the characteristics of local contexts can make specific issue dimensions cut across traditional party lines.

On the one hand, therefore, the thematic nature of complex policy issues gives political entrepreneurs the opportunity to selectively address certain aspects (most notably security and perceived insecurity), while ignoring others (economic and, less so, cultural impact). On the other hand, local political actors seize the opportunities and features of the media and political environment where competition takes place, engaging on complex issues based on local circumstances, incentives and constraints affecting the expectations for success or failure of their strategies. Despite the specificities of the contexts under observation, this model can help make sense of ongoing debates on migration, providing empirical evidence, and conceptual and analytical tools, for understanding the political dynamics that led to the securitization of migration well beyond the Italian case. Processes similar to the ones outlined here can be observed in other European settings, where the actual content of migration debates is shaped by the real or perceived circumstances characterizing the context where competition takes place and the discursive strategies of the actors involved. The emphasis on the different dimensions of migration, therefore, will depend on the relative importance attributed to aspects such as economic migration and the ongoing Mediterranean refugee crisis, racial and Islamophobic discrimination and security panics following terrorist attacks, especially if involving second-generation migrants as in the case of Paris in January 2015.

Moreover, since increased salience enhances the similarity in mainstream actors' immigration discourse, an agenda logic seems to drive choices of politicization. The left in particular is often forced to bend the knee to right-wing strategies towards dimensional issue salience and positions, in particular when right-wing parties mobilize the law and order dimension. The success of blatantly anti-immigration actors such as Golden Dawn in Greece and Pegida in Germany, in this sense, comes as no surprise in contexts where migration is increasingly securitized in public and media discourse, at all levels of governance. As illustrated in this chapter, in fact the process of securitization of migration debates also permeates local political competition, since mediatized logics and public moods associated to critical junctures facilitate the consolidation of security arguments targeting the unwanted presence of ethnic minorities and illegal migrants in the local territory. Hence, not only do this chapter's analyses relate to the study of issue politicization (cf. Green-Pedersen, 2010), they also pave the way toward connecting with public opinion research, in particular that focusing on how elites' framing affects citizens' preferences and opinions (cf. Chong and Druckman, 2007a, 2007b). Similar to this stream of research, the present analysis suggests that parties may structure public opinion by offering different sets of choices to different publics (Sniderman and Theriault, 2004). The results of this chapter may therefore contribute to joint research on party politics with the study of mediatization and communication, which is the endeavour undertaken in the next chapters.

Notes

1 A notable exception to this is the study by Höglinger *et al.* (2012) focusing on the framing of globalization debates, and assessing empirically the circumstances that make the cultural logic or the economic logic prevail.

2 The detailed description of the candidates, lists, coalitions and their electoral results is reported in Appendix 2.

3 The results of the Chi-Square tests for the above table indicate that the dimensional issue attention is statistically different between parties: X^2 *(12, N = 2204) = 143.2, p <* *0.01* (Cramér's V = 0.18).

4 Next to the local-level factors discussed in the previous section, this can be partly explained by the post-fascist tradition of the Italian radical right, especially in Rome. Similar groups have a tendency to emphasize corporatist and social justice arguments in their political campaigning (Albanese *et al.*, 2015; Caldiron, 2009; Castelli Gattinara *et al.*, 2013; Froio and Castelli Gattinara, 2015).

5 In order to provide an exhaustive account of the differences reported in Table 5.3, we performed Chi-Square tests of goodness of fit. The results of the tests indicate that dimensional issue attention is not equally distributed across challenger and incumbent actors: X^2 *(6, N = 1783) = 104.9, p < 0.01* (Cramér's V = 0.17). Moreover, the results also confirm that the attention profile of the centre-right running as incumbent is not equal to its attention profile as a challenger: X^2 *(2, N = 1,130) = 28.0, p < 0.01* (Cramér's V = 0.16). Similarly, the attention profile of the centre-left as an incumbent and as a challenger is not equal: X^2 *(2, N = 653) = 63.8, p < 0.01* (Cramér's V = 0.31).

6 Due to inconsistent coalition choices across cases, political actors outside of the mainstream left and right coalitions participate quite irregularly to the electoral campaigns under study, and were therefore excluded from this section of the study.

7 Both measures are developed from Sigelman and Buell's (2004) measure of issue convergence among parties, which – in a two-party system – is calculated as follows:

$100 - (\sum_{i=1}^{n}|P_A - P_B|) / 2$. The logic of the *interparty overlap* is to average the absolute differences between issue (dimensional) emphases of parties (results are then standardized in order to range between 0 and a 100 and subtracted from 100 in order to measure similarity rather than dissimilarity). From the example of Green-Pedersen and Mortensen (2010), moreover, the *intraparty similarity* index applies the same logic to consecutive campaigns. Instead of averaging differences across parties' attention profiles, this measure does so between a party's attention profile and its own profile at the previous time point (measuring the average summed distances between a party's campaign and that party's campaign at the previous election): $100 - (\sum_{i=1}^{n}|P_{t1} - P_{t2}|) / 2$.

8 The high values of overlap are explained by the low number of categories upon which the measurement of overlap is made. See: Sigelman and Buell (2004).

9 For this reason, the standard errors allow for intragroup correlation, relaxing the usual requirement that the observations be independent. That is to say, the observations are independent across groups (clusters) but not necessarily within groups.

10 These correspond to the mainstream coalitions and the lists that ran with independent candidates in the six election campaigns, as well as the minor list and the public interest groups' categories.

11 Model D in the appendix displays this separately for each dimension of the immigration issue.

12 In order to test for possible interaction effects, we ran additional models including interaction terms between specific actors and issue dimensions. Given that no result reached statistical significance, the models were excluded from the analysis.

13 The standard errors allow for intragroup correlation, relaxing the usual requirement that the observations be independent. The observations are independent across groups (clusters) but not necessarily within groups.
14 The difference with respect to the analysis presented earlier in this chapter is due to the missing values associated with no salience (salience = 0).
15 Model D in the appendix reports this separately for each dimension of the immigration issue.
16 In order to test for possible interaction effects, we ran additional models including interaction terms between specific actors and issue dimensions. Given that no result reached statistical significance, the models were excluded from the analysis.

References

Albanese, M., Bulli, G., Castelli Gattinara, P. and Froio, C. (2015) *Fascisti di un altro millennio? Crisi e partecipazione in CasaPound Italia*. Rome and Acireale: Bonanno Editore.
Albertazzi, D., McDonnell, D. and Newell, J. (2011) 'Di lotta e di governo: The Lega Nord and Rifondazione Comunista in Office', *Party Politics*, 17(4), pp. 471–487.
Alonso, S. and Claro Da Fonseca, S. (2009) 'Immigration, Left and Right', paper prepared for presentation to the panel 'Immigrants vs. National Identity? The Problem of Integration in Europe' at the *Annual Meeting of the American Political Science Association*, Toronto, ON, 3–6 September 2009. Available at: www.wzb.eu/sites/default/files/personen/alonso.sonia.312/apsa09_alonso-fonseca.pdf (Accessed 19 May 2014).
Andall, J. (2007) 'Introduction: Immigration and Political Parties in Europe', *Patterns of Prejudice*, 41(2), pp. 105–108, DOI: 10.1080/00313220701265478.
Arzheimer, K. (2009) 'Contextual Factors and the Extreme Right Vote in Western Europe, 1980–2002', *American Journal of Political Science*, 53(2), pp. 259–275. doi: 10.1111/j.1540–5907.2009.00369.
Bale, T. (2003) 'Cinderella and Her Ugly Sisters: The Mainstream and Extreme Right in Europe's Bipolarising Party Systems', *West European Politics*, 26(3), pp. 67–90.
Bale, T., Green-Pedersen, C., Krouwel, A., Luther, K.R., Sitter, N. (2010) 'If You Can't Beat Them, Join Them? Explaining Social Democratic Responses to the Challenge from the Populist Radical Right in Western Europe', *Political Studies*, 58, pp.410–426.
Caldiron, G. (2009) *La Destra Sociale: Da Salò a Tremonti*. Roma: Manifestolibri
Castelli Gattinara, P., Froio, C. and Albanese, M. (2013) 'The Appeal of Neo-Fascism in Times of Crisis: The Experience of CasaPound Italia', *Journal of Comparative Fascist Studies*, 2(2), pp. 234–258.
Chong, D. and Druckman, J.N. (2007a) 'Framing Public Opinion in Competitive Democracies', *American Political Science Review*, 101, pp. 637–655.
Chong, D. and Druckman, J.N. (2007b) 'A Theory of Framing and Opinion Formation in Competitive Elite Environments', *Journal of Communication*, 57, pp. 99–118.
De Lange, S.L. (2007) 'A New Winning Formula? The Programmatic Appeal of the Radical Right', *Party Politics*, 13(4), pp.411–435.
Ellinas, A. (2007) *Playing the Nationalist Card: Mainstream Parties, Mass Media and Far-right Breakthrough in Western Europe*. Unpublished PhD Dissertation, Princeton University.
Froio, C. and Castelli Gattinara (2015) 'Neo-fascist Mobilization in Contemporary Italy Ideology and Repertoire of Action of CasaPound Italia', *Journal for deradicalization*, Vol. 2 (1), pp. 86–118.

Gabardi, E. (ed.) (2012) *La Rivoluzione Gentile. La Campagna per Pisapia sindaco di Milano.* Franco Angeli: Milan, Italy.

Golder, M. (2003) 'Explaining Variation in the Success of Extreme Right Parties in Western Europe', *Comparative Political Studies,* 36, pp. 432–466.

Green-Pedersen, C. (2010) *New Issues, New Cleavages, and New Parties: How to Understand Change in West European Party Competition.* Working Paper University of Aarhus, 26 August 2010. Available at SSRN: http://ssrn.com/abstract=1666096 or http://dx.doi.org/10.2139/ssrn.1666096

Green-Pedersen, C. and Krogstrup, J. (2008) 'Immigration as a Political Issue in Denmark and Sweden', *European Journal of Political Research,* 47, pp. 610–634.

Green-Pedersen, C. and Mortensen, P.B. (2010) 'Who Sets the Agenda and Who Responds to it in the Danish Parliament? A New Model of Issue Competition and Agenda-Setting', *European Journal of Political Research,* 49(2), pp. 257–281. doi: 10.1111/j.1475–6765.2009.01897.x

Helbling, M. (2013) 'Framing Immigration in Western Europe', *Journal of Ethnic and Migration Studies,* 40(1), pp. 21–41.

Höglinger, D., Wuest, B. and Helbling, M. (2012) 'Culture versus Economy: The Framing of Public Debates Over Issues Related to Globalization'. In: Kriesi, H., Grande, E., Dolezal, M., Helbling, M., Höglinger, D., Hutter, S. and Wuest, B. eds. *Political Conflict in Western Europe.* Cambridge/New York: Cambridge University Press, pp. 229–253.

Ignazi, P. (1992) 'The Silent Counter-Revolution: Hypotheses on the Emergence of the Extreme Right-Wing Parties in Western Europe', *European Journal of Political Research,* 22, pp. 3–35.

Inglehart, R. (1977) *The Silent Revolution: Changing Values and Political Styles among Western Publics.* Princeton, NJ: Princeton University Press.

Inglehart, R. (2008) 'Changing Values among Western Publics from 1970 to 2006', *West European Politics,*

Ivarsflaten, E. (2008) 'What Unites Right-Wing Populists in Western Europe? Re-Examining Grievance Mobilization Models in Seven Successful Cases', *Comparative Political Studies* 41(1), pp. 3–23.

Kitschelt, H. (1995) *The Radical Right in Western Europe.* Ann Arbor: University of Michigan Press.

Kriesi, H., Bernhard, L. and Hänggli, R. (2009) 'The Politics of Campaigning – Dimensions of Strategic Action'. In: Marcinkowski, F. and Pfetsch, B. eds. *Politik in der Mediendemokratie.* VS Verlag für Sozialwissenschaften, pp. 345–365.

Kriesi, H., Grande, E., Dolezal, M., Helbling, M., Höglinger, D., Hutter, S. and Wuest, B. (2012) *Political Conflict in Western Europe.* Cambridge/New York: Cambridge University Press.

Kriesi, H., Grande, E., Lachat, R., Dolezal, M., Bornschier, S. and Frey, T. (2008) *West European Politics in the Age of Globalization.* Cambridge: Cambridge University Press.

Lahav, G. (2004) *Immigration and Politics in the New Europe: Reinventing Borders.* Cambridge: Cambridge University Press.

McDonnell, D. (2006) 'A weekend in Padania: Regionalist Populism and the Lega Nord', *Politics,* 26(2), pp. 126–132.

Meguid, B. (2005) 'The Role of Mainstream Party Strategy in Niche Party Success', *American Political Science Review,* 99(3), pp. 347–359.

Meguid, B. (2008) *Party Competition between Unequals: Strategies and Electoral Fortunes in Western Europe.* Cambridge: Cambridge University Press.

Mudde, C. (2007) *Populist Radical Right Parties in Europe.* Cambridge: Cambridge University Press.

Sides, J. (2006) 'The Origins of Campaign Agendas', *British Journal of Political Science,* 36, pp. 407–436.

Sigelman, L. and Buell, E.H. (2004) 'Avoidance or Engagement? Issue Convergence in U.S. Presidential Campaigns, 1960–2000', *American Journal of Political Science,* 48(4), pp. 650–661.

Sniderman, P. and Theriault, M. (2004) 'The Structure of Political Argument and the Logic of Issue Framing'. In: Saris, W.E. and Sniderman, P. eds. *Studies in Public Opinion: Attitudes, Non-Attitudes, Measurement Error and Change.* Princeton: Princeton University Press, pp. 133–165.

Van der Brug, W. and van Spanje, J. (2009) 'Immigration, Europe and the "New" Cultural Dimension', *European Journal of Political Research,* 48, pp. 309–334.

6 Framing local migration debates

Introduction

This chapter moves one step further in the analysis of electoral campaigns, investigating how political actors frame immigration across different local settings and election campaigns. Indeed, even if the dimensional analysis developed earlier in this book allowed for a closer look at the thematic structure of electoral debates from the point of view of city settings and party competition, it is still not apparent what the real arguments are that different local politicians mobilize in order to debate migration. Previous chapters helped unpack the immigration issue to expose its intrinsically multidimensional nature, yet could not assess how particular problems are defined, nor the justifications used to support the contrasting positions. Put differently, what are the concrete argumentations that local political entrepreneurs use when competing over the immigration issue? What are the actual motivations behind supportive and restrictive stances towards migration? Do political actors follow the same framing strategies under different campaign circumstances?

Developing the basic argument underlying this study, this chapter claims that the immigration issue may take multiple meanings. These alternative understandings change and develop because of variations in the type of actor involved in the campaign, as well as the circumstances of local debates. Contextual constraints related to the social and political environment in which competition takes place, as well as ideological and practical ones related to partisan differences, have an impact on the choice of particular frames to debate migration in local electoral campaigns. The present chapter therefore looks at the specific frames that municipal candidates mobilize to deal with and to express support for or against migration. Keeping the focus on electoral coalitions and municipal candidates, this chapter departs from partisan dimensional attention profiles to investigate the framing of each issue dimension in public discourse. Likewise, it will further investigate the motivations for supporting or opposing migration, or – more accurately – the motivations that electoral actors advance in public, across the three cases.

Previous literature has looked extensively at how migration is framed in general, while giving relatively little attention to the way in which different actors make use of alternative frames in order to build their electoral discourses (Helbling, 2013). As was discussed in the theory section, framing involves not only selection and salience, but also the definition of problems, the diagnosis of its causes, and the evaluation and prescription of possible remedies (Gamson, 1992). In this sense, if the previous chapter looked at how certain issue dimensions are emphasized in order to fix the public's attention while obscuring alternative ones, the present one provides an investigation into the framing choices of electoral actors within each specific aspect of the issue. In so doing I offer an in-depth analysis of the active efforts of political actors to construct immigration discourse, looking at how alternative frames are used, and how positions on immigration are taken and justified. I will examine the extent to which left-wing coalitions differentiate their discourse from the political right, based on the evidence on the preferences of the different actors that was obtained in the previous sections of this book and on the empirical data on electoral campaigning in Italian local elections. Subsequently, I look at each of the six electoral campaigns under study, in order to check for variation in actors' framing choices, due to the different circumstances in Milan, Prato and Rome. A final section looks at the evaluative judgement that actors put forth, in order to elucidate whether opposition and support to migration are framed differently by different actors and in different contexts.

Migration frames and strategic choice

Party logics

The choice of focusing on issue-specific frames (or attribute framing) rather than on general frame categories reflects a more general understanding of the relationship between political actors and the issue they mobilize. As was discussed in Chapter 2, I chose to look at substantive, issue-specific frames, linking them explicitly to an issue dimension and an evaluation (see: Entman, 2004). In terms of competition strategies in electoral campaigning, this implies understanding actors' strategies in terms of differentiation in problem definition between one actor's framing choices and those of their most direct competitors. Attribute framing and second-level agenda setting theory suggest that focusing on issue dimensions can shape public perceptions and choice, by prompting people to think about specific attributes of an issue, or – in other words – influencing not only *what* to think about, but also *how* to think about it (McCombs, 2004).

At a first level, however, parties' general understanding of social reality will inevitably influence their framing choices. As pointed out by, among others, Helbling (2013) and Sniderman and Theriault (2004), political actors are not completely free to develop framing strategies, but are constrained by their previous choices and by their broader ideological commitments. The choice of particular frames to describe a given social reality is thus likely to derive from a combination of tactical and ideological considerations, including sets of ideas, values and worldviews that are (at least presumably) shared within a party or coalition. Hence, concerning the immigration issue, and assuming that the ultimate goal of any political actor is to convince the public of her interpretation of the social reality, framing choices must resonate with the broader ideological understanding of the actor doing the mobilizing (Statham and Trenz, 2012). As was illustrated in the theoretical chapter and confirmed by the analyses carried on in the previous chapter, such ideological commitments are generally plotted along left–right scales, in which cosmopolitan and social security aspects characterize the left while nationalism and free-market liberalism characterize the right (Helbling, 2013; Knutsen, 1995). In terms of the cultural and religious dimension, therefore, previous studies suggest that the political left is more inclined to mobilize multicultural arguments (favouring cultural openness, living together among different groups and religions, and universal human rights), whereas the political right prefers nationalistic ones (stressing the importance of national identity and assimilation).

The socioeconomic dimension meanwhile is divisible into two frames, referring on the one hand to labour and social security (including unemployment and salary problems, reduction of welfare assets and social security), and on the other to economic prosperity (interpreting migration in terms of economic benefits, growth and improved societal well-being). Supporters of economic liberalization on the left and on the right could use economic prosperity arguments based on the need for a cheap labour force in order to improve the country's productivity, interpreting the advantages and disadvantages of migration in terms of economic growth. By contrast, labour and social security frames can emphasize the trade-off between national and immigrant welfare and employment, especially by labour protectionist actors. For the Italian case, however, previous researchers suggest that mainstream left actors faced little concerns of 'social dumping' among their constituencies, at least when compared to other European countries (Chaloff, 2005; Massetti, 2014).

Finally, with previous chapters in mind, it is reasonable to assume that law and order arguments are more appealing to right-wing actors, since radical right and populist parties in particular mobilize feelings of insecurity by linking immigration to crime and violence (Mudde, 2007). Yet, in some cases, left-wing actors are also susceptible to using similar frames. As was discussed earlier, similar arguments are not necessarily related to security problems at the urban level, but have often been grounded in more broad emergency logics, which tend to depict immigration-related problems as unexpected and immigration in general as a temporary phenomenon. At the local level, this has also involved the targeting of specific communities, in particular the Roma, who are held responsible for problems of security, receiving the etiquette of 'the Gypsy problem' (Sigona, 2005).

Table 6.1 below reports the share of attention given to each of the seven frame categories by the main actors in local electoral campaigns, as well as the relative importance of each actor in the debates by frame category. Data are reported for the mainstream left, the mainstream right and the radical right, alongside interest groups and a category encompassing the remaining parties in the elections under study.[1] As can be noticed, the centre-left mobilizes multiculturalist frames (20%) more often than the mainstream right (11.5%) and radical right (1.3%), which instead are much more prone to use nationalist arguments (10%) than the left (4%). In contrast, there are no clear-cut differences in the use of economic frames between mainstream parties, although the centre-left uses economic prosperity arguments somewhat more often than the centre-right (7.5% and 4.4%, respectively).

In line with the expectation that right-wing actors 'drive' immigration debates, moreover, the radical right consistently mobilizes both the labour and security frame (24%) and the prosperity one (14%). In terms of security, finally, centre-right parties are more inclined to mobilize what we have called the 'emergency logic' than the centre-left (30% and 21.7%, respectively). In line with the discussion in the previous chapters, looking at the table horizontally it also appears that the mainstream right is key in mobilizing all types of discourses on immigration, irrespective of the frame category. This is most evident for emergency frames, where the centre-right is responsible for more than 60% of claims making, and least so for economic prosperity and multiculturalist frames. Yet, the results illustrate that the centre-right is almost as important as the centre-left in terms of multiculturalist frames.

These results suggest that partisan ideological differences explain only part of the framing strategies in local electoral competition. A more accurate interpretation must also account for whether these frames are used to support or to oppose

Table 6.1 Immigration frames by actor (overall)

Frame	Centre-left	Centre-right	Radical right	Interest groups	Others	Total
Socioeconomic dimension						
Labour and security	8.2	7.1	24.1	7.6	10.4	-
% of frame	24.7%	39.2%	14.9%	9.8	11.4%	100%
Economic prosperity	7.5	4.4	13.9	8.8	6.4	-
% of frame	30.3%	33.0%	11.7%	15.4%	9.6%	100%
Cultural and religious dimension						
Nationalism	3.9	10.1	10.1	5.1	15.8	-
% of frame	12.1%	56.8%	6.4%	6.8%	17.7%	100%
Multiculturalism	20.0	11.6	1.3	20.9	20.1	-
% of frame	34.5%	36.8%	0.5%	15.6%	12.6%	100%
Law and order dimension						
Roma issues	19.5	17.3	15.2	14.5	5.4	-
% of frame	31.2%	50.6%	5.0%	10.0%	3.1%	100%
Urban issues	19.1	19.5	17.1	27.3	19.3	-
% of frame	24.7%	46.3%	4.6%	15.2%	9.1%	100%
Emergency issues	21.7	30.0	18.5	20.6	22.6	-
% of frame	22.7%	57.5%	4.0%	8.6%	7.1%	100%
Tot.	100%	100%	100%	100%	100%	-
N	764	1401	158	330	279	2653

Note: Share of core sentences dedicated to immigration in newspaper articles.

Source: Author's data (see Appendix 1).

migration, as it is likely the case for multiculturalist frames. Before moving to the analysis of frames' evaluative content, however, we shall look at whether framing strategies are associated with the context in which competition takes place, investigating whether cross-context differences outweigh partisan ones.

Campaign logics

Next to previous commitments and partisan ideologies, framing strategies by political actors are likely to be influenced by the characteristics of the context in which competition takes place. In line with the idea that electoral campaigns are driven by party-system agendas, in fact, the social and political environment of local campaigns is of utmost importance in setting up actors' campaigning strategies. Local characteristics and features can increase the legitimacy of certain arguments, or enhance the relative attractiveness of a specific understanding of immigration affairs (Hopkins, 2007; Hopkins *et al.*, 2014). Based on these considerations, this section will describe in detail the framing of migration debates in Milan, Prato and Rome. Table 6.2 displays the framing strategies of centre-left, centre-right and radical right actors in each of the three cities, during each of the six election campaigns. Overall, the results show that the framing choices of the three actors vary considerably across city settings, especially for the centre-left and the radical right.[2]

Concerning the framing of the socioeconomic dimension, the three cities showcase different framing strategies by political actors. In Milan both mainstream coalitions tend to focus on labour and security aspects, whereas little – if any – attention is given to economic prosperity aspects. The same holds for the centre-left in Rome in 2006 and for the radical right in 2008. By contrast, in Prato all actors shifted attention from prosperity frames in 2004 to labour and security ones in 2009. The in-depth analysis of the data collected might help illustrate the main messages in each election campaign.

Migration was framed in labour and security terms in Milan and, to a certain extent, in Rome since the mainstream right and left developed symmetrical, yet opposite, discourses. The centre-right questioned the access of foreign residents to social benefits, housing and open competitive exams for jobs within local institutions and offices. The left-wing coalition, on the contrary, focused on migrants' rights as workers, accusing the government of putting them in competition with precarious workers. In Prato, instead, the framing of the socioeconomic dimension changed towards labour and security following the lead of the radical right, which entered the competition in the latest election campaign. This dynamics of competition corroborate my anticipation that the radical right plays the role of agenda-setter, not only in terms of attention, but also with respect to the public interpretation of the issue. In 2004, immigration had to do with economic prosperity, referring to immigrant entrepreneurship either as 'a fundamental resource for Prato',[3] or as 'the origin of the crisis in our textile industry'.[4] Yet in 2009, the radical right list running for mayor emphasize the trade-off between foreign labour and social security, emphasizing the problems of sustainability of the local

Table 6.2 Immigration frames by city and election campaign

Party	Election campaign Issue frame	Milan 2006	2011	Prato 2004	2009	Rome 2006	2008
Centre-left	Labour and security	9.4	11.7	9.1	13.9	1.9	0.0
	Economic prosperity	6.2	0.5	22.7	15.3	0.0	3.0
	Nationalism	6.3	4.1	4.5	7.0	0.0	1.0
	Multiculturalism	50.0	35.5	7.6	15.4	19.6	9.4
	Roma issues	0.0	26.4	0.0	0.9	58.8	32.1
	Urban issues	21.9	7.1	24.3	13.5	11.8	35.4
	Emergency issues	6.2	14.7	31.8	33.9	7.8	18.2
	Tot.	100%	100%	100%	100%	100%	100%
Centre-right	Labour and security	11.1	8.0	8.5	12.8	8.2	2.8
	Economic prosperity	1.8	1.2	19.5	12.8	1.6	3.3
	Nationalism	20.4	8.3	19.5	17.6	11.5	6.1
	Multiculturalism	14.8	18.5	1.7	8.8	1.6	5.3
	Roma issues	16.7	19.8	0.0	1.6	45.9	18.8
	Urban issues	20.4	7.7	13.6	34.4	19.7	35.9
	Emergency issues	14.8	36.5	37.3	12.0	11.5	27.7
	Tot.	100%	100%	100%	100%	100%	100%
Radical right	Labour and security	-	-	-	35.6	-	8.8
	Economic prosperity	-	-	-	23.3	-	1.5
	Nationalism	-	-	-	5.6	-	16.2
	Multiculturalism	-	-	-	0.0	-	2.9
	Roma issues	-	-	-	0.0	-	35.3
	Urban issues	-	-	-	11.1	-	36.4
	Emergency issues	-	-	-	24.4	-	18.2
	Tot.	100%	100%	100%	100%	100%	100%

Note: Share of core sentences dedicated to immigration in newspaper articles.

Source: Author's data (see Appendix 1).

welfare system. The centre-right candidate picked up on this with claims that the wealth of the Chinese and that of Prato's citizens are mutually exclusive. Similarly, the left-wing coalition also ultimately accepted that, due to the increasing numbers of foreign residents, the municipal administration 'will not be able to guarantee resources to everybody'.[5]

Concerning the framing of the cultural and religious dimension, the interpretation of the results in the above table have to take into account that this issue is generally more salient in Milan than either in Rome or in Prato. Yet, three elements stand out concerning each of the observed party type. First, the centre-left: although the use of the multicultural frame is more frequent than that of nationalist ones in all three cities, there is variation across electoral campaigns, since this frame is used 50% of the time in Milan in 2006, compared to only 7.6% in Prato in 2004. Second, the radical right: across the three cities, the radical right used almost exclusively nationalist frames, but the overall importance of this frame is not as pronounced as one could assume before looking at the data. Third, the mainstream right: its profile in framing the cultural dimension is ambiguous, showing a preference for nationalist frames at earlier elections and for multiculturalist ones in the most recent campaigns. More in detail, left-wing multiculturalist frames were generally informed of cultural liberalism – 'it is our intention to build a centre for the Chinese culture'; 'our goal is to have a green, multi-ethnic munici-pality'.[6] Nationalist frames by the radical right have to do with loss of identity for the city and with the need to restore its traditional values. I refer here to proposals to show the crucifix in public buildings and claims opposing the introduction of Quran readings in public schools, and other nationalist arguments – 'we needed Chinese labour force, but we do not want to rebuild China in Prato'.[7] The shift towards multiculturalist frames by the mainstream right may be related to the unsuccessful strategy to radicalize the issue of diversity *vis-à-vis* Italian culture and tradition (Caponio, 2013), which have generally not been backed by Catho-lic and moderate public opinion in Italy (Bordignon, 2008). Nationalist frames include slogans such as 'Milanese people come first',[8] but also by calls to defend the traditional identity and 'Christianity' of cities from the excessive presence of alien immigrants.[9] Multiculturalist interpretations, instead, included pragmatic policy proposals, such as the construction of a 'Department of Identity and Citizenship to promote civil coexistence between natives and immigrants', but most frequently took the form of reactive counter-framing, especially when the issue at stake was the construction of the mosque in Milan.

If we turn the attention to security aspects, we can see that law and order frames were widely used in all the campaigns. Yet, the way in which this dimension was framed varied considerably across city contexts, especially in terms of Roma issues. This frame was completely absent in the debate in Prato, in both electoral campaigns.[10] On the contrary, it was widely mobilized in Rome in 2006 (but lost importance in the subsequent campaign) and in the second election campaign in Milan. Both the right and the left tend to associate the presence of Romani people with threats to individual and collective security. In Rome the right-wing candi-date Alemanno proposed to 'erase immigrant illegality: nomad camps and abusive settlements should be displaced away from urban areas',[11] whereas in Milan the Lega Nord proposed to 'reset all regular and irregular Roma camps'.[12] The radical right claimed with irony that the 'best mayor in Europe is the one of Bucharest, as he sent all of the Roma people here'.[13] Besides right-wing actors, however, the frequency by which the centre-left frames security issues in terms of Roma people is unexpected. The analysis of framing strategies shows that the centre-left takes the lead in promoting the Roma issue frame in immigration discourse. In Rome, this takes the form of blaming, especially by accusing the national government of being responsible for the regularization of thousands of Romanian Roma, which are described as the primary source of insecurity in the city. In Milan, instead, the Roma were targeted only in the 2011 election, and often in a reactive way since the challenger coalition was accused of being excessively permissive with respect to Romani settlements.

Concerning the urban issue category, this is widely mobilized by all parties in Rome in 2008, due to the previously mentioned crime-related event, which the can-didates framed in terms of urban problems such as the decay of the city's outskirts, the incapability of the city to integrate migrant residents, and the lack of security in specific areas of the city. In this sense, the right-wing candidate depicted the city as 'out of control' due to the inefficacy of its security policies.[14] The radical right described the city as insecure because 'it is always migrants who steal our bread and rob our houses'.[15] Similarly, the centre-right made extensive use of the crime stories in the media to support its campaign against the incumbents: 'the murder confirms what we have been denouncing: the escalation in immigrant criminality is shaking the everyday life of Rome'.[16] This, in turn, forced the left to react with promises of tightening the controls in dangerous districts, and by mobilizing counter frames such as 'the propaganda of our opponents does not help to fight crime and problems of integration in certain areas of the city'.[17]

Finally, emergency frames are frequent in all contexts under observation. Actors framed migration in terms of emergencies to discuss refugee and migrant crises, in which local administrations were expected to intervene. This frame characterized arguments about the management of humanitarian crises, especially in Milan. Although issues related to terrorist threats and amnesty proposals received only marginal attention, radical and centre-right actors also asked for special powers or special interventions. In particular, the radical right claimed 'the army is essential in Prato as a deterrent of violence'[18] and called for a 'sheriff'[19] rather than a mayor to restore the rule of law. The centre-left also mobilized emergency frames, mainly in a reactive way to defend the regional law on immigration and accusing the national government of indifference towards the 'emergency that Prato and Tuscany are facing with respect to the governance of legal and illegal immigration'.[20] These examples indicate that the emergency logic is a crucial dimension of migration debates, although it only surfaces when the conditions are appropriate. Visible humanitarian crises, the arrival of boats from North Africa and the Middle East, migration tragedies or stories such as those characterizing the current refugee crisis in Europe, are then described as unexpected phenomena and perceived as unstoppable events.

In sum, the findings support the general idea that framing choices vary across campaigns, as actors tend to use somewhat different frames in the three cities. First, candidates seem to take into account the specific necessities, conditions and priorities that characterize local economies and organize their framing of the socioeconomic dimension accordingly, so that debates on the presence and labour-market integration of migrants take quite different meanings in Prato when compared to Rome and Milan (Campomori and Caponio, 2013). Second, although the left–right differentiation is more noticeable for the framing of the cultural dimension, the propensity of radical right and mainstream right parties to use nationalist frames is lower than one could expect, as they increasingly prefer to use multicultural ones in a reactive way. Third, the relative importance of the law and order frames also changes across electoral campaigns, although I find that left-wing parties stand out in framing immigration in terms of Roma issues, and centre-right ones in terms of emergency and urban issues.

In order to elaborate further on the role of party-system agendas, this chapter follows the same approach as for the analysis of issue dimensions. I constructed two indexes for the consistency of the frames applied by the mainstream coalitions: the first measures the degree to which the framing choices of an actor overlap with the one of other actors in the same election campaign *(interparty overlap)*; the second measures the consistency of mainstream parties' framing choices across subsequent election campaigns *(intraparty similarity)*.[21] The two indexes reveal whether party strategies of framing migration are more similar to one another in any given election campaign (which would support the idea that party-system agendas influence individual actors' choices) than to a party's own discourse at previous elections (which would support, instead, the actor-driven logic). Table 6.3 displays the results for the two indexes.

The interparty overlap score indicates that, on average, the framing strategies of the competing parties at time *t2* coincided three-quarters of the time, whereas at time *t1* their convergence was lower. Similar to the results of Chapter 5, this confirms the agenda interpretation of the dynamics of electoral debates, since the choices of mainstream parties become increasingly similar when the salience of immigration increases. This implies that the more important migration is in electoral debates, the more actors have to 'respond' to one another, not only in terms of the attention that they attribute to specific issue features, but also in terms of the argumentations and justifications that they mobilize. Moreover, the intraparty similarity score indicates that the centre-left behaves somewhat more consistently than the centre-right in terms of issue framing, although the difference is very marginal. Combined to earlier findings concerning the disadvantage of left-wing actors in migration debates, this implies that the right enjoys an advantage in terms of driving the attention to its preferred issue dimension, and it is more flexible in the type of justifications it uses to discuss its dimensional positions. As I have shown previously for the case of the multiculturalism frame in Milan, this is mainly the result of 'trespassing' strategies by which the centre-right takes up the frames mobilized by the centre-left and uses them to discredit the proposed justification. Overall, the table indicates that, at both points in time, the interparty overlap scores are higher than intraparty similarity for the centre-left and for the centre-right. This suggests the prevalence of the agenda logic over the partisan one in driving framing choices with respect to the immigration issue. This is further confirmed by the fact that the gap between the two indexes increases as the level of attention to immigration grows.

Table 6.3 Interparty overlap and intraparty similarity in framing strategies

	Interparty overlap	Intraparty similarity	
		Centre-left	Centre-right
Time *t1*	69.1%		
Time *t2*	74.3%	68.7%	66.5%

Note: Degree of dimensional similarity across parties and elections.

Source: Author's data (see Appendix 1).

In conclusions, these findings suggest that when the immigration issue as a whole increases in salience, the degree of similarity between the frames applied by the mainstream right and left does too. This is likely because actors are increasingly forced to respond to one another once the issue has come to the core of election debates, as illustrated by the reactive use of multiculturalist frames by the mainstream right. As I have illustrated, the framing of the centre-left is somewhat more consistent than the one of the centre-right, which is at odds with the findings of Chapter 5 where the analysis showed that the dimensional attention profile of the right was more consistent than the one of the left. Together, these results indicate that whilst the left is more ready to change its migration discourse across issue dimensions, the right is more inclined to differentiate its framing choices within single dimensions. In other words, the centre-left is more prone to change its dimensional profile across electoral campaigns, whereas the right is more likely than the centre-left to put forth alternative interpretations of the same immigration dimension. A closer look at how different frames are used to support and oppose migration might help clarify these dynamics.

Framing opposition and support to migration

Party logics

So far the analysis looked at the degree of importance of alternative frames within electoral competitors' discourse, following the assumption that frame categories can be considered neutral from an evaluative point of view. As shown, agenda logics tend to prevail, since in interactive environments like election campaigns candidates feel the pressure to respond to one another, especially when they are engaged by the mass media. In these cases, looking at the salience of frames may not suffice to distinguish an actor's profile from his opponent's. In other words, when candidate a deals with issue x using frame i, candidate b may find himself obliged to respond to the frame used by a about issue x. In such cases, the only element enabling the differentiation between the competing actors would be their evaluative judgement about the political issue under debate.

This section looks therefore at the composition of the alternative partisan discourses, analysing the choice of frames to express evaluative judgements on migration. Since frames are justification of actors' positions on a given dimension, they are related with either pro- or anti-immigration positions. In this sense, nationalist and labour and security frames are generally mobilized by to oppose migration, whereas multiculturalist and economic prosperity ones characterize pro-immigration stances. Finally, as the law and order dimension is less prone to be mobilized to support migration, the corresponding frames also primarily express negative interpretations of migration and its consequences. Yet, emergency arguments can also play a different role, since moderate parties may use them to express neutral or humanitarian statements on forced migration and asylum issues. Table 6.4 below displays the extent to which each category is used in support of, or opposition to, migration by the main political actors.

Table 6.4 Opposition and support frames of immigration by actor

Parties	Centre-left		Centre-right		Radical right	
Issue frames	Anti-	Pro-	Anti-	Pro-	Anti-	Pro-
Labour and security	3.4	11.5	7.1	6.3	23.6	100
Economic prosperity	5.0	8.8	3.3	15.9	14.0	0
Nationalism	1.3	5.8	10.5	6.3	10.2	0
Multiculturalism	2.0	32.4	9.3	32.5	1.3	0
Roma issues	32.7	10.8	18.4	6.3	15.3	0
Urban issues	36.0	7.9	21.2	4.8	17.2	0
Emergency issues	19.1	22.9	30.2	27.8	18.5	0
Tot.	100%	100%	100%	100%	100%	100%
N	303	445	1262	126	157	1

Note: Share of core sentences dedicated to the migration issue in newspapers.

Source: Author's data (see Appendix 1).

The table provides two main insights. On the one hand, it shows that mainstream actors choose substantively different frames depending on whether they express support for or opposition to migration.[22] On the other, it indicates that the framing choices to express opposition to migration change depending on the actor doing the mobilizing,[23] whereas the justification for supportive arguments is rather similar among mainstream left and right actors.[24] To support migration, both mainstream parties use primarily the multiculturalism and the emergency frame. In contrast, opposition is articulated primarily in terms of urban and Roma issues by the centre-left, and in terms of emergency issues by the centre-right. Unexpectedly, the centre-left stands out as the main actor targeting the Roma community in terms of migration problems, conspicuously more than its right-wing competitors. The radical right meanwhile mobilizes in particular labour issues to oppose migration, in line with the welfare chauvinism that characterizes this party family.

I now address the framing of each issue dimension separately, starting from the framing of the socioeconomic dimension and its two frame categories. The above table shows that the mainstream right prefers labour and security frames to oppose migration and economic prosperity ones to support it. If the left tends to use both socioeconomic frames mainly to support migration, the radical right, on the contrary, mobilizes both frames in a restrictive fashion. In terms of the framing of the cultural dimension, my data shows that the radical right uses exclusively nationalist frames, naturally to oppose migration, whereas the centre-right criticizes migration also in terms of multiculturalism. This frame category, however, is also used when the centre-right engaged in pro-migration discourse. Reciprocally, the centre-left uses nationalistic frames more in the pro-category than in the anti- migration one. Again, this suggests that competing actors are highly responsive to one another when it comes to framing this issue dimension. Finally, the security frames express mainly negative attitudes towards migration, for all actors. Despite this general tendency, however, emergency frames also allow parties, political entrepreneurs and other social actors engaging in migration debates to emphasize 'temporary' actions, exceptional interventions and the 'unexpected' nature of migration. In this sense, these frames can justify shelter policies for refugees and asylum seekers in case of international emergencies and exceptional circumstances. In a pro-immigration fashion, this frame is used by competing actors in order to suggest putting aside political differences in favour of either a pragmatic, problem-solving approach, or a more universalistic understanding of international solidarity.

Campaign logics

Similar to previous chapters, I now focus on framing strategies in each of the contexts under investigation, looking at whether the composition of electoral campaigns, and the presence and framing choices of radical right actors influence debates as a whole, and the behaviour of the other competing actors. Figure 6.1 below displays actors' positions on each immigration frame in Milan's two election campaigns. As can be noticed, the pattern is approximately the same: in both elections, the centre-right framed migration positively only in terms of namely economic prosperity, which is also the least mobilized frame (used in only 2% of the cases). The centre-left, conversely, mobilized negatively only through urban issues frames, which are used quite frequently, especially in 2006. The average position on multiculturalism by the left and the right remained unchanged and highly polarized over time, while the frame gained in importance.

The strategy of the mainstream left coalition in the 2011 elections included using emergency framing in a more negative fashion than in 2006, whilst also directly engaging in competition with its opponents over Roma issues. This strategy is quite different from the one followed in 2006, when the left avoided campaigning on Roma affairs. This time, instead, Roma issues were mobilized reactively, since the left denounced the inefficacy of the mayor's policies of 'zero tolerance' against Roma camps, and claimed that dismantling Romani settlement could only displace the problem, rather than solving it. This was a clear attempt at delegitimizing the local government over the outcomes of its policies. The mainstream right responded to its opponents by framing security problems in terms of emergency. It placed the emphasis on the security threats emerging from a supposed 'Islamic invasion' that Milan would face in the aftermath of the Arab Spring, and defended the conduct of the municipal government by arguing that immigrant criminality was due to the extraordinary inflow of clandestine migrants.

Figure 6.2 reports pro and contra framing of immigration in Prato. First, the two election campaigns differ due to the presence of a radical right party in 2009, which wholeheartedly challenged migration and the municipal policies on immigration and integration. Possibly, because of this, the comparison over time shows that both mainstream actors decisively changed their framing strategies between

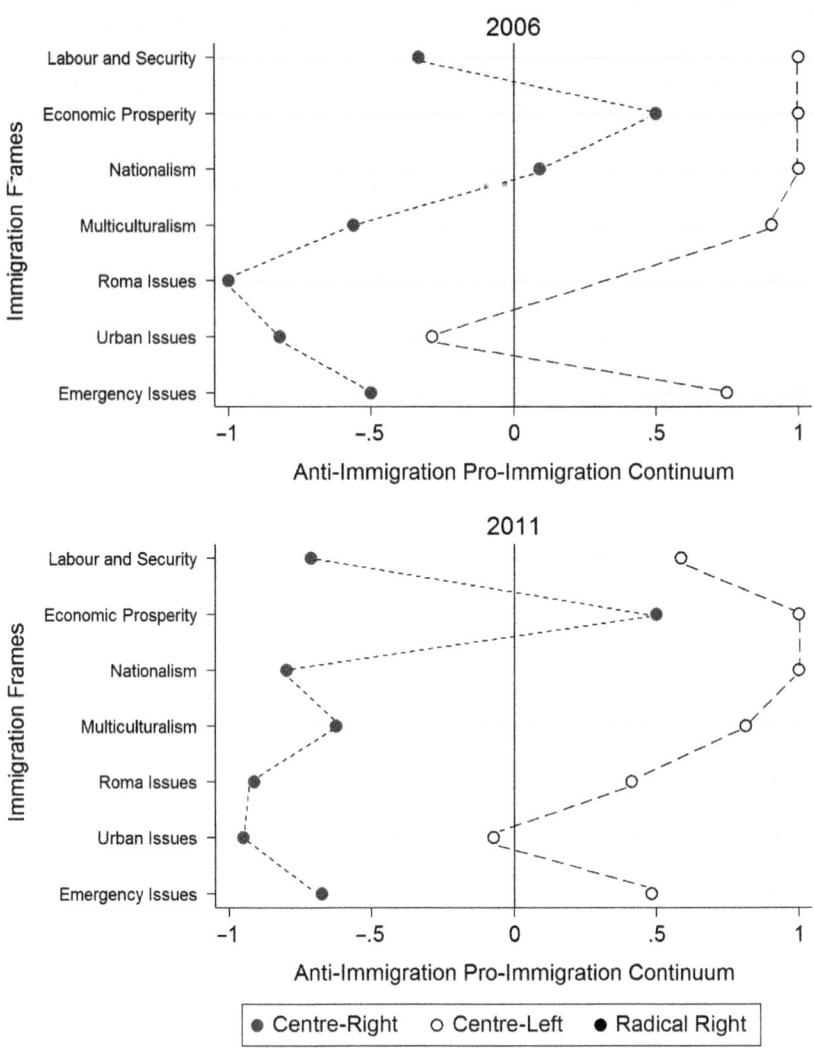

Figure 6.1 Framing of support and opposition to immigration in Milan by actor 2006 and
2011

Source: Author's data (see Appendix 1).

the two election campaigns. In particular, the centre-right remained opposed to migration across all issue frames except for multiculturalism, on which it nuanced considerably its position (whilst simultaneously increasing salience). Since this happened in combination with the appearance of a radical right competitor, it seems safe to conclude that this strategy aimed at attracting moderate voters.

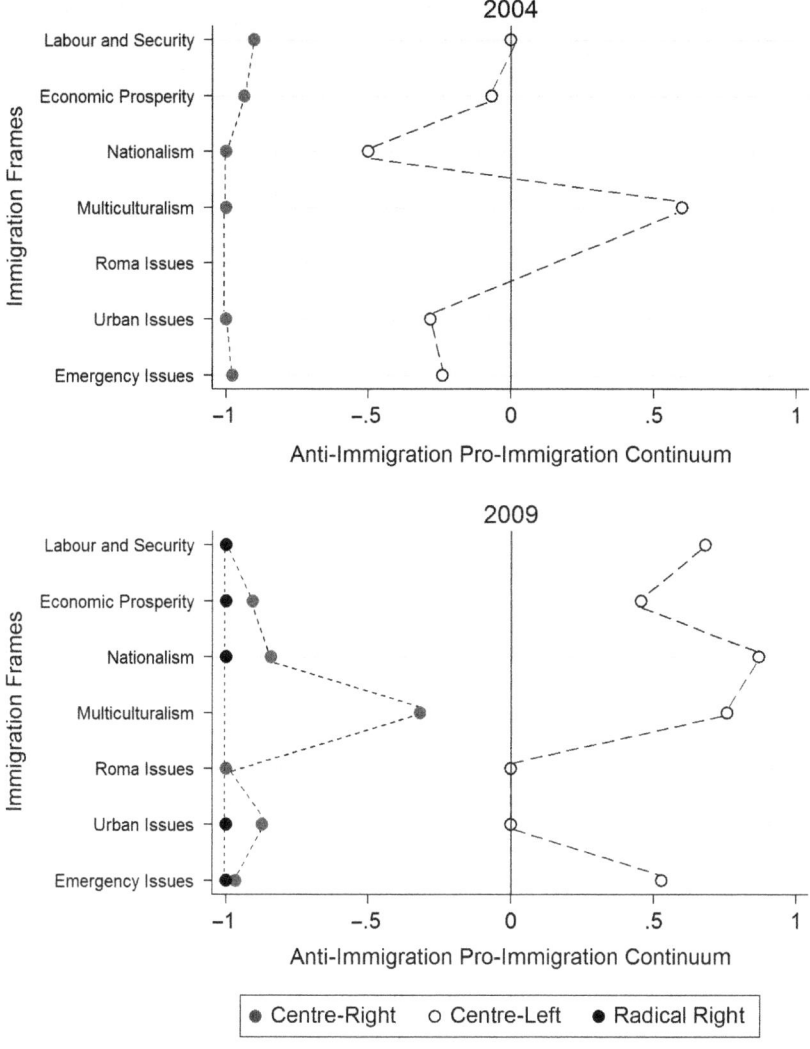

Figure 6.2 Framing of support and opposition to immigration in Prato by actor 2004 and 2009

Source: Author's data (see Appendix 1).

By contrast, the centre-left changed its strategies *vis-à-vis* all issue frames, most of which expressed considerably more supportive stances towards migration in 2009 than in 2004: this applies to the two socioeconomic frames and to the nationalist and emergency frames. The left in fact framed security problems mainly by reference to clandestine migration and regulations of the inflow of migrants, challenging the proposal of the radical right to expel illegal residents from the city.

This strategy seems oriented at differentiating its profile from that of the right-wing competitors, in the attempt to put pressure on the mainstream right which had to decide whether to compete with the left for moderate voters or with the radical right for less moderate ones. This approach, in other words, confirms previous findings on the strategy of the left-wing coalition that I illustrated in the previous chapter.

Figure 6.3 presents the data for the case of Rome. As can be noticed, both time points display a skewed distribution of positions, with centre-left and centre-right

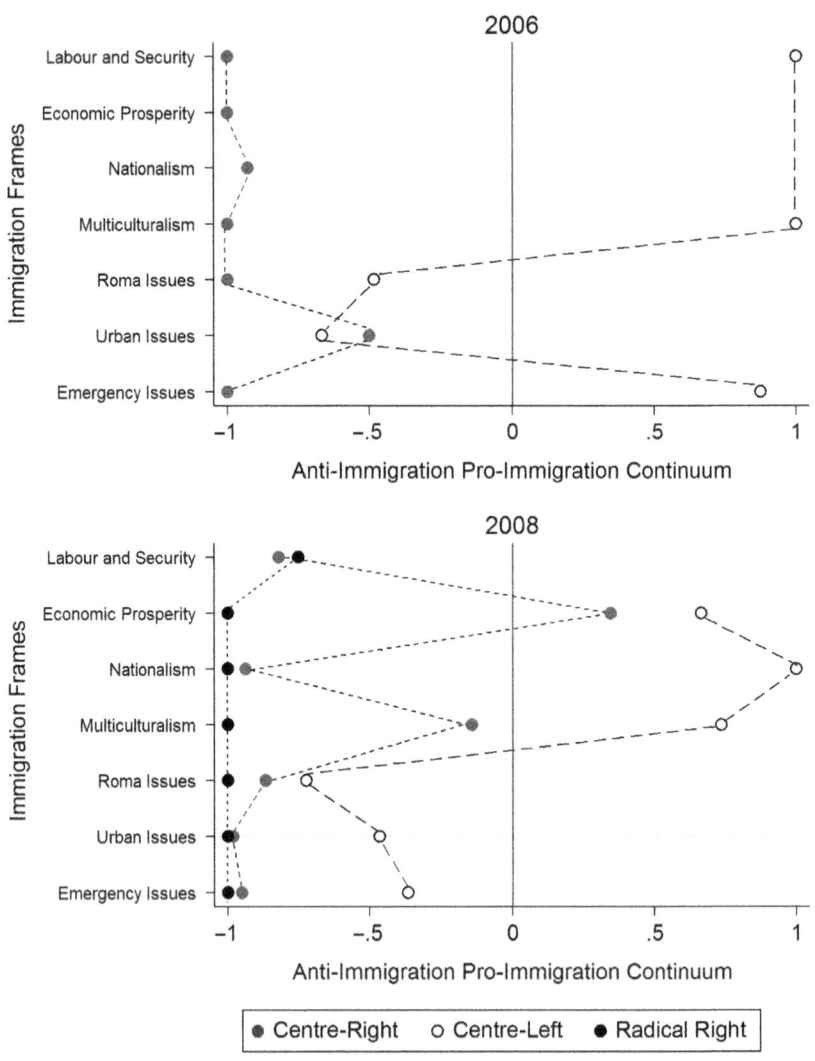

Figure 6.3 Framing of support and opposition to immigration in Rome by actor 2006 and 2008

Source: Author's data (see Appendix 1).

articulating opposition to migration primarily through security frames. Similar to Prato, the radical right, participating in the 2008 campaign, offered a consistently anti-immigration discourse across all seven frames. Again, this seems to have forced the centre-right to nuance positions justified by multiculturalism and economic prosperity (these frames also receive more attention in 2008 than in 2006, although the difference is marginal). The three law and order frames, instead, consistently express opposition to migrants and immigration. This pattern is most likely attributable to the centre-right's need to avoid alienating electorates with mixed preferences, i.e. voters who approved immigration in terms of cultural and economic enrichment, yet were afraid of its consequences in terms of security.

In contrast, by looking at the centre-left strategy in 2006 and 2008, one can notice that this remained largely unchanged in terms of cultural framing of migration, and with respect to the targeting of Roma people in highly restrictive terms. Instead, dimensional choices changed substantially in the use of emergency frames. Pressed by the centre-right and radical right on security affairs because of the mass media coverage of crime stories, and anticipating high levels of perceived insecurity among the electorate, the centre-left preferred to frame migration concerns as emergencies in order to avoid being held responsible as the party in office. Put differently, the centre-left coalition supporting the outgoing mayor strategically framed the news stories about crime as unexpected and exceptional events, which needed firm handling (hence the increasingly anti-migration tone), yet for which the incumbent administration was not responsible.

In sum, the results outlined in this section show that mainstream actors choose substantively different frames depending on whether they express support for or opposition to migration, whereas the radical right mobilizes the most consistently anti-immigration discourse across the various elections. Supportive arguments mobilize above all multiculturalist frames, although tactical considerations often induce left actors to frame immigration in terms of emergencies. Similarly, the results show that the left uses Roma frames restrictively much more frequently than the centre-right, targeting a specific community rather than migrants as a whole when immigration focuses on security matters.

Conclusive remarks

The previous chapters analyzed the multiple dimensions that comprise parties' understanding of, and public discourse on, immigration. Recognizing the relevance of studying electoral competition within inherently multidimensional models, however, triggered a number of additional questions: what arguments do actors set out in order to defend their positions on immigration? What frames do they use under different circumstances? To answer these questions, the analysis not only looked into how issues are framed, but also into who was responsible for the frames, i.e. the choices of the various electoral candidates and coalitions. Therefore, I not only investigated the context of issue framing, but I also looked at partisanship and other forms of constraints on discursive choices by strategic actors. In sum, by showing the justifications and the underlining interpretations of actors' claims and positions on migration, this chapter sought to contribute to a better understanding of migration politics in electoral campaigning.

In line with the broader theoretical framework of this study, the chapter's empirical analysis shows that the way in which migration is debated can take various meanings and forms, depending on the type of actor participating in the campaign, the contextual circumstances of the electoral campaign, and whether a certain frame is deployed seeking to support or oppose immigration. In fact, even if there is considerable variation in framing strategies across actors and contexts, I find additional evidence for an agenda-based interpretation of immigration debates, since increasing salience of immigration as a whole reduces the leeway of political actors, which are constrained to focus on a more limited set of aspects and justification types.

The results show that framing strategies at the aggregate level are influenced only marginally by the ideologies of the political actors involved in the construction of public discourse, as no major differentiation could be identified between the mainstream left and right. Yet, framing strategies follow an actor-driven logic in two interrelated aspects: the left is substantially more prone to support immigration than the right, and it tends to prefer multiculturalist frames over nationalist ones, unlike its right-wing competitors. In this sense, a clearer left–right pattern emerged in terms of cultural and religious aspects, which was confirmed across the different election campaigns and despite city-level specificities. As I showed earlier, moreover, it was precisely by changing its position on the multicultural frame that the centre-right tried to differentiate its discourse from that of the radical right, when necessary.

In contrast to the idea that issue-position justifications resonate with previous commitments by the actors, my analysis shows that tactical considerations play a crucial role in setting up partisan framing strategies at the local level. These considerations and the disadvantage of the left on security matters explain the generally negative tone and the attention this actor provides to Roma issues. Similarly, the pro-immigration framing of the law and order dimension often uses emergency arguments, since these enable developing a pragmatic discourse without endorsing restrictive tones. The finding that increasing salience of migration leads to increasing similarity in the framing choices of mainstream left and right parties suggests that, when the issue is at the core of electoral debates, parties are increasingly forced to respond to one another. Moreover, the presence of the radical right in the campaigns had an impact on framing choices by, and the positions of, the centre-right and centre-left coalitions alike.

Beyond the specific findings of this chapter, this analysis provides additional insights for the study of the politics of migration and the changing nature of electoral competition. To begin with, they tend to corroborate the idea of an increasing securitization of migration debates across Europe, illustrating that this takes place not only at the national level, but also in local elections (Buonfino, 2004). Beyond emergency logics, community-based and context-specific security frames stand out as fundamental elements shaping electoral debates. In particular, the centre-left framing of the law and order dimension shows that the left is still unable to construct a pragmatic discourse on migration autonomously. Its framing strategy relies heavily on responses to the arguments of its opponents, and on the targeting of specific communities as the main cause of immigration-related problems and conflicts.

Second, these results provide further information on the dynamics by which issues that were previously outside the core of contentious politics are integrated into political campaigning agendas.[25] Actors do not simply aim at ideological consistency when faced with immigration as a campaign issue, but also consider contextual circumstances and tactical opportunities, and are constrained by the behaviour of their competitors as well as by unexpected events. At least at the local level, in fact, only cultural frames are articulated in a somewhat consistent way, in line with the general ideological orientations of the competing coalitions. Concerning the other dimensions comprising the migration issue, by contrast, framing strategies appear to be set up based on different types of considerations. This makes it fundamental to account for other types of factors that may change the relationship between the different actors and the immigration issue during the actual campaign, especially the nature of the mediatized system of political communication, and the difference between actors' pledges in the electoral platforms and the coverage of these by the media (Esser and Matthes, 2013). Whether or not these elements are able to explain further migration debates across local election campaigns in Italy is the subject of the next chapter.

Notes

1 The Chi-Square analysis indicates that framing choices are also statistically different across the observed parties: X^2 *(24, N = 2653) = 234.4, p < 0.01* (Cramér's V = 0.15).
2 The Chi-Square indicates that framing choices are statistically different across the election campaigns for the centre-right: X^2 *(30, N = 1401) = 427.6, p < 0.01* (Cramér's V = 0.25). The same applies also to the centre-left and radical right: X^2 *(30, N = 764)= 363.4, p < 0.01* (V = 0.31); X^2 *(6, N = 158) = 72.1, p < 0.01* (V = 0.67).
3 Declaration by Mauro Vannoni (Rifondazione Comunista) to *Il Tirreno*, 01/06/2004.
4 Declaration by Filippo Bernocchi (Alleanza Nazionale) to *Il Tirreno*, 02/06/2004.
5 Declaration by Massimo Carlesi (Partito Democratico) to *Il Tirreno*, 14/05/2009.
6 Declaration by Lanfranco Nosi (Sinistra RossoVerde) to *Il Tirreno*, 15/05/2009.
7 Declaration by Aldo Milone (Prato Libera e Sicura) to *Il Tirreno*, 09/06/2009.
8 Declaration by Davide Boni (Lega Nord) *Il Giorno*, 12/04/2011.
9 Declaration by Gianni Alemanno (PDL) to *Il Messaggero*, 09/05/2006.
10 One could consider this a consequence of the demographics of Prato, which is a medium-sized industrial city that did not experience a conspicuous settlement of Roma people, unlike Milan and Rome. As was illustrated earlier, however, the actual number of Roma residents is neither the primary nor a sufficient cause for discrimination, since the overall amount of Romani in Italy is very limited and much lower than that of other communities.
11 Declaration by Gianni Alemanno (PDL) to *Il Messaggero*, 05/03/2008.
12 Declaration by Matteo Salvini (Lega Nord) *Il Giorno*, 02/04/2011.
13 Declaration by Francesco Storace (La Destra) to *Il Messaggero*, 10/04/2008.
14 Declaration by Gianni Alemanno (PDL) to *Il Messaggero*, 27/02/2008.
15 Declaration by Francesco Storace (La Destra) to *Il Messaggero*, 05/04/2008.

16 Declaration by Gianni Alemanno (PDL) to *Il Messaggero,* 16/04/2008.
17 Declaration by Goffredo Bettini (PD) to *Il Messaggero,* 01/04/2008.
18 Claim by Lega Nord reported in *Il Tirreno,* 25/04/2009.
19 Declaration by Aldo Milone (Prato Libera e Sicura) to *Il Tirreno,* 23/05/2009.
20 Claim by PD in *Il Tirreno,* 31/05/2009.
21 Both measures are developed from the measure of issue convergence that was presented in Chapter 6 (Sigelman and Buell, 2004).
22 The Chi-Square test shows framing choices in support and opposition to immigration are statistically different for the centre-left: X^2 *(6, N = 748) = 226.9, p < 0.01* (Cramér's V = 0.55); and for the centre-right: X^2 *(6, N = 1388) = 122.4, p < 0.01* (Cramér's V = 0.30).
23 The Chi-Square test shows that framing opposition to immigration is statistically different between actors: X^2 *(12, N = 1722) = 207.5, p < 0.01* (Cramér's V = 0.25). The results are stable also when I excluded the radical right and run the Chi-Square for the two mainstream parties only. Statistical significance is instead not confirmed for framing support to immigration: X^2 *(6, N = 571) = 11.6, p < 0.1* (Cramér's V = 0.14).
24 No pro-immigration category is reported for the radical right, as I could retrieve only one observation for this category, namely pertaining to the labour and security frame.
25 De Vries *et al.* (2011) refer to this process as *issue bundling,* and address it as the process by which issues that remain high in the political agenda are integrated in parties' existing ideological profiles in the attempt to preserve ideological consistency and avoid voters' flight.

References

Bordignon, F. (2008) 'Ritorno alla penisola della paura'. In Demos & Pi, *IV rapporto su immigrazione e cittadinanza in Europa.* Vicenza: Demos & Pi. Available at: www.demos.it/2008/dossier/pdf/dossier_immigrazione_2008 (Accessed 21 January 2011).

Buonfino, A. (2004) 'Between Unity and Plurality: The Politicization and Securitization of the Discourse of Immigration in Europe', *New Political Science,* 26(1), pp. 23–49. doi: 10.1080/0739314042000185111

Campomori, F. and Caponio, T (2013) 'Competing Frames of Immigrant Integration in the EU: Geographies of Social Inclusion in Italian Regions', *Policy Studies,* 34(2), pp. 162–179.

Caponio, T. (2013) 'Multiculturalism Italian Style: Soft or Weak Recognition?' In: Taras, R. ed. *Challenging Multiculturalism: European Models of Diversity.* Edinburgh: Edinburgh University Press, pp. 216–235.

Chaloff, J. (2005) 'Italy'. In: Niessen, J. and Schiebel, Y. eds. *Immigration as a Labour Market Strategy: European and North American Perspectives.* Brussels: Migration Policy Group, pp. 111–128.

De Vries, C., Hakhverdian, A. and Lancee, B. (2011) 'The Dynamics of Voters' Left/Right Identification: The Role of Economic and Cultural Attitudes', Paper prepared for the *ECPR General Conference 2011,* Reykjavik.

Entman, R. (2004) *Projects of Power: Framing News, Public Opinion, and U.S. Foreign Policy.* Chicago: University of Chicago Press.

Esser, F. and Matthes, J. (2013) 'Mediatization Effects on Political News, Political Actors, Political Decisions, and Political Audiences'. In: Kriesi, H., Boschsler, D., Matthes, J., Lavenex, S., Bühlmann, M. and Esser, F. eds. *Challenges to Democracy in the 21st Century. Democracy in the Age of Globalization and Mediatization.* Hampshire, UK: Palgrave Macmillan, pp. 177–201.

Gamson, W.A. (1992) *Talking Politics.* Cambridge: University Press.

Helbling, M. (2013) 'Framing Immigration in Western Europe', *Journal of Ethnic and Migration Studies*, 40(1), pp. 21–41.

Hopkins, J. (2007) *Threatening Changes: Explaining Where and When Immigrants Provoke Local Opposition*. Working Paper, Centre for the study of American politics: Yale University.

Hopkins, D.J., Tran, V.C. and Williamson, A.F. (2014) 'See No Spanish: Language, Local Context, and Attitudes Toward Immigration', *Politics, Groups and Identities,* 2(1), pp. 35–51. Available at: http://dx.doi.org/10.1080/21565503.2013.872998

Knutsen, O. (1995) 'Party Choice'. In: van Deth, J.W. and Scarbrought, E. eds. *The Impact of Values*. Oxford: Oxford University Press, pp. 461–491.

Koopmans, R., Statham, P., Giugni, M. and Passy, F. (2005) *Contested Citizenship: Immigration and Cultural Diversity in Europe*. Minneaopolis, MN: University of Minnesota Press.

Massetti, E. (2014) 'Mainstream Parties and the Politics of Immigration in Italy: A Structural Advantage for the Right or a Missed Opportunity for the Left?' *Acta Politica*, advance online publication 22 August 2014; doi: 10.1057/ap.2014.29

McCombs, M. (2004) *Setting the Agenda. The News Media and Public Opinion.* Malden, MA: Blackwell.

Mudde, C. (2007) *Populist Radical Right Parties in Europe.* Cambridge: Cambridge University Press.

Sigelman, L. and Buell, E.H. (2004) 'Avoidance or Engagement? Issue Convergence in U.S. Presidential Campaigns, 1960–2000', *American Journal of Political Science,* 48(4), pp. 650–661.

Sigona, N. (2005) 'Locating "The Gypsy Problem"'. The Roma in Italy: Stereotyping, Labelling and "Nomad Camps"', *Journal of Ethnic and Migration Studies,* 31(4), pp. 741–756.

Sniderman, P. and Theriault, M. (2004) 'The Structure of Political Argument and the Logic of Issue Framing'. In: Saris, W.E. and Sniderman, P. eds. *Studies in Public Opinion: Attitudes, Non-Attitudes, Measurement Error and Change*. Princeton: Princeton University Press, pp. 133–165.

Statham, P. and Trenz, H.J. (2012) *The Politicization of Europe: Contesting the Constitution in the Mass Media.* London and New York: Routledge.

7 Controlling campaign agendas

Introduction

So far, this study has looked at the ways in which debates on immigration were reported in the news, analysing electoral campaigning based on actors' positions emerging from media reports. Hence, the analysis focused on the electoral agenda only once it had already become public. In this chapter, I look more in detail at the way in which the agenda is constructed, by evaluating the attention given to the immigration issue dimensions by political actors in their electoral manifestos and in their public statements during electoral campaigns. Policy platforms are the most formalized way in which electoral actors communicate their positions about policy issues, yet they might or might not be fully consistent with the actual campaign messages of mayoral candidates. Manifestos provide complementary information on parties' relationship with the immigration issue, generally reproducing the main views of party elites. Hence, the advantage of using party manifestos is that the positions expressed in there can be considered as unmediated by media attention (at least to a certain extent, since parties might also anticipate media reactions). In contrast, party positions in the media are filtered by media agendas and newsworthiness considerations (Koopmans *et al.*, 2005).

Hence, I compare here two different stages of electoral agenda building: the one of political actors' promises and pledges prior to the campaign, and the one of the actual electoral rhetoric as reported in national and local newspapers. In line with previous contributions from the field of political communication (Hänggli and Kriesi, 2010; Wolfsfeld, 1997), campaigning is thus conceived as a multistage process in which political actors first communicate with the media and then – through the media – interact with voters. In other words, this chapter investigates the variation in the way in which political actors deal with the various dimensions of migration in their electoral manifestos and in their public statements during the electoral campaign.

Similar to the previous chapters, I do not focus on *what* issues manage to enter the agenda and set public priorities, but on *how* they are discussed in electoral actors' manifestos and media agendas. In line with research on second-level agenda setting (Huckins, 1999; Kiousis *et al.,* 2006; McCombs and Ghanem, 2001; McCombs and Shaw, 1993; Tan and Weaver, 2007; Wirth *et al.,* 2010), the idea is that actors not only try to influence the attention given to particular issues in the composing of the news agenda, but are also interested in manipulating the way in which those are discussed in the media. In fact, there are certain issues in certain periods and contexts that simply cannot be excluded from agendas, irrespective of partisan efforts and preferences (Walgrave *et al.,* 2006). In such cases, actors do not compete over which issues are worth being discussed during the campaign, but rather on how their constitutive dimensions must be publicly understood.

By looking at actor preferences for salience, dimensions and positions as reported in electoral platforms and in the media, the remainder of this chapter focuses on the degree to which the original preferences in electoral manifestos correspond to the contents of electoral debates in the news. The construction of electoral agendas is explored from the point of view of migration as a single issue, for each of its constitutive dimensions and for the positions that political actors take with respect to each of these. Based on the evidence on electoral competition in the three city contexts developed earlier, and considering the interplay between actor strategies and media preferences, this chapter discusses patterns of variation in the way in which actors deal with migration politics in their ideal agendas compared to the rhetoric of their public statements to the media during the campaigns.

The mass media in electoral campaigns: ideal and tactical agendas

This study makes use of content analytical data from electoral manifestos in order to compare actors' preferences in terms of electoral promises to those emerging from the news media coverage of their electoral rhetoric. Hence, similar to the technique employed in studies on party pledges and on programme-to-policy linkages (Mansergh and Thomson, 2007), I identify the proposed electoral agendas according to the policy positions and preferences the actors outline in their electoral platforms. Electoral manifestos are issued at the very beginning of the official campaign, and are therefore severely limited when the aim is to analyze the dynamic relationship between parties and the media in the course of election campaigns (Hänggli, 2010; Walgrave *et al.,* 2006). A similar analysis would have required data enabling to capture the dynamic interaction between political actors and the media, such as press releases and other types of communication produced and divulged on a daily basis (Brandenburg, 2002; Froio and Castelli Gattinara, 2015), which was not available at the local level in Italy for the observed period.

Consistent with previous literature, therefore, I use electoral manifestos as benchmarks for the understanding of partisan preferences and promises (Budge, 2001; Budge and Fairle, 1983; Helbling and Tresch, 2011; Morales *et al.,* 2014). Previous studies have underlined that different channels of campaign communication are associated with different sets of issue preferences, since actors adjust their issue focus to the logics of communication and newsworthiness, and to their respective strategies of competition (Elmelund-Præstekær, 2011). Norris *et al.* (1999) distinguish between two types of partisan electoral agendas, identifying an 'ideal agenda' corresponding to the preferences emphasized at the beginning of the campaign within election manifestos, and a 'tactical agenda' which instead results from the continuing modification of the ideal one through the interaction with the media, ongoing events and political competitors.

In sum, the idea is that parties' policy preferences and promises may vary depending on the channel of communication and on the phase of the election campaign (Elmelund-Præstekær, 2011). Given that electoral manifestos are generally negotiated *within* parties and coalitions rather than *between* them and the outside world, they offer a valuable measurement of partisan position before they engage in active competition and develop strategies to interact with the media. In other words, party manifestos offer a reliable measure of actors' initial, or ideal, sets of preferences. Although the news media generally reproduces quite accurately the positions that actors take in their manifestos (Helbling and Tresch, 2011), this is not likely to be confirmed for issue salience, since active campaigning means focusing selectively on specific topics. This aspect is of particular importance when studying the multiple dimensions of policy issues. By analysing the gap between the attention provided to specific elements or sub-issues in party manifestos and in the media, I shall provide additional information on the nature of electoral campaigning.

Three main processes may explain the difference between actors' discourses on migration in their original manifestos and in media reports. The first argument concerns the influence that the media exerts on politics, based on media outlets' own preferences and on the fact that parties need the media in order to gain visibility and, eventually, support (Altheide and Snow, 1979; Kepplinger, 2002; Mazzoleni and Schulz, 1999; Mazzoleni *et al.,* 2003; Walgrave and van Aelts, 2006). The second argument deals with actors' strategies of competition, and investigates the extent and nature of the adjustments of party strategies over the course of the election campaigns (Green-Pedersen and Stubager, 2010; Soroka, 2002; Van der Pas, 2014; Walgrave *et al.,* 2008). Finally, the third argument is that both media and partisan strategies are subject to the influence of exogenous events and context-specific characteristics that may change the rules of the game and, as such, the strategic choices of the actors and the way these are reported in the news (Birkland, 1997). Since the design of this study does not enable assessing systematically the explanatory power of each of the three interpretations, I shall use them as my main reference points within an exploratory analysis of the association between ideal and tactical agendas in migration debates.

In particular, my attention is devoted to understanding the extent to which actors' strategies and characteristics can explain the difference between the issues that are emphasized in their manifestos and those they discuss during the campaign. Campaign strategies may be fundamental for the reproduction of specific understandings of a given issue. As previous chapters demonstrated, in fact, the competition between electoral candidates for the control of the news agenda does not only involve a struggle over the attention to alternative political issues, but also a struggle between different aspects of the same issue, as over the meaning of issues. In other words, actors may support and promote specific understandings of issues in the media when the definition of the problem and the suggested solutions suits their policy programme (Van der Pas, 2014).

As discussed in Chapter 2, the reputation of an actor in dealing with a specific issue or issue dimension may provide advantages in terms of setting the media agenda. Accordingly, I envisage that the immigration issue is overrepresented in the media for mainstream right and radical right actors, since they enjoy easier access to the media when debates focus on this issue. Similarly, although ideal agendas cannot be considered fully isolated from anticipations of media reactions, I have illustrated that incumbent parties are more subject to campaign-specific constraints, since the actors in opposition are advantaged in setting the party-system agenda. Hence, during the campaign challenger parties can force incumbents to take up issues or (issue dimensions) that they had deliberately avoided in their 'ideal' agendas and, more broadly, it is likely that the difference between the dimensional attention profiles in the manifestos and in the electoral rhetoric will be higher for incumbent actors than for challengers.

Although these hypotheses will constitute the main guidelines of this chapter, the analysis offered here will also provide additional insights on electoral agenda building dynamics, further illustrating the way in which certain actors come to dominate local migration debates. In particular, I suggest that the difference attributed to each issue dimension in party manifestos and in electoral rhetoric should be explored from the point of view of the different 'publics' that the two types of agendas address. It is known from previous studies that the media is not equally attentive to all types of issues, and generally prioritizes issues that appeal to the broad public (Hallin and Mancini, 2004; Swanson and Mancini, 1996). In terms of dimensional attention in media coverage, therefore, one should also consider the newsworthiness of the various aspects of migration (Altheide and Snow, 1979; Hallin and Mancini, 2004; Mazzoleni *et al.*, 2003).[1] In his categorization of policy issues, Soroka (2002) distinguishes between *obtrusive, sensational* and *government issues* based on two main characteristics that influence agenda setting. On the one hand is the degree of direct experience that citizens have with a given issue, or aspect of an issue; on the other, the dramatic and/or emotive nature of its content, which determines the extent to which an issue can be considered newsworthy.

Sensational issues clearly correspond to the law and order dimension, since despite their concreteness they have 'little observable impact on the vast majority of individuals' (Soroka, 2002, pp. 20–21). In addition, this aspect of migration is also the one most likely to express dramatic, emotional and intense tones. As a result, one may consider security as the most newsworthy aspect of migration debates. The socioeconomic dimension meanwhile corresponds to Soroka's obtrusive issues, since people have high levels of everyday, direct experience with it. This makes media attention less necessary for citizens to evaluate the (negative and positive) socioeconomic implications of migration.[2] Nonetheless, political entrepreneurs have to account for this dimension in order to increase their appeal to voters, to defend their policy choices while in office and/or to propose alternative ones. Finally, the cultural and religious dimension does not fit neatly into Soroka's issue attributes. Cultural aspects are generally unobtrusive,[3] yet they may take concrete forms, since identity issues can easily take dramatic and sensationalistic tones. If this is the case, then cultural aspects gain concreteness and newsworthiness, and media coverage is likely to amplify further their visibility.

Ideal and tactical agendas: similarity and difference

As a first step, this section shall look at the news coverage of migration affairs across all election campaigns, in order to see whether and to what extent it reflects partisan issue preferences in electoral manifestos. Overall, the degree to which immigration was salient in party manifestos and in electoral rhetoric in the media was approximately the same: 10.4% in party manifestos across cities and election campaigns, and 11% in the news media. In contrast, positions were considerably more supportive of migration in electoral manifestos (with a mean slightly superior to 0.1) than in media reports (−0.4). National and local news outlets diverged marginally in terms of level of attention provided to the issue (9.5% of national media attention; 12.3% in local coverage), but not in terms of the average tone of the debate (−0.3 and −0.4, respectively).

Beyond aggregate data, a closer look at salience and positions is necessary, since preferences expressed in electoral manifestos cannot be analyzed and understood without taking into consideration differences between political actors. To this end, Table 7.1 below reports the salience of the immigration issue as expressed in coalition manifestos, compared to the news coverage of their election campaigns, differentiating between aggregate news coverage and national and local media outlets. The results indicate that there is a certain degree of difference in salience across different communication channels. As shown in columns A and B, for the centre-left, and to a lesser extent the radical right, the immigration issue receives roughly the same importance in the manifestos and in the news media. By contrast, the visibility of migration in news coverage of the centre-right is twice as high as in the actor's electoral manifestos. A lower degree of attention for migration affairs instead characterizes the news coverage of the radical left.

Moving the focus to column C and D, moreover, the table shows that the access to the news media is not equal for all actors involved in electoral campaigns: smaller actors seem to be disadvantaged in reaching national channels of communication, at least compared to local media (column D). In particular, the radical right discourse on migration is largely downsized in national news (only 5% of the relative attention), compared to the attention in the election manifestos (25%), and in local outlets (24.6%). The results thus show that mainstream actors, especially the centre-right, are advantaged in terms of access to national news coverage. In line with previous research (Hänggli, 2010, 2012), this suggests that the media can influence public debates by following the campaign of one candidate (generally the most powerful organizations and the most relevant parties) more closely than the one of its competitors (Brants and Van Praag, 2006; Hänggli, 2010; Hopmann *et al.*, 2012).

In line with the abovementioned expectations, the results show that the discourse on migration of the mainstream right is largely overrepresented in the

Table 7.1 Salience of immigration in party manifestos and news media

Party		*Salience of immigration*			
		A	*B*	*C*	*D*
		Electoral	*Aggregate*	*National*	*Local*
		Manifestos	*News media*	*News media*	*News media*
Centre-right	%	6.4	12.8	11.9	13.5
	N	128	1131	482	649
Centre-left	%	8.2	8.1	6.9	10.2
	N	278	653	264	389
Radical left	%	8.2	4.6	-	4.6
	N	76	14	-	14
Radical right	%	26.3	20.3	5.3	24.6
	N	62	123	8	115
Total	%	10.4	11.0	9.5	12.3
	N	570	1977	760	1217

Note: Share of core sentences dedicated to immigration in newspaper articles and party manifestos.

Source: Author's data (see Appendix 1).

media compared to the party manifesto, since this issue receives in the news (local and national) two times the attention that it receives in electoral manifestos. In contrast, the media gives roughly as much attention to the centre-left's discourse as the coalition does in its own party platform. Concerning the radical right, although its discourse is not overrepresented, it is fairly well represented at least in local news coverage, where it receives substantial attention.

In other words, it appears that centre-right actors engage in migration politics much more frequently in terms of electoral rhetoric than in their party manifestos, whereas other actors have more balanced profiles. Strategically, this may be due to the advantage that mainstream right actors enjoy in migration debates, as shown in previous chapters. Compared to party platforms, which are a low-key form of communication with the electorate, addressing the media allows political actors to concentrate further their attention on advantageous issues. From the point of view of the media, instead, reporting the migration stances of the centre-right may be more newsworthy and appealing than for other actors. This may be because of the focus of the campaign or because of the reputation on migration affairs of the actor doing the mobilizing, which would also explain the importance attributed to the radical right in local media. The two explanations are not contradictory and may have a mutually reinforcing effect, since radical and mainstream right actors have incentives to further stressing the issues on which they have an advantage during the electoral campaigns, being confident that the media would be responsive and grant them access to the public agenda. In this sense, the reputation of a given actor on a specific issue may be the result of the actor's own communication as well as of the cognitive link that the mass media create between the actor and the issue in the coverage of everyday affairs (Walgrave and De Swert, 2007).

In order to investigate this further, it is useful to look at the relationship between the positions expressed by actors in their manifestos and the ones emerging from the news media coverage of election campaigns. Figure 7.1 shows that the increased visibility that migration receives in media coverage does not necessarily imply a change of tone. Positions in the media (considering both local and national outlets) tend to be less supportive of migration than in party programmatic documents (with the exclusion of the radical left). Yet, the figure also shows that the positions expressed by right-wing actors are quite similarly anti-immigration across channels of communication, whereas those of the mainstream left are much less pro-migration in the media than in the electoral manifestos. As it turns out, the centre-left approaches immigration with quite different tones in its electoral programmes and in public statements to the media, whereas the gap is less wide for the actors in the anti-immigration camp and, to a certain extent, the radical left. Electoral calculations and anticipations of public reactions may explain why the mainstream left preferred to tone down its stances during the campaign, especially since it faced strong opposition to migration from its radical right, centre-right and centrist competitors. For the same reasons, the radical left opted to move to the pro-immigration end of the continuum, as to differentiate further its positions from those of the mainstream left.

The analysis outlined so far supports the hypothesized mechanism, underlining that the relationship between tactical and ideal agendas is not homogeneous for all actors, due to media preferences, strategic calculations by the involved actors and their reputation on migration affairs. In a similar fashion, the difference between

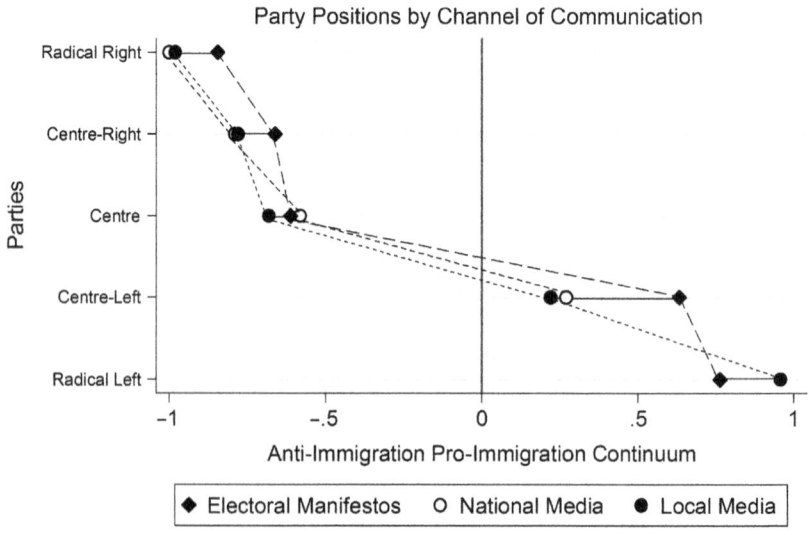

Figure 7.1 Party positions by channel of communication

Source: Author's data (see Appendix 1).

the preferences expressed in the manifestos and in news coverage might have to do with the leeway that different actors have *vis-à-vis* the party-system agenda. As was illustrated in earlier chapters, in fact, party-system agendas represent constraints on the freedom that different parties enjoy in focusing on their preferred issues and issue dimensions. More specifically, although party manifestos often incorporate anticipations of media reactions and campaign dynamics, challengers can force incumbents to take up issues that they had deliberately avoided in their 'ideal' agendas, because parties in office have to respond to most issues included in the party-system agendas.

To explore this, Table 7.2 below reports the degree of attention dedicated to the immigration issue in the different channels of communication by incumbent and challenger actors. In line with the expectations, the degree of attention to the issue is lower in incumbents' party manifestos than in those of challengers, for both mainstream left and right coalitions. This likely has to do with the fact that parties in office prefer to dismiss highly contested issues in their electoral platforms, in the attempt of reducing their overall salience in the electoral campaign. Since migration is mainly discussed in negative terms, candidates that have to defend the incumbent coalition's handling of migration and integration affairs generally prefer to avoid the issue altogether, at least when it is only up to them to choose what to focus on. In other words, incumbents prefer dismissal rather than having to choose between two disadvantageous discursive strategies: on the one hand, popular arguments criticizing the conduct of the outgoing administration; and on the other, unpopular arguments that promote its conduct. Hence, upon drafting

Table 7.2 Immigration attention in incumbent/challenger manifestos and in the media

| Role | Party | | Salience of immigration | | | |
| | | | A | B | C | D |
			Electoral Manifestos	Aggregate News media	National News media	Local News media
Incumbent	Centre-right	%	3.5	13.3	11.8	16.4
		N	34	580	337	243
	Centre-left	%	5.6	8.4	6.2	9.7
		N	114	459	143	338
Challenger	Centre-right	%	9.0	12.2	14.4	12.2
		N	94	551	145	406
	Centre-left	%	12.0	7.5	7.7	7.1
		N	164	194	121	51

Note: Share of core sentences dedicated to immigration in newspaper articles and party manifestos.

Source: Author's data (see Appendix 1).

electoral manifestos, which is prior to interacting with the media and engaging their opponents, incumbents tend to make fewer policy promises on migration than challengers.[4] Incumbents provide considerably more attention to migration in the media than in their election manifestos, irrespective of whether they belong to right-wing or left-wing coalitions. On the contrary, the difference between media and manifestos agendas is smaller for the mainstream right, and reversed for the mainstream left, when they run as challengers. The results also display a more pronounced gap in local outlets than in national ones (columns C and D).

Additional evidence on the different treatment of migration affairs across the two agendas emerges from the analysis of issue positions. Figure 7.2 below illustrates the positions of mainstream coalitions on the anti-immigration pro-immigration continuum, differentiating between incumbent and challengers and between electoral manifestos and local and national media outlets. The figure shows that the positions of actors vary substantially depending on their role in the election campaign. Both the centre-left and centre-right are subject to the same incumbency mechanism, as the position they take on migration varies across agendas when they are incumbents, whereas it remains the same when they run as challengers. When in office, both the right- and left-wing actors change their positions to adopt stronger anti-immigration tones once they interact with the media. This suggests that the disadvantage of being incumbents forces actors to change their strategic choices during the election campaign. The left does so by taking up positions that are more similar to the ones of their opponents (moving in the direction of opposition to migration), following what Meguid has called accommodative strategy (2005). The right by contrast opts for an adversarial strategy, meaning that it moves away from the position proposed by the main challenger.

By looking at party manifestos only, moreover, the figure shows that both actors adopt moderate positions when they are in office compared to when they run as challengers. This suggests that incumbents initially try to tone down their arguments in order to defend the policies and decisions that they have taken while in office. In contrast the positions of challengers tend to be polarized (the centre-right towards the anti-immigration end, and the centre-left towards the pro-immigration end) and consistent across the different agendas.[5]

Overall, these results tend to support the incumbency dynamics outlined in previous chapters, since the gap between the positions on migration in electoral manifestos and in the news media is larger for incumbent than for challenger actors. Actors in opposition are more consistent in their strategies, whereas incumbents are more moderate in the manifestos and then change their position once the actual competition has started. The nature of this change depends on the reputation of actors on migration affairs, so that the left follows an accommodative strategy, moving towards its opponent, whereas the right follows an adversarial tactic aiming at increasing interparty distance and distinguishability. In either case, the campaigning of incumbent actors on migration turns more negative once we account for media agendas. Although the limited amount of observations and the specificity of certain local contexts do not allow drawing systematic conclusions on the effects of incumbency, my exploratory analysis shows that consideration of

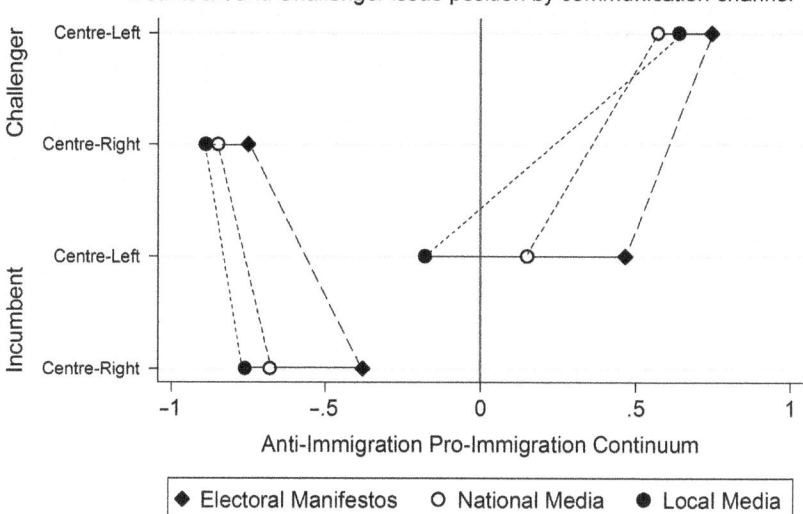

Figure 7.2 Incumbent and challenger positions by channel of communication
Source: Author's data (see Appendix 1).

newsworthiness and media preferences contribute to explaining these differences, since the strategy of challenger appears to force incumbents to focus on issues that they would otherwise avoid. In order to explore this process further, the next section looks at party and media agenda in a dimensional perspective.

Issue dimensionality across agendas

The analysis now turns to the relationship between ideal and tactical agendas from the point of view of issue dimensions, based on my previous suggestion that migration attributes differ in terms of newsworthiness. Table 7.3 below shows data on attention to the three constitutive dimensions of the immigration issue in electoral manifestos and in the public statements during election campaigns. The results are discussed first at the aggregated level and then in relation to each city.

To begin with, the table shows that the law and order dimension is considerably more important in the news media than in actors' electoral platforms, which supports the idea that these arguments are particularly appealing for the news media due to their dramatic and sensational characteristics.[6] Although the pattern is relatively stable across the three case studies, the results are not homogeneous across actors and cities. The centre-right in Prato does not follow this pattern, whereas in Milan it does so only marginally, given that security arguments receive substantial attention already in party manifestos. Rome shows the widest gap between attention in the media and in manifestos, suggesting that the focusing event provided the law and order dimension with additional news value. Conversely, it

Table 7.3 Dimensional salience of immigration in party manifestos and the media, by city

Dimension	Centre-right		Centre-left		Radical left		Radical right	
	Manifestos	Media	Manifestos	Media	Manifestos	Media	Manifestos	Media
Aggregate								
Socioeconomic	20.7	11.5	26.8	15.7	56.6	5.6	36.5	38.0
Cultural and religious	19.5	21.7	48.1	23.9	26.4	61.1	23.1	11.4
Law and order	59.8	66.7	25.1	60.3	17.0	33.3	40.4	50.6
Total	100%	100%	100%	100%	100%	100%	100%	100%
N	87	1401	183	764	53	18	52	158
Milan								
Socioeconomic	23.8	9.5	29.1	12.7	–	–	–	–
Cultural and religious	14.3	27.4	40.9	41.9	–	–	–	–
Law and order	62.9	63.1	30.0	45.4	–	–	–	–
Total	100%	100%	100%	100%	–	–	–	–
N	21	704	110	229	–	–	–	–
Prato								
Socioeconomic	15.1	26.7	22.4	29.9	59.6	5.6	40.0	58.9
Cultural and religious	18.4	23.9	60.3	19.9	21.3	61.1	20.0	5.6
Law and order	66.5	49.2	17.2	50.1	19.1	33.3	40.0	35.5
Total	100%	100%	100%	100%	100%	100%	100%	100%
N	33	243	58	281	47	18	20	90
Rome								
Socioeconomic	24.3	6.6	26.7	2.7	–	–	34.4	10.3
Cultural and religious	24.1	11.7	53.3	12.2	–	–	25.0	19.1
Law and order	51.5	81.7	20.0	85.1	–	–	40.6	70.6
Total	100%	100%	100%	100%	–	–	100%	100%
N	33	454	15	254	–	–	32	68

Note: Share of core sentences dedicated to immigration in newspaper articles and party manifestos.

Source: Author's data (see Appendix 1).

turns out that the socioeconomic dimension is generally more salient in programmatic documents than in the news media, which confirms the obtrusive nature of this issue dimension.[7] While in Rome and Milan the socioeconomic dimension is systematically more salient in manifestos than in media coverage, however, in Prato the opposite relation holds. Lastly, the attention to the cultural dimension varies between the two types of agendas, but do not show a clear pattern across parties and cities.[8]

Nonetheless, the limited amount of observations on manifesto attention at the local level calls for particular caution in drawing general conclusions on the differential news value of the three issue dimensions. At the least, these results provide informative insight into how the strategies of electoral candidates change across the two agendas. By looking at each party separately, Table 7.3 confirms the findings of previous chapters, in that the attention profile of the right-wing parties is much more homogeneous between the manifestos and the media coverage than that of left-wing ones.[9] The centre-left, in particular, tackles migration in its manifesto in a very different way from the way it does in its public statements. In party platforms, it dedicates almost 50% of the attention to cultural and religious arguments, which are generally the ones to which the core of its constituency is more sensitive. In the media agenda, instead, these security arguments outweigh cultural ones, since probably the left-wing candidate considered these more appealing when addressing a broader public. The dynamics of the debate and the interaction with the media seem to define the increasing importance that the mainstream left attributes to the security dimension, in particular in Rome. Accordingly, it shall be instructive to look at the positions that actors take on the three migration dimensions in their public statements and election manifestos (Figure 7.3).

As noted earlier in Figure 7.1, party positions in the media are generally less positive than in manifestos. To begin with, both media and manifesto data show that the positions of the radical right are the most coherent across the three dimensions in the two agendas. Conversely, the positions of the mainstream left are the least so, and the centre-right is located somewhere in the middle. More generally, centre-left actors turn out to follow a considerably different pattern than their right-wing counterparts. Right-wing political actors, which tend to be markedly opposed to migration, display coherent positions, particularly in the media. In other words, right-wing positions in active campaigning are more negative and more similar across issue dimensions than they are in party manifestos. The opposite takes place for the centre-left: its dimensional positions are not only the least coherent across the two agendas, but they are also more distributed across dimensions in the media than in the election manifestos. This result points at a general contradiction in the way in which the mainstream left organizes its campaigning on migration, as it sends remarkably different messages depending on the channel of communication it uses. This is mainly due to the law and order dimension. In fact, while most parties' positions on security do not vary substantially across the two channels of communication, the mainstream left shows a substantial shift from pro-migration to opposition to migration in law and order affairs. Contrarily, the positions of the mainstream right and of the centrist party remain unchanged on security, whereas the radical right moves towards even more restrictive positions in media coverage. The opposite relation characterizes the radical left: it shows a more pro-migration discourse on security in the media than in its platforms, displaying, however, high levels of support for migration in both channels.

In addition, the results indicate that the socioeconomic dimension takes very different meanings when dealt with in party manifestos compared to the media. With the exception of the radical left, all parties adopt significantly more negative positions on socioeconomic aspects in the news media than in their electoral platforms. The analysis of dimensional positions by city showed that this result is not only due to party positions across media and manifestos in Prato, where the socioeconomic dimension is most salient. Rather, the socioeconomic dimension is one aspect of migration on which actors are very incoherent between media and electoral platforms, in terms of salience and positions.

Overall, this analysis corroborates previous results pointing to a substantial difference in the way actors deal with the immigration issue and its constitutive dimensions at different stages of electoral campaigning. The change in the degree of attention provided to the three dimensions of the immigration issue, and the change in the positions by which political actors discuss these, turns out to increase further the advantage of anti-immigration actors. Disadvantaged actors such as the mainstream left sets out considerably different messages during the electoral campaign, depending on whether it addresses its own constituency in the party manifesto, or the public in general through the mass media. Although this study does not focus on the outcomes of campaign strategies, this differentiation

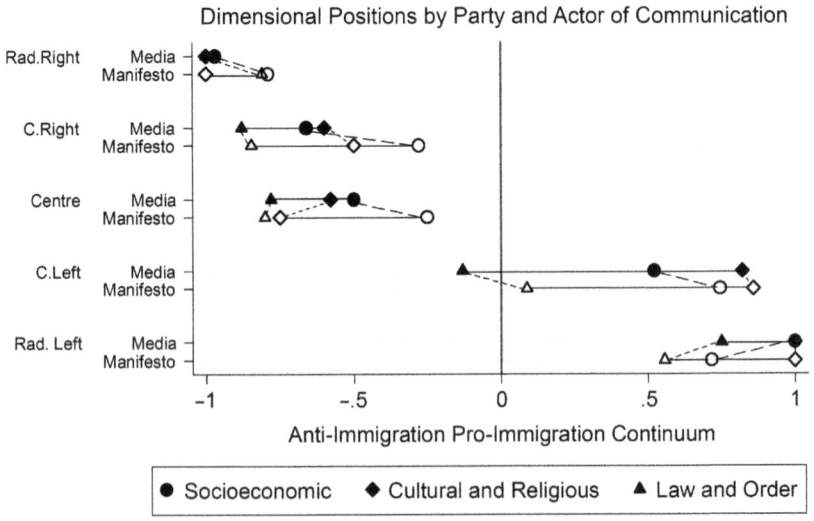

Figure 7.3 Dimensional positions by party and actor of communication

Source: Author's data (see Appendix 1).

hints at a general contradiction in the relationship with migration politics. Moreover, the results provided here cannot fully disentangle the respective role of political actors and the media in this process, since changing tones and issue emphases may be the result of anticipation strategies by political actors, media biases or other forms of interaction between competitors and the media environment. Yet, I have provided exploratory evidence suggesting that, given the attractiveness of sensationalistic news stories in the media, actors that invest in securitization discourse in their electoral platform have an advantage in accessing news media channels, whereas centre-left and incumbent parties in particular have to substantially change the tone and the emphases they set up in their ideal agendas.

Conclusive remarks

This chapter set out to investigate competition on migration politics from the point of view of the different agendas that comprise electoral campaigning. By looking at the way in which parties refer to this issue in their ideal agendas and in the news media, it has sought to reveal the difference between how political actors *would* discuss migration before engaging in competition, and how they *actually do* in electoral campaigns. As was discussed, the best way to assess processes of agenda is by means of data tackling in a direct way the struggle among campaigners over the control of the news agenda, whereas the comparison between party manifestos and media reporting does not allow fully disentangling the respective roles of actor and media preferences. In contrast, I explored the different ways in which political actors deal with migration when they address their own constituency, and when, instead, they interact with media agendas and their newsworthiness considerations. In this sense, although the analyses performed here are mainly exploratory in nature, they point to the continued need to examine the relationship between policy promises and actual electoral rhetoric on the different dimensions of the immigration issue.

In this sense, building upon the multidimensional model proposed in this study, I suggested that the different forms of political communication characterizing electoral campaigning (from the formalized positions expressing the range of views prevalent within party elites, to actors' views emerging from media reporting of campaign activities) interact with the constitutive dimensions of migration. In other words, the reciprocal efforts of political actors and the media to manipulate the electoral agenda, and their respective issue preferences influence the relative importance of issue dimensions. Hence, not only immigration as a whole, but also each of its constitutive aspects receive quite different levels of attention, and are discussed in different ways, in the two channels of communication.

To this end, the chapter investigated the variation in attention to, and issue positions on, the three dimensions of migration across six local electoral campaigns in Italy, looking at news coverage compared to the preceding issue preferences by political actors in election manifestos. The empirical analysis confirmed the idea of a structural disadvantage of mainstream left parties in migration debates. The results showed that right-wing, anti-immigration parties enjoy a particular its own set of preferences and priorities. Second, the reciprocal strategies of competition of political actors, including the adjustment of these based on anticipation of media reactions. Third, the effect of exogenous events and context-specific factors that may change the relative news value of different items in a communication process. My exploratory analyses suggest that neither party strategies nor media preferences *por so* can fully explain the unfolding of public debates in any electoral campaigns. Rather, I have proposed that the construction of campaign agendas depends on the strategies of politicization of the actors involved in competition, which try to anticipate, and end up being shaped by, the preferences of the mass media *vis-à-vis* migration and its attributes.

Notes

1   The concept of media logics is used in political communication literature to refer to the set of imperatives driving the production of news, ranging from professional to commercial ones (see: Altheide and Snow, 1979; Green-Pedersen and Stubager, 2010; Hallin and Mancini, 2004; Mazzoleni *et al.*, 2003; Soroka, 2002; Walgrave *et al.*, 2008).

2   Unless – obviously – external events or macro-level circumstances change the intrinsic value of debating these issues, such as in case of low economic performances, high unemployment rates or general economic crises.

3   Even in the case of the Islamic centre in Milan, citizens had to rely on the media and political entrepreneurs to learn about it, as otherwise only the inhabitants of one neighbourhood of the city would have had direct experience with it.

4   The difference in attention between manifestos and public statements for incumbents and challengers is also statistically significant: X^2 $(3, N = 2190) = 266.0, p < 0.01$ (Cramér's V = 0.33).

5   In terms of different media outlets, results show only minimal differences, with the notable exception of centre-left incumbent actors, since their positions are significantly more anti-immigration in national outlets than in local ones.

6   The results of the tests indicate that the attention to the law and order dimension is statistically different in the news media and in party manifestos: X^2 $(3, N = 1566) = 46.1, p < 0.01$ (Cramér's V = 0.17).

7   X^2 $(3, N = 450) = 48.3, p < 0.01$ (Cramér's V = 0.33).

8   X^2 $(3, N = 757) = 57.6, p < 0.01$ (Cramér's V = 0.27).

9   In line with the measures of consistency outlined earlier (Sigelman and Buell, 2004), I calculated an index of similarity by averaging the absolute differences between issue (dimensional) emphases. I standardized the results in order to range between 0 and a 100 and subtracted from 100 in order to measure similarity rather than dissimilarity. The results confirm that consistency across agendas is highest for right-wing parties (79% and 75% for centre-right and radical right parties) and considerably lower for centre-left (59%) and radical left parties (46%).

References

Altheide, D. and Snow, R.P. (1979) *Media Logic*. Beverly Hills, CA: Sage.

Birkland, T.A. (1997) *After Disaster: Agenda Setting, Public Policy, and Focusing Events*. Washington: Georgetown University Press.

Brants, K. and van Praag, P. (2006) 'Signs of Media Logic: Half a Century of Political Communication in the Netherlands', *Javnost-The Public* 13(1), pp. 25–40.

Budge, I. (2001) *Mapping Policy Preferences: Estimates for Parties, Electors and Governments, 1945–1998*. Oxford: Oxford University Press.

Budge, I. and Fairle, D. (1983) 'Party Competition: Selective Emphasis or Direct Confrontation? An Alternative View with Data'. In: Daalder, H. and Mair, P.eds. *West European Party Systems: Continuity and Change*. London: SAGE, pp. 267–305.Brandenburg, H. (2002) 'Who Follows Whom? The Impact of Parties on Media Agenda Formation in the 1997 British General Election Campaign', *International Journal of Press/Politics*, 7(34), pp. 34–54.

Elmelund-Præstekær, C. (2011) 'Mapping Parties' Issue Agenda in Different Channels of Campaign Communication: A Wild Goose Case?', *Javnost-The Public*, 18(1), pp. 37–52.

Froio, C. and Castelli Gattinara, P. (2015) 'The Agenda-building Practices of Social Movement Organizations of the Extreme Right: Mobilization Strategy, Issue Attention and News Media Coverage', Paper presented at the *Livewhat Summer School*, Scuola Normale Superiore, Florence, Italy.

Green-Pedersen, C. and Stubager, R. (2010) 'The Political Conditionality of Mass Media Influence. When Do Parties Follow Mass Media Attention?', *British Journal of Political Science*, 40, pp. 663–677.

Hallin, D.C. and Mancini, P. (2004) *Comparing Media Systems: Three Models of Media and Politics*. Cambridge: Cambridge University Press.

Hänggli, R. (2010) *Frame Building and Framing Effects in Direct-Democratic Campaigns*. Unpublished PhD dissertation. Faculty of Political Science, University of Zurich, Switzerland.

Hänggli, R. (2012) 'Key Factors in Frame Building: How Strategic Political Actors Shape News Media Coverage', *American Behavioural Scientist*, 56(3), pp. 300–317.

Hänggli, R. and Kriesi, H. (2010) 'Political Framing Strategies and Their Impact on Media Framing in a Swiss Direct-Democratic Campaign', *Political Communication*, 27(2), pp. 141–157.

Helbling, M. and Tresch, A. (2011) 'Measuring Party Positions and Issue Salience from Media Coverage: Discussing and Cross Validating New Indicators', *Electoral Studies*, 30, pp. 174–183.

Hopmann, D.N., Elmelund-Præstekær, C., Albaek, E., Vliegenthart, R. and De Vreese, C.H. (2012) 'Party Media Agenda-Setting: How Parties Influence Election News Coverage', *Party Politics*, 18(2), pp. 173–191.

Huckins, K. (1999) 'Interest-Group Influence in the Media Agenda: A Case Study', *Journalism and Mass Communication Quarterly*, 76(1), pp.76–86.

Kepplinger, H.M. (2002) 'Mediatization of Politics: Theory and Data', *Journal of Communication*, 52, pp. 972–986.

Kiousis, S., Mitrook, M., Wu, X. and Seltzer, T. (2006) 'First and Second-Level Agenda-Building and Agenda-Setting Effects: Linkages Among Candidate News Releases, Media Coverage, and Public Opinion During the 2002 Florida Gubernatorial Election', *Journal of Public Relations Research*, 18, pp. 265–285.

Koopmans, R., Statham, P., Giugni, M. and Passy, F. (2005) *Contested Citizenship: Immigration and Cultural Diversity in Europe*. Minneaopolis, MN: University of Minnesota Press.

Mansergh, L. and Thomson, R. (2007) 'Election Pledges, Party Competition, and Policymaking', *Comparative Politics*, 39, pp. 311–329.

Mazzoleni, G. and Schulz, W. (1999) '"Mediatization" of Politics: A Challenge for Democracy', *Political Communication*, 16, pp. 247–261.

Mazzoleni, G., Stewart, J. and Horsfield, B. (2003) *The Media and Neopopulism: A Contemporary Comparative Analysis*. Westport: Praeger Publishers.

McCombs, M. and Ghanem, S. (2001) 'The Convergence of Agenda Setting and Framing'. In: Reese, S., Gandy, O. and Grant, A. eds. *Framing Public Life: Perspectives and our Understanding*. Mahwah, NJ: Lawrence Erlbaum Associates, 2001, pp. 67–81.

McCombs, M. and Shaw, D.L. (1993) 'The Evolution of Agenda-setting Research: Twenty-five Years in the Marketplace of Ideas', *Journal of Communication,* 43(2), pp. 58–66.

Meguid, B. (2005) 'The Role of Mainstream Party Strategy in Niche Party Success', *American Political Science Review,* 99(3), pp. 347–359.

Morales, L., Pardos-Prado, S. and Ros, V. (2014) 'Issue Emergence and the Dynamics of Electoral Competition around Immigration in Spain', *Acta Politica,* advance online publication: doi:10.1057/ap.2014.33

Norris, P., Curtice, J., Sanders, D., Scammell, M. and Semetko, H.A. (1999) *On Message. Communicating the Campaign.* London: SAGE.

Soroka, S.N. (2002) *Agenda-setting Dynamics in Canada.* Vancouver: UBC Press.

Swanson, D.L. and Mancini, P. (1996) 'Patterns of Modern Electoral Campaigning and their Consequences'. In: Swanson, D.L. and Mancini, P. eds. *Patterns of Modern Electoral Campaining and their Consequences.* Westport, CT: Praeger Publishers, pp. 246–276.

Tan, Y. and Weaver, D.H. (2007) 'Agenda-Setting Effects among the Media, the Public, and Congress, 1946–2004', *Journalism and Mass Communication Quarterly,* 84, pp. 729–744.

Van der Pas, D. (2014) 'Making Hay While the Sun Shines: Do Parties Only Respond to Media Attention When the Framing Is Right?', *The International Journal of Press/Politics,* 19(1), pp. 42–65.Walgrave, S. and De Swert, K. (2007) 'Where Does Ownership Come From? From the Party or from the Media? Issue-party Identifications in Belgium, 1991–2005', *The International Journal of Press/Politics,* 12, pp. 37–67.

Walgrave, S., Soroka, S.N. and Nuytemans, M. (2008) 'The Mass Media's Political Agenda-Setting Power: A Longitudinal Analysis of Media, Parliament, and Government in Belgium (1993 to 2000)', *Comparative Political Studies,* 41(6), pp. 814–836.

Walgrave, S. and Van Aelts, P. (2006) 'The Contingency of the Mass Media's Political Agenda Setting Power: Toward a Preliminary Theory', *Journal of Communication,* 56(1), pp. 88–109.

Walgrave, S., Varone, F. and Dumont, P. (2006) 'Policy With or Without Parties? A Comparative Analysis of Policy Priorities and Policy Change in Belgium: 1991 to 2000', *Journal of European Public Policy* 13(7), pp. 1021–1038.Wirth, W., Matthes, J., Schemer, C., Wettstein, M., Friemel, T., Hänggli, R. and Siegert, G. (2010) 'Agenda Building and Setting in Referendum Campaign: Investigating the Flow of Arguments Among Campaigners, the Media and the Public', *Journalism and Mass Communication Quarterly,* 87(2), pp. 328–345.

Wolfsfeld, G. (1997) *Media and Political Conflict: News from the Middle East.* New York: Cambridge University Press.

Part 3

Conclusion

8 Conclusions

Introduction

When migration becomes a stable part of electoral agendas, all the actors involved in campaigning have to choose how to address the issue in public debates. Times of high migration salience and critical junctures of different nature affect how political actors approach this issue, since they have to cope with issues as varied as the Mediterranean refugee crisis, sudden outburst of racist violence, terrorist attacks involving second-generation migrants, or the emergence of blatantly anti-immigration actors such as *Golden Dawn* in Greece and *Pegida* in Germany. Dismissive tactics do not always pay off, and parties that would otherwise prefer to stay out of these debates have nonetheless to develop their own strategies of politicization and campaigning. While the histories of different countries are often hard to compare to one another, the Italian case displays a pattern of politicization that is similar to the one experienced in other European contexts. In particular, even though the size and visibility of the foreign population in Italy is still much lower than in many traditional countries of immigration, this study confirms that political actors are crucial in driving the politicization of public debates on this issue (van der Brug *et al.*, 2015). Politicization in Italy implies that political actors engage not only on asylum seeker and border control issues, but also on the socio-economic and cultural tensions resulting from the presence of migrants, which is again in line with general trends in Western European societies. Besides this, the mechanism behind the increased securitization of migration in Europe find confirmation in Italy as well, where the discursive nexus between migration and security emerges from the interplay between political actors in the construction of public agendas.

By dissecting the immigration issue in a number of different issue dimensions, and by analysing processes of framing in local electoral campaigning and agenda building, this study has tried to find answers to questions about the supply side of issue competition on migration. In so doing, it has asked how actors holding different predispositions with respect to migration compete with one another, why they compete the way they do and what explains varying strategies and preferences across different electoral contexts. My main argument has been that, instead of emphasizing or de-emphasizing the issue as a whole, actors' campaigning entails strategic framing and selective emphasis of issue dimensions, which allow them to develop distinctive profiles and engage in public debates on aspects of the issue that are relatively favourable to them. In order to assess the dimensionality of campaigning on migration, I have analyzed debates from several interrelated angles, looking at the weight of different issue dimensions across local contexts; investigating how actors tackle these depending on available opportunities and constraints and by means of strategic framing; and assessing the varying news value of the multiple aspects of the issue.

Following the assumption that the politics of campaigning are a fundamental aspect in the functioning of contemporary democracies at different levels in the decision-making process, the book analyzed framing and electoral agenda building on migration in six local campaigns across three cities in Italy. The focus on electoral periods follows the idea that campaign decisions are too important for political scientists to ignore (Rohrschneider, 2002), and combines the study of party strategic attention to policy issues with the investigation of framing choices. These analyses unpacked the process by which political actors, relying on the media to convey frames to the public, define political problems and compete with one another over the meaning of public issues. Electoral campaigning not only involves a struggle over the attention to alternative political issues, but also encompasses a struggle between different definitions, so that candidates compete over alternative ways of understanding social reality and public problems.

The main argument put forward is therefore that the immigration issue must not be understood as a homogeneous category that parties endorse or dismiss, support or oppose. This argument found support in the empirical evidence, as I illustrated how debates in different local settings deal with migration in substantively different ways, and how parties rely upon the thematic structure of the issue, exploiting framing and issue dimensions to increase the appeal of their messages. This is this volume's most general conclusion. It has sought to offer one of the first comprehensive analyses of an issue that has too often been considered *new*, that has been generally approached as a single category and that therefore has been predominantly analyzed through a fixed framework of competition between 'established' and 'emergent' actors. Rather, this study suggests that migration may be less exceptional than often implied, and may resemble any other political issue in electoral campaigning. Other issues like the environment, EU integration or civil rights, which also first appeared as part of the politicization strategies of parties wishing to increase the salience of then largely neglected issues in electoral and public debates, may have followed a similar trajectory.

This process of 'issue bundling' refers to the sets of mechanisms by which the dominant political discourse progressively integrates a previously non-salient political issue (De Vries *et al.*, 2011). So far, the literature interpreted this process in terms of integration of issues within the left–right dimension. When public events and the strategies of parties succeed in politicizing a new controversy and in establishing it within the public agenda, parties tend to opt for the safest strategy and to ensure ideological consistency by assimilating the new issue into their already established profile. This book, however, looked empirically at the path towards normality and at how new issues reshape the competitive dynamics of party systems, illustrating that this process also involves the development of a set of sub-categories and dimensions characterizing the framing of the issue in public debates. The incorporation of new policy issues into the dominant political debate, in fact, besides integration into the left–right dimension, also means dis-integration into a number of alternative dimensions, aspects and frames. It is with these, as I show, that electoral actors set up their strategies of competition, since parties do not simply aim at ideological consistency but also consider contextual and tactical opportunities available across election campaigns.

Beyond competition over saliency of policy issues, electoral actors interact with one another based on issue dimensions, positions and interpretations. Strategic campaigning aims at shifting the focus of debates to alternative dimensions and meanings of migration, manipulating the content of electoral agendas in order to gain a relative advantage. My study suggests that context, campaign and party level conditions jointly drive the choices of politicization by competing political actors, but that their strategies of politicization of migration are far from uniform, whether we consider the substance of the debates, its tone or its scope. Depending on local circumstances and structures of opportunity, the competing actors take up sections and aspects of policy issues, while neglecting others. Next to framing the immigration issue based on consistency with their ideological profiles, they also carry out cost-benefit calculations based on their role in the election campaign and on the resonance of alternative interpretations with common understandings of immigration. By recognizing this, the findings pave the way toward connecting this field of research with other promising areas within the social and political sciences, such as electoral and public opinion research and the study of mediatization and communication, opening new avenues for the understanding of contemporary party politics.

The dimensionality of policy issues

In line with a growing amount of research, this book suggested that political issues may encompass multiple policy dimensions (Baumgartner *et al.,* 2008; De Vries and Hobolt, 2012; Helbling *et al.,* 2010; Höglinger *et al.,* 2012), and that migration represents a prototypical example of a multidimensional political issue. As a result, it suggested that any understanding of the strategies used by political actors to politicize migration must include an account of its multiple issue dimensions, and the variety of framing strategies to address each of these. In fact, although every public policy of substance is inherently multidimensional, its public understanding at any given time is only partial (Baumgartner and Jones, 2002).

The book advanced three interrelated reasons behind the multidimensionality of electoral issues and their selective politicization in party competition. *Inherent complexity* refers to the substantial complexity of policy problems and the multiple implications they have that cut across policy areas. *Cognitive factors* explain that the fragmentation of issues into distinct dimensions facilitates their processing and understanding for the public. And *strategic factors* account for the fact that political entrepreneurs have neither the resources, nor the incentives, to address all aspects of policy issues simultaneously.

Expecting increased electoral returns, political actors strategically mobilize certain aspects rather than others in order to promote specific understandings and perspectives on policy problems. Chapter 2 thus put forth a model of party competition based on a categorization of migration into three issue dimensions, and empirically accounted for each dimension by further differentiating seven alternative frames used in newspaper coverage of electoral debates. This approach implies that each separate attribute of migration provides distinct opportunities to campaigners, so that electoral agendas are the results of their struggle over conflict dimensions within policy issues. Once issues reach electoral agendas, alternative frames serve political actors in attempting to drive attention away from aspects that they perceive as disadvantageous towards advantageous ones. Accordingly, I have presented, discussed and empirically tested hypotheses concerning the politicization of migration, proposing to take into account the complexity of political debates and analysing how the separate aspects of issues are taken up, contextualized and framed in partisan and media agendas. I have demonstrated that strategies oriented at manipulating electoral agendas vary depending on the interaction between context, campaign and party level factors, and the features of the issue at stake. Political decisions tend to encompass a multiplicity of dimensions of choice, so that political actors do not only choose whether they will address one issue in the electoral campaign or not, but they can also decide which aspects of that issue they want to highlight, and how.

This study has therefore primarily focused on the empirical analysis of the strategic framework of issue multidimensionality, investigating the choices of political actors confronting complex policy issues. In so doing, I have illustrated the varying approaches that local political actors have followed depending on strategic opportunities and constraints with respect to each distinctive dimension of the issue. By focusing on the supply side of competition, however, a main limitation of my approach is that it could not account for cognitive factors in the context of multidimensional issue competition. In this sense, my results provide initial evidence that could be developed in future research assessing dynamically how attitudes towards migration can generate different electoral effects, conditional on the specific dimension of the issue that is mobilized as well as on its predominant framing, and how – in turn – political actors respond to changing public perceptions of migration.

Local migration debates

I have proposed to study the dimensionality of migration in a very specific context, namely Italian local electoral campaigns. The decision to investigate local electoral campaigns in Italy matched the focus of this study on competitive strategies *within* multidimensional issues, which requires the in-depth investigation of the construction of immigration discourse by the competing actors. The three city contexts that I have selected differ systematically with respect to the features of the migrant population and the corresponding public problems, allowing me to study the implications of some key situational conditions influencing electoral campaigning. The observed electoral campaigns represent ideal-typical situations in terms of available opportunities to mobilize on migration, corresponding to the three constitutive dimensions of the issue.

Inevitably, the disadvantage of a natural-setting design implies that the observed campaigns and actors differ in many respects, which makes comparing them more complex. In this sense, the timing, composition of the party systems and the coalitions opposing each other in Rome, Milan and Prato vary considerably. Additionally, a disadvantage of this design is that I have focused on a set of specific local electoral campaigns in Italy, so that my results are heavily tainted by the context of the Italian political and communication system. I acknowledge, of course, that the Italian context might have influenced my results in many ways, and that one must replicate this study in other local contexts in order to be better able to assess the generalizability and external validity of my findings. Most notably, the volatility of the Italian party system and the specificity of Berlusconi's populist political style, but also the lack of a significant immigrant vote and the particular competences of the municipal governments in Italy, are all issues that can have influence on the specific campaign strategies observed in the cases under study.

Yet, although the results of social science research in natural settings are always context-bound, they may still point beyond the specificities and idiosyncrasies of a given context, if they succeed in characterizing it in analytical terms, and recognize how this conditions the results. In other words, if the specific circumstances of local migration politics in Italy might explain the stronger presence of one dimension over another in the case under study, the logics of competition unfolded throughout the study apply beyond this specific context. I shall therefore in this conclusive chapter attempt to indicate how my results do not only speak of campaigning in three Italian cities, but say something more general on migration politics and on electoral campaign strategies over multidimensional policy issues. The comparative analysis of the three city contexts in Italy showed that understanding the supply side of electoral competition over migration cannot avoid accounting for local dynamics, as local factors can be responsible for substantial differences in how the issue is politicized. To explain this, however, the analysis showed the crucial role of the complex nature of policy issues, which are made of a thematic network of alternative aspects and dimensions that can be mobilized independent from one another. The varying levels of attention towards migration affairs are associated with the relative emphasis on each of its constitutive dimensions across different local debates and election campaigns. Studies on the composition of electoral agendas should focus not only on the traditional questions about the *when* and *whether* of attention to immigration, but also on the more detailed investigation of those aspects that determine the salience of different issue dimensions in electoral debates, since these lead to the overall importance that is attributed to the issue.

Security arguments dominate electoral debates on migration in Italy. This has primarily to do with the special responsibilities of Italian local administrators in the enforcement of law and order. Yet, securitization is not stable across cases and over time, showing that the actual competences of administrators cannot explain the full complexity of local debates on immigration. In fact, my analysis identified substantial differences in the framing of the issue across local settings. Structures of opportunity influence the composition of migration debates in a substantial way, as the nature of debates depends on the way in which events and controversies interact with local characteristics, the actual competences of administrators and the type of actors involved in debating immigration. The comprehensive analysis of migration debates presented in Chapter 5, and the following frame analyses of Chapter 6, confirm not only the appropriateness of studying politicization dynamics at the local level, but also the need to account for the various aspects and frames of policy issues that can be simultaneously mobilized.

Such findings point to a first set of conclusions about the comparative study of migration politics, beyond the specificities of the local electoral campaigns under investigation and the high degree of territorial, cultural and socioeconomic differentiation in Italy. To begin with, the thematic understanding of policy issues that I suggested enables accounting for the concrete aspects of migration that make it matter in contentious politics, improving the understanding of its politicization and how political debates unfold. In addition, approaches based on political and institutional factors at the national level risk overlooking the multifaceted development of migration debates, which unfold according to the characteristics of local settings. Although this study did not analyze debates on different levels of governance, and therefore cannot draw conclusions in this sense, future research might look into whether, and to what extent, national politicization dynamics influence local discursive opportunities, and *vice versa*.

Moreover, my results incontrovertibly demonstrate that the broader process of securitization of immigration politics is increasingly permeating to the local level as well. A mix between symbolic security politics and actual competences of local administrators, alongside sensationalistic stories and transformative events at the local level, explains why law and order overwhelmingly dominates public debates on migration. Especially when unexpected events are highly mediatized, all actors at the local level endorse a law and order, highly restrictive approach to migration affairs, so that insecurity is primarily framed in terms of the presence of ethnic minorities, in particular Roma communities, on the local territory. These results echo the mechanisms illustrated in the main models of securitization, positing that security emerges from speech acts legitimizing exceptional policies (Buzan, Waever *et al.*, 1998), the routinized practices of security professionals (Bigo, 2002), or the combination between elite discourse, audience mobilization and governmentality (Balzacq, 2011; Bourbeau, 2011). Building upon these models, my empirical results suggest that securitizing moves by strategic actors take advantage of local characteristics to develop their public discourse, so that strategies are set up based on the thematic nature of policy issues. In so doing, this book not only offers an innovative exploration of party competition on migration at the local level, but it also provides the conceptual and analytical tools for understanding the political dynamics that led to the securitization of migration well beyond the Italian case.

Campaign strategies: issue emphasis and framing

The empirical analyses presented in Chapters 5, 6 and 7 tackled the strategies of politicization of the immigration issue put forth by the actors in electoral campaigning in the three cities. This framework builds on the threefold assumption that the public learns about candidates mainly in the course of election campaigns, that political actors rely on the media to reach citizens and to win the support of electorates, and that political actors' strategic choices are not fully free. I suggested that in the course of electoral campaigns the conflict between political actors unfolds, as the actors involved form coalitions, compete and craft messages based on alternative arguments, frames and worldviews, with the goals of getting public and media attention and of mobilizing support. Hence, a comprehensive account of political conflict in electoral campaigns requires analysing not only partisan strategies across issues, but also strategies of politicization within issues, i.e. the strategies that parties adopt toward issues that they cannot avoid or cannot afford to dismiss.

I have demonstrated that the type of debate varies substantially depending on the strategies of the actors involved, the characteristics of specific electoral campaigns, as well as the socio-contextual features of local settings. By conceptually dividing policy choices into distinctive dimensions and frames, my model of electoral campaigning conceived partisan strategies as successive steps in the process of competition with other parties in the system, accounting for the constraints posed by the features of the issue under debate and the opportunities of the context where competition took place. Accordingly, actors must first decide whether to take up the immigration issue or discard it altogether from their electoral campaign. If they engage in immigration affairs, multidimensional competition follows three basic strategic clusters, depending on whether parties are interested in capitalizing on support or opposition to immigration. First, they have to decide whether to take up the same issue dimension as their competitors or rather shift the debate to alternative aspects. By mobilizing alternative dimensions they try to raise attention for aspects that they deem electorally rewarding, while avoiding direct competition with their opponents. When instead focusing on the same issue dimensions as their competitors, parties have to decide whether to take up the same frames as the opponents or to mobilize alternative ones. Mobilizing alternative frames means an attempt to persuade voters of an alternative interpretation of a given aspect of migration, whereas providing the same frame as their competitors entails a direct competition with them.

My analyses have shown the importance of party-system agendas and campaign-level factors in explaining local debates on immigration. Dimensional profiles and issue positions do not vary only across parties on the left–right scale, but especially between local settings within the same coalitions. Mainstream parties' accommodative and adversarial strategies depend on dimensional emphasis and on the presence and electoral strength of radical right competitors. Moreover, the behaviour of a mainstream opponent also explains strategic responses and campaigning choices *vis-à-vis* specific issue dimensions. Hence, immigration debates do not appear to be only actor-driven but also agenda-driven. When it comes to migration, therefore, actors seem to be ready to mix their strategies with those of the opponents, whilst matching them with respect to other issue aspects. They try to stay competitive by tackling primarily the issue dimensions that do not contradict their values, and hoping not to have to surrender too much of their credibility when disadvantageous aspects gain visibility in public debates. Although so-called *proprietal* issues may be increasingly exceptional due to the tendency of parties to dedicate attention to the same policy problems (Froio *et al.*, 2013; Greene *et al.*, 2014), patterns of issue advantage and disadvantage emerge in the framework of their multiple dimensions and aspects.

Framing, in this sense, represents a crucial instrument to manipulate the public understanding of policy issues especially when actors have to take a stance on disadvantageous issues. By involving both selection and diagnosis, evaluative framing enables to define issue dimensions and to provide them with specific meaning. Chapter 6, looking at substantive, issue-specific frames, shifted the focus of the analysis on the aspect of the problem definition by strategic political actors. The empirical analyses presented therein showed that ideological profiles explain framing strategies only marginally, whereas tactical considerations, and the degree to which election debates are consensual, conflictual or blurred, are crucial factors. In fact, the public discourse of the mainstream left and right, whether in support of or in opposition to immigration, was found to be remarkably similar, with little substantive evidence that parties framed migration in line with their ideological commitments. Against this background, I illustrate that the centre-right is better able to provide a consistent discourse on immigration than the centre-left. The political right enjoys issue ownership, whereas the 'structural' disadvantage of left-wing actors in immigration debates is persistent and formidable, relegating them to the role of followers. By emulating the dimensional attention profile of the centre-right, and by taking up law and order aspects, therefore, mainstream left actors often turn into agents of securitization in times of high salience of migration affairs.

Advantaged and disadvantaged actors

Based on a twofold differentiation of the actors involved in electoral competition, I looked at patterns of advantage and disadvantage on migration debates starting from, on the one hand, parties' positions along the left–right scale, and, on the other, the role they play in the election campaign, that is, as incumbents or challengers. Although the limited amount of cases of this study enabled me to draw only preliminary conclusions to be tested in future research, the empirical analysis confirmed that incumbent actors tend to be generally disadvantaged and more hesitant when dealing with migration debates. This implies that parties tend to focus more on the dimensions that they perceive as advantageous when they are challengers than when they are in office, whilst governing actors are less able to avoid dimensions unfavourable to them, since they have to respond to the issues their competitors bring into the agenda. Opposition parties have strong incentives to introduce new alternatives in order to win office, whereas governing actors, in turn, are compelled to respond to them in order to stay in power.

Challengers make use of 'heresthetic' devices in order to divide the majority with a new alternative, or to reframe existing problems in order to win a majority of votes (Klingemann *et al.*, 1994; Riker, 1986). This is in line with previous research suggesting that government rhetoric is not only shaped by public preferences, but also by the oppositions' agenda setting (Hobolt *et al.*, 2008; Walgrave and Nuytemans, 2009). The electoral campaigns of incumbent actors (irrespective of their left–right ideological profile) tend to discuss migration most vigorously by means of issue dimensions and frames that enable them to defend their decisions against challengers' disruptive campaigning. Incumbents try to construct a pragmatic discourse of solidarity that conveniently minimizes government responsibility for policy failure, using emergency logics that insulate incumbent actors from voter sanctions. Conversely, challengers enjoy more leeway in attributing importance to migration issue aspects and in taking a position on these. I recommend scholars in the future to look into this process further, investigating whether other cases confirm the finding that challengers are freer in their choices when they set up the agenda of contested policy issues.

Based on my empirical data, moreover, I have tentatively suggested that although parties in opposition tend to focus more on convenient dimensions than incumbent ones, right-wing actors benefit more from being in opposition than left-wing ones. To put it differently, the advantage of being a challenger is more evident for right-wing parties than for left-wing ones, and the left appears to be more ready to change its dimensional profile than the right when incumbent. In this sense, I have further confirmed the general disadvantage of the left in migration debates. Most notably, the investigation of the overlap between the dimensional and framing choices of mainstream parties has illustrated that leftist parties' disadvantage has been aggravated by securitization. Looked at from that angle, these findings corroborate the conclusions of previous research on party competition suggesting that the Downsian 'if you can't beat them join them' is not the only strategy that disadvantaged parties may follow (Bale *et al.*, 2010). On the contrary, more differentiated agenda setting strategies are at stake, since parties do not consider all issue dimensions as equally important, and emphasize dimensions on which they have a strategic advantage depending on the opportunities available at the campaign level and the strategies adopted by their mainstream opponents.

In this context, the left first had to take up unwillingly the issue as a whole, before then turning out to be unable to participate in increasingly restrictive debates based on the issue dimensions on which it enjoyed relative credibility. The inability to keep the focus on advantageous aspects, such as social and economic arguments and universal values, explains why its attention profile experienced so much variation. However, the media tends to reward coherence, which is why political consistency matters for agenda friction and for explaining how issues emerge in, and disappear from, the public agenda (Jones and Baumgartner, 2005). As I have illustrated in Chapter 7 by comparing migration debates in newspaper coverage and in election manifestos, the media tends to prioritize simplified and consistent messages. I have shown that established features of party competition at the national level persist in local arenas, so that political debates in the media tend to give priority to securitized and simplistic messages that are more attractive for mediatized audiences.

More broadly, the relative importance of the different dimensions of migration is conditional on the type of political communication in electoral campaigning. In this sense, the reciprocal efforts of political actors and the media to manipulate the electoral agenda, and their respective issue preferences influence the relative importance of the various dimensions of policy issues. Immigration as a whole, and each of its constitutive aspects, receive quite different levels of attention, and takes different meanings across different channels of communication. Again, this process is particularly evident for centre-left parties, whose discourse on migration changes considerably after interaction with the mass media. Conversely, right-wing, anti-immigration parties enjoy a particular advantage in the news media coverage of migration debates, especially in terms of visibility, but also in terms of consistency across different channels of communication. This means that interaction with the media allows advantaged parties to concentrate further their attention on advantageous issues, triggering additional issue-prioritization. Mediatized discourse on migration, therefore, contributes to the capacity of security frames to trump economic and cultural ones in public debate, since commercial media are not equally attentive to all types of issues and overemphasize sensationalistic coverage that appeals broader publics.

The discussion so far beg the question whether parties on the pro-migration side of political competition, the mainstream left in particular, can ever find a way out of their disadvantage. By only looking at the supply side of competition, my empirical results do not tell much about how successful the different strategies are. As suggested in previous studies, in fact, there are multiple patterns of strategic adjustment to new political conflicts and challenges, so that political scientists should beware of 'winning formulas' as explanations of, or prescription for, party behaviour in the long run. Nevertheless, the analysis of the dimensionality of migration clearly suggests that agendas depend primarily on the formulation of coherent discourses on issue dimensions, or at least ones that are familiar to, and resonant with the values of specific constituencies of national or local electorates. Hence, the disadvantage of the pro-migration camp also has to do with the inconsistency of its campaign rhetoric over time and across contexts. Although the press seems to respond predominantly to sensational news stories and to the stimuli of issue owners, rhetorical clarity also plays a pivotal role. In this sense, at least in the Italian case, the mainstream left and right seem to have taken very different directions.

The Italian right has responded to the dilemma between economic liberalization and social and cultural nationalism decisively, fully opposing integration and the opening up of borders when it comes to immigration affairs. Even more importantly, it has successfully understood and interpreted media logics and language, offering a coherent anti-immigration discourse and framing perceived threats to the national identity in security terms. Its discourse has been readily translatable into news stories and securitizing discourses by professionals, thus gaining further currency within its electorates and beyond. Next to resonating with its voters, this choice enabled the right to frame immigration in light of common arguments, making it familiar and accessible to mediatized audiences, giving it a further advantage in electoral struggles. The main problem with this strategy is one of accountability: if security issues and threats arise when the political right is in government, it may be held accountable over the aspect of migration that it prioritized during the electoral campaign. This, however, would require that independent and threatening radical right actors challenge the mainstream right on its own territory, something that has been very uncommon in the Italian political landscape of the recent years. One could even raise the question whether this strategy could inadvertently contribute to the emergence of a competitive anti-immigration actor on the extreme right of the political spectrum, especially today when the far-reaching alliances in the right-wing field seem to have ended. Alternatively, it should be the left and the centre-left to point at the failures of the right in terms of migration and security.

Instead, pro-immigration actors and the centre-left in particular generally opt for a strategy of differentiation. First, left-wing parties often reconsider their policy preferences from one electoral campaign to the other and across different local contexts. Second, their positions vary across issue dimensions: tolerance and openness in the cultural dimension go alongside neutral positions on socioeconomic integration and support for tough migration policies in terms of internal and international security, in particular concerning Roma affairs. On the one hand, this indicates that the increasing importance of the issue in political conflict opens up substantial room for strategic manoeuvres by the left. On the other hand, however, this may be interpreted as the image of a weak and procrastinating left, unable or unwilling to fully engage in migration politics, and undecided in terms of the values it wants to represent in public debates. In other words, the Italian centre-left has mainly followed the dynamics of party-system and media agendas, without being able to take the lead and to shape issue debates and policy-making in its most favourite direction. The volatility in terms of dimensional selection and issue positions and across channels of communication indicates that the left is quite uncertain on *how* to address the immigration issue and on the type of electorate (or public) that it should be addressing.

This points to how the migration issue and its dimensions are likely to undergo a continuous number of re-framings by the centre-left, because its electoral strategies are highly shaped by the prevailing definitions and meanings of the issue among right-wing competitors. There seems to have been a partial contagion from the right in migration-related issues, so that the preservation of tolerant stances on cultural aspects goes alongside the endorsement of repressive policies in security matters. In so doing, moderate pro-migrant actors have tried to straddle both camps; they raised attention over their own issue dimensions whilst simultaneously acknowledging the importance of those discussed by their opponents. In order to come to terms with electorates with mixed preferences (such as working-class authoritarians), the centre-left has taken up the discourse of its opponents, emphasizing emergency logics. This seem to have been a self-defeating strategy, as it contributed to validating right-wing narratives, reproduced the idea of immigration as exceptional and temporary, and de-legitimized the left's own efforts to politicize immigration in terms of long-term socioeconomic and cultural benefits. As a result, the mainstream left in Italy now finds itself in a political *cul-de-sac.*

To come out of it, the results of this study suggest it should approach migration affairs as a function of its multiple dimensions. The growing salience of the agenda of order and anxiety has shifted public priorities, overtaking the economic and social agendas; the left must decide whether it wants to build a new profile in terms of security, or instead whether it prefers to restore the centrality of its traditional worldview. This requires coming to terms with the cleavage over the value of security in migration affairs, which should not be understood as a cleavage between the left and the right, but within the left itself (Sniderman *et al.,* 2000).

If the left really aimed at capitalizing on security threats associated with migration and crime, then the most appropriate strategy would be to drop the discussion of economic and cultural benefits of immigration from the agenda. Their politicization, combined with substantial attention on security aspects, in fact seems detrimental, as security concerns benefit from higher media coverage and therefore tend to be prioritized by voters. This choice, however, would mean engaging in direct confrontation with the anti-immigration camp, by giving up a theoretically advantageous position in managing social and economic integration in favour of a platform that is, at least in terms of dimensional attention, the same as the political right. Hence, one could question whether this would be electorally rewarding. As the case of Rome has shown, when this is the case it is increasingly difficult for the centre-left to preserve its pro-immigrant positions within a security frame. Alternatively, it may realize – as this study implicitly suggests – that becoming an agent of securitization does not necessarily yield electoral gains (van der Brug and van Spanje, 2009). Adapting their policy positions to what electorates think, or what the left thinks they think, may prove beneficial only in the short-term. Over the long run, instead, this strategy has only contributed to strengthening even further the advantage of the political right, by bringing to the fore values of authority, order and discipline to which the left is vulnerable.

Left-wing parties might be better off cultivating egalitarian constituencies than constructing securitized agendas, focusing on long-term socioeconomic and cultural benefits of migration rather than on short-term fears and threats. In so doing, it fails to highlight favourable dimensions, it fails to address the contradictions of its adversaries and it actually contributes to reinforcing the perceived need of 'tough' immigration policies. Ideological consistency channelled through egalitarianism, instead, would engage the left in a more comprehensive struggle over the meaning of migration. Otherwise, moderate pro-migrant actors would find themselves increasingly dragged into the securitization discourse whenever the migration issue gains visibility in the media, and even more so when this happens as a result of dramatic events or critical junctures such as with the ongoing Mediterranean crisis. By choosing to follow the right and focus on public anxieties and security concerns, the left contributes to consolidating further the credibility of securitized discourses in migration debates.

Future research directions

This study has revealed that neither party strategy nor media preferences *per se* can fully explain how public debates will unfold in electoral campaigns. Rather, it shows that the construction of campaign agendas in terms of issue dimensions depends on multiple factors, ranging from the politicization strategies of the actors involved in competition, through the issue-specific preferences of media actors and socio-contextual factors, to focusing events and opportunities affecting the environment of electoral competition. The aim of this study was to link partisan strategic options with contextual circumstances, while introducing a thematic conceptualization of migration policy debates. It is up to the reader to assess the extent to which the evidence provided is convincing, and to judge whether the study has been successful in meeting its goals.

The dimensional dynamic of party competition that I have outlined, however, also gives rise to additional questions that need to be addressed in future studies. These questions concern the degree to which this trend can be generalized beyond the case of migration politics, in order to assess whether this issue maintains a certain degree of exceptionality in party competition. Moreover, since my results show that political actors are selective with respect to the aspects of migration they choose to highlight, a cross-national comparative design could assess the strategic advantage and spatial location of actors depending on the type and nature of migration across countries. The analysis of the media coverage of electoral campaigns reveals much about strategies of politicization, and about the nature of the relationship between parties and the media system. However, it certainly does not provide an entire picture of the dynamics of electoral campaigning. To provide a more exhaustive assessment, one would have to combine these findings with data on how political actors acquire media attention. The most common way parties produce events that the media find attractive are press conferences and press releases, but also demonstrations and other explicitly staged events. Because of this, this study has avoided drawing general conclusions on the reciprocal influences between parties and the media, which could only be assessed based on indicators that tackle the struggle among campaigners over the control of the news agenda more directly.

Future research could apply the theoretical framework that was developed in this study to models based on more complete figures of issue attention, to begin with by accounting for other issues susceptible to a process of issue bundling similar to the one described here. Indeed, one limitation of this study is that assessing the relevance of a political issue based solely on its own salience is never preferable to looking at the distribution of attention across all issues discussed in a campaign. The coexistence of distinct dimensions within single policy issues, as well as the conditional relationship between issue dimensions and electoral strategies, might in fact be specific to immigration. Yet, the multiple analytical steps and the conceptual framework developed in this study referred to general processes of electoral campaigning. The changing importance of issue dimensions across local contexts, the tendency of migration to polarize debates, and the specific patterns of issue ownership that it generates, helped illustrate the dynamics of the incorporation and subsequent normalization of new policy issues in political competition, through mechanisms of dimensionality and framing. More generally, I hope that my typology of migration issue dimensions will open the way for new developments in the study of issue competition, with a better integration of salience and positions, in a dynamic perspective. Another potentially important direction for future research may be to use the multidimensional model proposed here to uncover general dynamics of politicization and framing. To provide a more systematic analysis of issue incorporation, future studies might account for longer periods and tackle not only cross-national convergence and divergence but also multi-level interactions between actors in local, national and supranational arenas.

My analysis also provided additional evidence of the increasing securitizing tide of migration debates in Europe, illustrating that this takes place not only at the national level, but also in local elections. Inevitably, as I discussed, this is also the result of the larger context of the Italian media and political system, which means that future cross-national research must look at questions that could not be addressed in this study. Unanswered questions are whether party systems characterized by different levels of fragmentation and volatility result in alternative strategic choices by political actors mobilizing migration issue dimensions, and whether contexts in which municipal governments have less competences in matters of internal security than in the Italian case are displaying different campaigning and dimensional preferences.

These are just some of the obviously important aspects that can help the understanding of electoral campaigning, which this research could not address. Nonetheless, this study has provided a first comprehensive analysis that combines parties' strategic advantages and issue multidimensionality. Thus, it provided an innovative understanding on the reasons why 'the immigration issue' has been difficult to assimilate within existing conflict dimensions, remove addressing the need for a systematic, comparative analysis of how parties handle and engage with policy issues and their constitutive dimensions in the public sphere.

References

Bale, T., Green-Pedersen, C., Krouwel, A., Luther, K.R. and Sitter, N. (2010) 'If You Can't Beat Them, Join Them? Explaining Social Democratic Responses to the Challenge from the Populist Radical Right in Western Europe', *Political Studies,* 58, pp. 410–426.

Balzacq, T. (ed.) (2011) *Securitization Theory. How Security Problems Emerge and Dissolve.* London: Routledge

Baumgartner, F.R., De Boef, S. and Boydstun, A.E. (2008) *The Decline of the Death Penalty and the Discovery of Innocence.* Cambridge: Cambridge University Press.

Baumgartner, F.R. and Jones, B.D. (2002) *Policy Dynamics.* Chicago: University of Chicago Press.

Bigo, D. (2002) 'Security and Immigration: Toward a Critique of the Governmentality of Unease', *Alternatives* 27(2): 63–92.

Bourbeau, P. (2011) *The Securitization of Migration. A Study of Movement and Order.* London: Routledge.

Buzan, B., Wæver, O. and de Wilde, J. (1998) *Security: A New Framework for Analysis.* Boulder: Lynne Rienner.

De Vries, C, Hakhverdian, A. and Lancee, B. (2011) 'The Dynamics of Voters' Left/Right Identification: The Role of Economic and Cultural Attitudes', Paper prepared for the *ECPR General Conference 2011,* Reykjavik.

De Vries, C. and Hobolt, S.B. (2012) 'When Dimensions Collide: The Electoral Success of Issue Entrepreneurs', *European Union Politics,* 13(2), pp. 246–268.

Froio, C., Bevan, S. and Jennings, W. (2013) 'Party Mandates and the Politics of Attention: Party Platforms, Party Priorities and the Policy Agenda in Britain', Paper presented at *6th Annual Conference of the Comparative Agendas Project,* Antwerp, University of Antwerp, 27–29 June, 2013.

Greene, Z., Froio, C. and Bevan, S. (2014) 'The Electoral Consequences of Government Accountability: Evidence from the United Kingdom', Paper presented at the *APSA Annual Meeting.* Available at SSRN: http://ssrn.com/abstract=2455509.

Guinaudeau, I. and Persico, S. (2014) 'What is Issue Competition? Conflict, Consensus and Issue Ownership in Party Competition', *Journal of Elections, Public Opinion and Parties,* 24(3), pp. 312–333, DOI: 10.1080/17457289.2013.858344

Helbling, M., Höglinger, D. and Wüest, B. (2010) 'How Political Parties Frame European Integration', *European Journal of Political Research,* 49(4), pp. 495–521. doi: 10.1111/j.1475–6765.2009.01908.

Hobolt, S., Klemmemsen, R. and Pickup, M. (2008) *The Dynamics of Issue Diversity in Party Rhetoric.* OCSID Working Paper OCSID_03. Available at: http://ocsid.politics. ox.ac.uk/publicatio ns/index.asp (accessed 02 October 2014).

Höglinger, D., Wuest, B. and Helbling, M. (2012) 'Culture versus Economy: The Framing of Public Debates over Issues Related to Globalization'. In: Kriesi, H., Grande, E., Dolezal, M., Helbling, M., Höglinger, D., Hutter, S., Wuest, B. eds. *Political Conflict in Western Europe.* Cambridge/New York: Cambridge University Press, pp. 293–253.

Jones, B. and Baumgartner, F. (2005) *The Politics of Attention: How Government Prioritizes Attention.* Chicago: University of Chicago Press.

Klingemann, H.-D., Hofferbert, R.I. and Budge, I. (1994) *Parties, Policies, and Democracy.* Boulder: Westview Press.

Riker, W.H. (1986) *The Art of Political Manipulation.* Yale: Yale University Press.

Rohrschneider, R. (2002) 'Mobilizing versus Chasing: How Do Parties Target Voters in ElectionCampaigns?', *Electoral Studies* 21, pp. 367–382.

Sniderman, P.M., Peri, P., De Figueiredo, R.J.P. and Piazza, T. (2000) *The Outsider: Prejudice and Politics in Italy.* Princeton: Princeton University Press.

Van der Brug, W., D'Amato, G. Berkhout, J. and Reudin, D. (2015) *The Politicisation of Migration.* Abingdon and New York: Routledge.

Van der Brug, W. and van Spanje, J. (2009) 'Immigration, Europe and the "New" Cultural Dimension', *European Journal of Political Research,* 48, pp. 309–334.

Walgrave, S. and Nuytemans, M. (2009) 'Friction and Party Manifesto Change in 25 Countries', *American Journal of Political Science,* 53(1), pp. 190–206.

Appendix 1

Technical appendix

In this appendix, I outline the approach that was followed for the choice of newspapers and electoral manifestos, and the selection of articles and relevant actors. I then present the codebook for the dimensions and frames, and the general codebook used for the coding of the collected material. The sections below also complement some of the statistical data that was presented in the empirical chapters of the book

Selection of newspapers and articles

The news media are treated in this study as the main source from which to observe framing and politicization strategies taking place during local electoral campaigns. For each city, I chose one local newspaper, selecting the most widely read in each location. Moreover, I also included the local section of the national newspaper *La Repubblica,* which is the largest quality newspaper per circulation in Italy (ADS, 2010). Given the size of the city of Prato, however, this type of data was not available, and local newspaper coverage had to suffice.[1] The focus on quality newspapers rather than tabloids or television programmes was based on the awareness that these kinds of papers are the main media of political coverage. It is information papers that generally report on political debates and influence the editorial decisions of several other news outlets and organizations. With respect to local media, these are also supposed to report more often and with more precision the state of the local political debate.

In Rome I chose *La Repubblica* as a national outlet, and *Il Messaggero* as a local newspaper.[2] The latter paper is distributed all over Italy, but it was founded in Rome, it generally focuses on Rome's chronicle and it is the most popular daily newspaper in the city (ADS, 2010). For Prato, as a local newspaper, I selected the local section of *La Nazione,* which is a Tuscany-based newspaper, and the most widely circulated newspaper in the province of Prato (ADS, 2010).[3] For Milan, it was *La Repubblica* and *Il Giorno,* which is one of the main local newspapers in Milan. Other Milan-based newspapers were not considered even though their distribution is higher than that of *Il Giorno,*[4] because of their strong ideological affiliation with a given party (most notably, *Il Giornale* and *Libero* are outlets belonging to Silvio Berlusconi's editorial group), and because they were more 'sensationalistic' than quality broadsheets.[5]

The media content analysis considered all news items in the selected local newspapers and in the local section of national newspapers, focusing on articles pertaining to the electoral campaign during the two months preceding the election. The choice for this time span is based on examples from previous literature that inform much of this section, most notably the codebook of the Media Study of the *European Election Survey* (EES) 2009 (Schuck *et al.*, 2010), and of Kriesi *et al.* (2008). Given that Italian law sets a minimum period of 30 days for campaigning before elections, the choice of focusing on two months of media coverage ensured a comprehensive description of candidates' activities, including coalition negotiations, and enabled accounting for possible variations in their strategies over the campaign period.

I defined the unit of coding for the selection of relevant articles as a 'news story': an article within a newspaper. In other words, a news story is each individual editorial news item. There was no minimum length for an item to be considered a news story. The content analysis focused on news stories that had an explicit or implicit reference to the electoral campaign at the city level. Generally, such analyses exclude commentaries. However, these were included since articles from prominent journalists and opinion articles represent some of the main elements defining the electoral agenda.

The stories were identified by means of keyword searches in the electronic databases of the selected newspapers. Two main criteria were used to identify stories on the basis of their reference to the electoral campaign: first, stories directly covering politics at the city level, the electoral campaigns and the candidates; and second, stories covering the immigration issue in the city where the election took place, during the time of the electoral campaign, but unrelated to the electoral campaign *per se*.

The most notable keywords were the names of all the candidates and lists running for mayor in each of the electoral campaigns considered. The word search was refined with a set of keywords specifically referring to the immigration issue, which I developed inductively from the preliminary analysis of immigration-related events in the three cities: these did not yield substantial additions to the original keyword search, suggesting that in times of electoral campaigns political actors are conspicuously monopolizing immigration debates, at least at the local level.[6] In sum, I am confident that all stories about immigration politics in Prato, Milan and Rome or about the municipal election campaign in the newspapers were taken into consideration for coding. This amounted to a total of 1,596 news stories and 21,680 core sentences.

Choice of electoral platforms and manifestos

Concerning the analysis of parties' and candidates' framing of the immigration issue before interaction with the mass media, I relied upon the platforms produced by mayoral candidates and their lists *(Programmi del Sindaco)*. According to Italian law, when a list or party decides to participate in a local election, it is requested to submit an official document to the prefecture office *(Commissione*

Elettorale Circondariale) reporting the list of all the candidates for that list/party and the administrative programme of the main candidate. Some lists present their own programme despite being part of a coalition of parties, whereas others submit only the coalition program. In order to gather these manifestos, I contacted the archives of the municipality of the three cities under observation and made an official request to obtain the *Programmi del Sindaco* of all the organizations taking part in the campaigns. In all six campaigns, I then conducted a content analysis of the manifestos, making use of the same codebook as for media coverage.

When available, the in-depth content analysis was first performed on the sections of the electoral programmes dealing with issues related to immigration and integration. The remaining textual part of the programmes is instead coded in such a way as to allow one to measure the importance of the immigration issue relative to all other issues in a party's programme. In total, I coded 23 coalition programmes across the 12 election campaigns, comprising a total of 3,800 core sentences.

The choice of referring to party and coalition manifestos is often criticized in this field of research, since it is considered a conservative tool for the approximation of partisan preferences. This is because, especially in the case of coalition programmes, these may represent the outcome of a long and difficult bargaining process inside the party and/or between different parties within a certain coalition. In this sense, party programmes would not really represent the ideological preferences of political actors, but rather a compromise solution, reached in order to pacify struggles internal to the party or the coalition (Janda *et al.,* 1995).

Even acknowledging this limit, framing strategies are always the result of a balance of power between different factions within the same group, and my interest lies exactly with identifying the dimension (or frame) that eventually prevails. Put differently, the puzzle is the strategic choice that is made by a given actor or coalition, not the set of possible choices that could have been made, had the coalition been more homogeneous. Moreover, one additional element that is generally conceived as a limitation of party manifestos makes this source of data particularly appealing given this study's purposes. Scholars studying the political market of electoral programmes, indeed, have often indicated that the preferences expressed in the manifestos are biased by the electoral context in which they are to be used. In this sense, certain issues may be overrepresented because they are expected to be particularly convenient in a given context at a given point in time. It is exactly this type of strategy, and this type of situation, that the present research refers to.

Hence, using this type of data was done both for theoretical and practical reasons. From a theoretical point of view, platforms are likely to provide an overview of the general positions and preferences of a political actor prior to engaging in active competition with his or her opponents, and before interacting with the mass media. In other words, this data can be considered exempt from the possible effects resulting from media logics. From a practical point of view, relying upon party programmes and manifestos allows one to cope with the difficulty of data collection, which is further exacerbated by the focus on local rather than national electoral campaigns. Even in as short a time span as the one considered here, there was a significant amount of change in terms of the party system's composition. As a result, relying on less accessible types of data (most notably press releases from mayoral candidates), was simply impossible, since local headquarters do not always keep records or archives of their activities, whereas electoral lists often disappear as soon as the electoral campaign is over.

In sum, party programmes remain one of the best available sources of data on the different political platforms that are supplied to the electorates at any given election campaign. Based on the core-sentence approach, a new dataset was built from the electoral programmes of the candidates in the municipal elections in the three case studies and six election campaigns. In this way, it will be possible to identify changes across local elections within and between the different cases.

The coding procedure

Similar to political claims analysis (PCA), core sentence analysis (CSA) uses newspapers to generate indicators of party positions and issue salience, and its unit of analysis is elements within articles (rather than news stories). CSA is based on the notion that the content of every written document can be described as a network of relationships between objects (Helbling and Tresch, 2011). Hence, party positions are analyzed from relationships between political objects within a text. Every sentence of the selected articles was reduced into a core sentence indicating the subject (actor), the object (the immigration issue and its dimensions), and the direction of the relationship between the two.[7] The number of core sentences in an article does not equal the number of grammatical sentences, as one sentence can include none, one or several core sentences.

In other words, each sentence within a news story was reduced to the basic semantic structure of the core sentence, consisting of a subject-actor (a party or politician), an object (an issue, then issue dimension and frame), and the direction of the relationship between the subject and the object (i.e. a polarity score ranging from -1 to $+1$ with three intermediary positions). The direction between subject and object is always quantified using a scale ranging from -1 to $+1$, with three intermediary positions indicating a 'potential' or an ambiguous relation. If, for example, a politician says that in the future he might be in favour of a certain position, we coded 0.5. Ambiguous relations – no direction at all – were coded 0. Here I like to give an illustrative example of what a core sentence looks like on the basis of the following sentence:

> Storace supports special laws for fighting crime in the city, and says 'no' to the study of Quran in schools.

While the subject is the same for both elements in the grammatical sentence, its object changes, as the first element is connected to the issue of security (in general, unless previous sentences make clear that the reference is to immigration), whereas the second is related to the immigration issue and the cultural dimension of immigration. In the example above, the second core sentence is associated to a restrictive, negative position on the cultural dimension of immigration, and would therefore be coded as −1. Figure A1 below summarizes graphically the approach followed for the content analysis in order to assess actor-issue relationships and framing. Due to practical constraints, I only coded core sentences that referred to the immigration issue, whereas all other core sentences were accounted for but not coded, so that they could be used in order to measure the relative salience of the immigration issue.[8]

This coding strategy allows for several types of comparisons. First, it permits one to evaluate the relative importance of immigration in the electoral campaign, relative to all alternative issue debates (although this study does not differentiate among the rest of the issues). Moreover, it allows for the calculation of the relative salience (i.e. the share of sentences) of a certain dimension in the total amount of immigration-related news stories. That is, it allows one to identify different types of debates across local electoral campaigns, and different types of discourse among the mayoral candidates' coalitions. Similarly, it permits one to evaluate the degree to which each frame and argumentation is utilized within a debate on immigration. Finally, it enables one to investigate which frames and dimensions are mobilized to support, and which ones to oppose, immigration (again across cases and mayoral candidates). The next sections illustrate in detail the coding procedures of subject, objects and polarity relationships within actor-issue sentences.

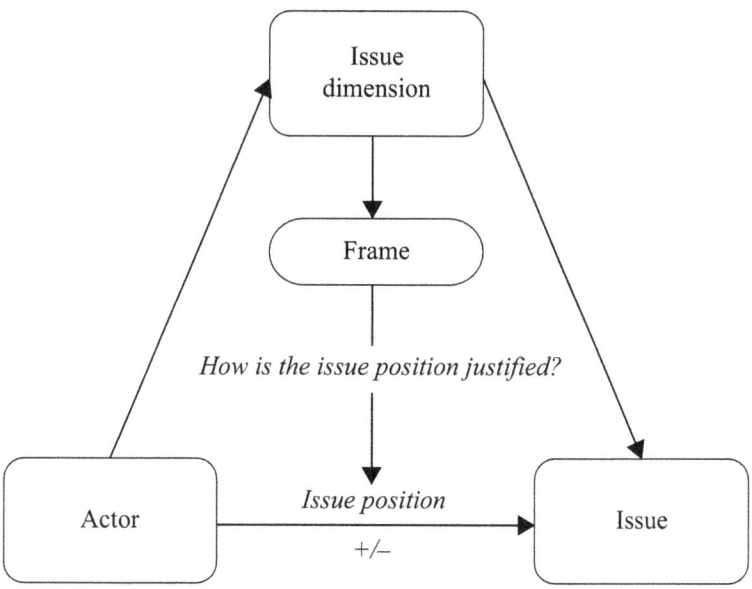

Figure A1 The core-sentence approach and the actor-issue network of relationships

Selection and coding of subject actors

The subjects of core sentences were coded on the basis of their party, list and coalition affiliation, differentiating between candidates running as independents, challengers or incumbents. Given that coalitions are crucial in local electoral campaigns in Italy, lists and candidates were grouped within separate categories: *radical left, centre-left, centre, centre-right* and *radical right.* Non-partisan actors belonging to public interest groups, or individuals and experts that are not members of any given party or coalition, were coded in the independent category *public interest groups*. Finally, all minor lists and candidates that did not reach the threshold of 2% but received considerable attention in the media were aggregated, independently of their ideological orientation, in the category *Minor lists.*[9]

This choice was made necessary because municipal elections are characterized by the participation of a multitude of local, groupuscular and often temporary political organizations: candidates often do not belong to structured organizations, they change their affiliation over time and their electoral committees disappear after the election. This forced a limit on the number of political organizations to be considered in the study, focusing on actors that could be considered relevant in local electoral competition. Relevant organizations were identified by first distinguishing between actors and lists who reached the threshold necessary to get a seat in the city council, and those who did not. This threshold is very low, generally about 2% of the votes, so the actors that have been excluded based on this criterion are generally very small ones. Subsequently, this list was cross-checked with the content of media reports, so that whenever an actor was consistently mentioned in the news media, selection was reconsidered on an *ad hoc* basis.

Despite the high fragmentation of the Italian political system, municipal elections in the observed period are characterized by the convergence of most parties in two main coalitions. The names and composition of local electoral lists are extremely volatile, but the main coalitions characterizing the 2004–2011 period can be identified as the groups of parties and lists clustering around the centre-right *(Alleanza Nazionale* and *Forza Italia,* subsequently *Il Popolo della Libertà),* and the centre-left *(Democratici di Sinistra* and *La Margherita,* subsequently *Partito Democratico).* Although in most occasions these coalitions involved political organizations at the extremes of the ideological spectrum (the radical right-wing *La Destra* and/or *Fiamma Tricolore,* and the euro-communist *Rifondazione Comunista*), and electoral lists affiliated with centrist parties at the national level (the *Unione di Centro – UDC*), independent candidates are not uncommon, as the electoral system allows for negotiations and endorsements after the first round of elections.[10]

Coding of the objects and frames

Objects within written documents (news stories and electoral manifestos) were selected based on whether the documents were implicitly or explicitly related to the electoral campaign or the issue of immigration (including asylum seekers and illegal migration) and integration (including ethnic and religious minorities and minority policies).

The objects and arguments proposed by each actor were coded in terms of the dimensions and frames of the immigration issue that were introduced in the theory chapter. Each coded core sentence included the dimension of immigration that the actor referred to, and the specific frame that was used in order to push forward a certain argument: Labour and Security as opposed to Economic Prosperity (Socioeconomic Dimension); Nationalism, as opposed to Multiculturalism (Cultural and Religious Dimension); and Roma Issues, Urban Issues and Emergency Issues (Law and Order Dimension). Concerning frames, however, several core sentences made reference to more than one type of argumentation. For this reason, I added an additional category reporting, when applicable, the second frame characterizing a given core sentence.[11]

In order to quantitatively account for the double frames, the data was reshaped in the long format, adjusting the unit of analysis (core sentences) to the number of immigration frames. This reshaping of the dataset into the long format greatly increased the number of observations. In terms of the media material, the amount of immigration-related sentences increased to match the sum of the first and second frames included in the original dataset (2,408 + 524 = 2,932). Given the increase in observations, the dataset in the long format could not be used for the measurement of the (relative) salience of issue dimensions in the general electoral debate. Instead it was utilized to look at the relative importance of each frame within the share of the debate dedicated to a given issue dimension.

Coding the relationship between subject and object

As was illustrated earlier, the theoretical assumption of core-sentence approaches is that every text is composed of a network of relationships between subjects and objects. The unit of analysis is therefore sentences reduced to their basic structure, expressed in terms of a relationship between a political actor and an object/issue. Each object refers to an attribute of the immigration issue, which is then characterized by the actor in terms of the various frames comprised in the socioeconomic, cultural-religious and law and order dimensions. In other words, each actor is connected (positively or negatively) to each one of the three dimensions of the immigration issue, and the argument that is provided is then coded in line with the framing typology.

With respect to each of the dimensions of immigration, political actors were given a score ranging from −1 to +1, with three intermediate positions indicating a potential (+0.5 and −0.5) and a neutral position (0). In this way, the data resulting from the content analysis offers detailed information on the positions of all candidates and parties with respect to each of the dimensions of the immigration issue. These are measured on a continuum ranging from full opposition to immigration (in any dimension) to full support for immigration (again in any dimension), and differentiating between mild support, mild opposition and neutrality.

In this way, the main characteristics defining each observation included in the dataset (next to contextual codes such as 'date', 'article id', 'title', etc.) are the following: the specification of a subject (type of actor, coalition and incumbent/challenger); the specification of the object (immigration-related sentence, non-immigration sentence); the specification of the dimension and frame within the immigration category (the three dimensions and seven frame categories); and the direction of the relationship between the subject and the object (from −1 to +1).

Notes

1 The search on the local section of the closest metropolitan area, Firenze, produced no results.
2 Periods: 28/03–28/05/2006; 26/02–26/04/2008.
3 Periods: 11/04–11/06/2004; 20/04–20/06/2009.
4 Periods: 28/03–28/05/2006; 28/03–28/05/2011.
5 Cf. the media study of the European Election Survey (Schuck *et al.*, 2010): www.piredeu.eu.
6 The list of keywords is reported in Appendix 3.
7 Whenever applicable, we also mentioned whether the subject-object relation also included a subject-actor reference. In other words, we coded cases in which Actor X addressed Object Y by making reference to Actor Z.
8 In order to identify core sentences on issues other than immigration, I used as a benchmark the set of issue categories included in Kriesi *et al.* (2012).
9 Despite its scarce relevance in terms of partisan competition, this category provides substantial information in terms of salience and characteristics of debates at the party-system level.
10 As will be discussed in the empirical chapters, the composition of electoral coalitions at the local level often (yet not always) reflects national-level strategies. This is particularly the case in Rome and Milan, which represent the most prominent administrative elections in Italy, and often assume importance and resonance at the national level.
11 For the media material, on 2,408 immigration-related core sentences, 524 employed two frames and were given a value corresponding to the second frame's category. This choice also reduced considerably the amount of core sentences that were not pertinent to any frame category (residual category).

Appendix 2
Italian local elections 2004–2011

In this section, I introduce the parties and coalitions that took part in the six electoral campaigns under consideration in this study, and provide a succinct overview of the main candidates and campaigns for each city.

Overview

The Italian electoral system for the election of the mayors in cities with a population higher than 15,000 inhabitants allows voters to express either a direct choice for the mayor by voting for the name of one of the candidates, or an indirect choice by voting for one of the parties and lists within the candidate's coalition. After the first round, if no candidate receives at least 50% of the preferences, the top two candidates are admitted to the second round of elections, which takes place two weeks later. The election of the City Council is based on a direct choice for the candidate with a preference vote, and the number of the seats for each list is determined proportionally.

Due to this electoral law for municipal elections, and in line with the increasingly bipolar tendencies of the Italian party system (cf. Chiaramonte, 2007; Cotta and Verzichelli, 2008; Fabbrini, 2009), each city presents two main candidates representing the centre-left and centre-right coalitions. The overall picture, however, is far less straightforward than this. The composition of the two coalitions varied over time and across cases, as a consequence of the extreme volatility of the Italian party system in general, and of local electoral lists in particular. What is more, the number of independent candidates running outside the mainstream coalitions varied across cases and over time, as a consequence of both partisan negotiations and local political dynamics (see: Baldini, 2002; Pasquino, 2001).

A radical left list of considerable size *(Rifondazione Comunista)* ran independently from the centre-left on only one occasion (the elections in Prato in 2004), whereas in all other cases radical left parties ran in support of the mainstream left coalition. These generally comprise a combination of post-communist, social-democratic, liberal-democratic and Catholic traditions – which is often the case in recent Italian political history (see: Cotta and Verzichelli, 2008; Newell and Bull, 1997). Prato in 2004 also saw the presence of the *Nuovo PSI* ('New Italian Socialist Party'), which is a centrist party that has been progressively integrated into the new party of the centre-right camp, *Popolo della Libertà* (PDL). The main Italian centrist party (*Unione di Centro* – UDC) runs in coalition with the centre-right parties in some occasions but not in others, mainly because of a combination of national politics and local dynamics (see: McDonnell, 2013). After bitter internal conflicts, in fact, the UDC decided to run on its own in the national elections of 2008, which made local alliances with the PDL unsuitable. Again, however, the elections of 2009 in Prato present an exception to this trend.

On the right-wing side of the political spectrum, local elections reproduce the longstanding national alliance between the mainstream right parties and the regionalist populist party, the Lega Nord (McDonnell, 2013). Being a regionalist party, however, the Lega Nord is not present in Rome, whereas it appears in the 2009 elections in Prato in coalition with the centre-right.[1] In addition, radical right parties participated in virtually all the elections considered, but only in two cases did they gain a substantial amount of voters. The 2008 elections in Rome provide another example of a national-local political intersection. The newly formed party *La Destra* was born out of a conflict over the birth of the PDL, and represented a new radical right actor which built an electoral alliance with a traditional party of that area: *Fiamma Tricolore.* Prato's radical right, by contrast, is a small munici-pal list, created as a single-issue movement (pro-security and against Chinese residents) for the occasion of the 2009 elections.

The sections below discuss electoral results in detail for the six electoral cam-paigns in the three municipal settings, specifying the type of coalition in each local setting. Tables A1 to A3 below indicate the coalitions, candidates and votes obtained by the elected mayors and main opposition candidates. As can be seen, in the second election in each city no candidate reached the required 50% quota, so that there was the need for the second-round voting *(ballottaggio)* in order to elect one of the two top candidates. Moreover, each city experienced an alternation in power between the mainstream left and right coalition over the period considered: Milan shifted from a centre-right administration to a centre-left one in the elec-tions of 2011, whereas both Rome and Prato followed the opposite trend in 2008 and 2009.

Milan

The 2006 elections in Milan coincided with the end of the second mandate of the mayor Gabriele Albertini, supported at first by *Forza Italia* and subsequently by *Casa delle Libertà*. As the Italian law does not allow more than two consecutive mandates, the mainstream right coalition (involving multiple centre-right lists, as well as Lega Nord, the radical right of *Azione Sociale* and *Fiamma Tricolore,* and moderates from *UDC* and *Nuovo PSI*) appointed Letizia Moratti, at the time Minister for School and University, in the incumbent Berlusconi government. The mainstream left coalition largely reproduced party agreements reached at the national level between the centre-left, the Greens, the radical left *(Rifondazione* and *Comunisti Italiani),* and multiple centrist actors (*UDEUR,* IDV). The coali-tion chose former city prefect Bruno Ferrante after a primary election. Some other candidates also considered the candidacy, but they eventually allied with the two main coalitions. Although the race was close, the centre-right candidate Moratti ultimately succeeded in keeping the centre-right in office in Milan, without the need of a second round of elections.

At the end of her mandate in 2008, Letizia Moratti was confirmed as the mayor candidate of the centre-right for the May 2011 elections, supported by Lega Nord, the radical right of *La Destra* and a number of lists belonging to centrist parties at the national level *(Nuovo PSI, Alleanza di Centro, Popolari)*. Yet, the main centrist party presented an independent candidate (Manfredi Palmeri) in line with the political strategy of autonomy undertaken by the *Unione di Centro* at the national level. Concerning the challenger coalition, the primary elections of the centre-left led by the *Partito Democratico* in November 2010 were won by Giuliano Pisapia. The left also supported his candidacy *(Rifondazione Comunista* and *SEL)*.

Table A1a Municipal elections in Milan, 2006

	Candidate	Party lists	Vote %	Coalition programme	Tot. %
Mainstream right coalition	**Letizia Moratti**	Forza Italia*	32.2%	Programma Coalizione	**54.3%**
		Alleanza Nazionale*	8.5%		
		Lista Moratti*	5.1%		
		Lega Nord*	3.7%		
		UDC*	2.4%		
		Pensioni e Lavoro	0.6%		
		DC per autonomie	0.4%		
		Azione Sociale – Muss.	0.4%		
		Fiamma Tricolore	0.3%		
		Giovani per Milano	0.2%		
		Nuovo PSI	0.1%		
		Pensionati Invalidi	0.1%		
		SOS Italia	0.1%		
Mainstream left coalition	**Bruno Ferrante**	L'Ulivo*	22.0%	Un'altra Milano comincia da qui	**44.6%**
		Lista Ferrante*	7.5%		
		Rifondazione Comunista*	4.2%		
		Federazione Verdi*	3.4%		
		Uniti con Dario Fo*	2.1%		
		Comunisti Italiani	1.5%		
		Di Pietro – IDV	1.5%		
		La Rosa nel Pugno	1.4%		
		Partito Pensionati	0.6%		
		UDEUR Popolari	0.3%		
		Lista Consumatori	0.1%		
Other	All other candidates below 1%				

Source: Italian Ministry of Internal Affairs – Electoral Archive (http://elezionistorico.interno.it) and *Archivio Elettorale del Comune di Milano* (www.comune.milano.it/).

* Indicates whether parties obtained seats in the city council.

Since Milan was a stronghold of conservative vote, many observers described the election in Milan as a poll of the popularity of the national cabinet of Silvio Berlusconi. This contributed to attracting the attention of national media and national political figures to this election. Although at the beginning of the campaign incumbent mayor Letizia Moratti was leading largely the polls, the centre-left coalition enjoyed a number of successes across local elections in Italy in 2011, and Pisapia ultimately defeated his competitor in the second round of elections in Milan (29–30 May 2011).

Prato

Prato used to represent a stronghold of the Italian Communist Party and – subsequently – of the centre-left. The procedure to appoint the 2004 mayoral candidate for the left was not smooth, with several important figures of the party proposing themselves and being supported by the different 'wings' of the centre-left party *Democratici di Sinistra* (DS) in Prato. Ultimately, the regional leadership in Florence appointed an outsider: Marco Romagnoli, an important figure at the regional level (yet loosely linked to politics at the city level), who secured a coalition with both moderate *(Margherita, UDEUR)* and radical leftist actors *(Comunisti Italiani)*. Yet, the choice of the candidate also resulted in a fraction with the left-wing of the city administration, which decided to support the candidate of the radical left Mauro Vannoni *(Rifondazione Comunista)*. Similarly, the centre-right was also unable to reach a shared decision: the appointment of Filippo Bernocchi (a member of *Alleanza Nazionale* considered closer to the most right-wing area of the *Casa delle Libertà)* led to a split with the centrist fraction of Massimo Taiti *(Nuovo PSI,* who ran as an independent) but not with the other centrists of *UDC.* Eventually, despite several observers expecting the left to be sanctioned electorally, the vote saw the success of the mainstream left already in the first round; the centre-right coalition and the radical left did not meet the expectations in terms of electoral scores and actually retrenched compared to the 1999 consultations.

In October 2008, since Romagnoli announced that he would not run for the upcoming Prato elections, the party appointed as candidate Massimo Carlesi, who was a prominent member of the outgoing *Partito Democratico* administration at the city level. The coalition supporting Carlesi this time involved a vast list of centrist *(Partito Liberale, IDV, Repubblicani)* and left-wing actors *(SEL, Comunisti Italiani)*, so that there were no sizable independent lists and candidates to his left. By contrast, the centre-right appointed Roberto Cenni: a local entrepreneur who presented himself as independent from local politics, but who was actively supported by PDL. In fact, Silvio Berlusconi came in person to Prato during the campaign. Cenni's coalition involved a wide set of lists and parties of the centre *(UDC)* and right-wing *(La Destra, Lega Nord),* as well as civic lists of consumers and young entrepreneurs. The main trait of the campaign of the centre-right was the challenge to the centre-left establishment that had administered the city of Prato for the previous 60 years. In this respect, the centre-right rhetoric could take advantage of a small anti-immigration list, led by a former member of the

Table A1b Municipal elections in Milan, 2011

	Candidate	Party lists	Vote %	Coalition programme	Tot. %	2nd Round
Mainstream left coalition	**Giuliano Pisapia**	Partito Democratico*	28.6%	Programma del candidato sindaco Giuliano Pisapia e delle liste che lo sostengono	**47.3%**	**55.1%**
		Sinistra Ecologia Libertà*	4.7%			
		Milano Civica per Pisapia*	3.9%			
		Rifondazione Comunista – Comunisti Italiani*	3.1%			
		Di Pietro – IDV*	2.5%			
		Lista Pannella – Bonino*	1.7%			
		Verdi Ecologisti	1.4%			
		Milly Moratti per Pisapia	1.3%			
Mainstream right coalition	**Letizia Moratti**	Il Popolo della Libertà*	28.7%	Per una Milano sempre più bella da vivere	**43.3%**	**44.9%**
		Lega Nord*	9.6%			
		Milano al Centro*	2.4%			
		Io amo MilanoIo amo l'Italia	0.5%			
		Progetto Milano Migliore	0.5%			
		Pensioni e Lavoro	0.3%			
		La Destra	0.3%			
		Unione Italiana	0.3%			
		Giovani per l'EXPO	0.2%			
		Nuovo PSI	0.2%			
		Popolari Italia Domani	0.1%			
		Alleanza Di Centro	0.1%			
Other	**Manfredi Palmeri**	Nuovo Polo per Milano*	2.7%	La Primavera di Milano Palmeri sindaco	**5.5%**	
		Unione di Centro	1.9%			
Other	**Mattia Calise**	Movimento 5 Stelle*	3.4%	Programma per la nostra città	**3.4%**	
Other		All other candidates below 1%				

Source: Italian Ministry of Internal Affairs – Electoral Archive (http://elezionistorico.interno.it).

* Indicates whether parties obtained seats in the city council.

Source: Archivio Elettorale del Comune di Milano (www.comune.milano.it/).

Table A2a Municipal elections in Prato, 2004

	Candidate	Party lists	Vote %	Coalition programme	Tot. %
Mainstream left coalition	**Marco Romagnoli**	Democratici di Sinistra*	35.2%	Per una Prato da Primato	**53.5%**
		La Margherita*	9.6%		
		Lista Di Pietro*	2.8%		
		Comunisti Italiani*	2.2%		
		Federazione Verdi*	2.0%		
		SDI	1.2%		
		Alleanza Pop. – UDEUR	0.3%		
Mainstream right coalition	**Filippo Bernocchi**	Forza Italia*	16.7%	Un futuro per Prato, un cambiamento per tutti	**33.0%**
		Alleanza Nazionale*	12.7%		
		UDC	2.5%		
		Insieme per Prato	0.86%		
Other	**Mauro Vannoni**	Rifondazione Comunista*	6.3%	Programma Coalizione	**8.1%**
		Sinistra per Prato	1.8%		
Other	**Massimo Taiti**	Nuovo Partito Socialista Italiano*	3.0%	Programma Nuovo PSI	**3.1%**
Other	All other candidates below 1.5%				

Source: Italian Ministry of Internal Affairs – Electoral Archive (http://elezionistorico.interno.it).

* Indicates whether parties obtained seats in the city council.

Source: *Ufficio Elettorale del Comune di Prato* (www.comune.prato.it).

centre-left administration (Aldo Milone) and supported by the groups of the local radical right *(Prato Libera e Sicura)*. Although the list's electoral appeal was limited (about 3% in the first round) the alliance with the mainstream right in the second round of elections was decisive, as Roberto Cenni was elected mayor with a 50.88% majority, and a surplus of only 1,500 votes over Carlesi.

Rome

For the 2006 elections in Rome, the two coalitions reproduced the sets of alliances supporting Romano Prodi and Silvio Berlusconi in the general elections of the same year. The incumbent mayor of the city Walter Veltroni *(L'Ulivo)* ran

Table A2b Municipal elections in Prato, 2009

	Candidate	Party lists	Vote %	Coalition programme	Tot. %	2nd Round
Mainstream right coalition	**Roberto Cenni**	Il Popolo della Libertà*	32.5%	Il PDL Cambia l'Italia: anche a Prato dalle parole ai fatti	**47.4%**	**50.9%**
		Lega Nord*	5.1%			
		Unione di Centro*	3.2%			
		La Destra	1.1%			
		Giovani Pratesi	0.9%			
		Prato Civica	0.8%			
		Taiti per Prato	0.5%			
		Socialisti Riformisti	0.4%			
Mainstream left coalition	**Massimo Silvano Carlesi**	Partito Democratico*	39.9%	Programma Coalizione	**48.1%**	**49.1%**
		Di Pietro – IDV*	4.3%			
		Sinistra e Libertà	2.5%			
		Comunisti Italiani	1.2%			
		Partito Liberale Europeo	0.1%			
		Repubblicani Europei	0.1%			
Other	**Aldo Milone**	Prato Libera e Sicura*	2.7%	Programma Prato Libera e Sicura	**2.7%**	*Supports Cenni*
Other		All other candidates below 1%				

Source: Italian Ministry of Internal Affairs – Electoral Archive (http://elezionistorico.interno.it).

* Indicates whether parties obtained seats in the city council.

Source: *Ufficio Elettorale del Comune di Prato* (www.comune.prato.it).

for a second mandate supported by a wide coalition of lists, ranging from radical left actors *(Rifondazione Comunista)* to centrist and moderate ones *(Moderati)*, in line with the coalition agreement that was formed at the national level. The main opposition party, the *Casa della Libertà* of Silvio Berlusconi, opted for Gianni Alemanno, prominent member of *Alleanza Nazionale* (the party that emerged from the neo-fascist *Movimento Sociale Italiano*) and Minister for Agriculture in the second Berlusconi cabinet. The candidature of Alemanno rapidly gathered the support of most parties and lists within the centre *(Unione di Centro, Nuovo PSI)* and right-wing area in the city *(Azione Sociale Mussolini)*. As predicted by a majority of pollsters, Veltroni obtained an easy victory in the first electoral round.

Two years later, however, municipal elections were held again in Rome (13–14 April 2008) as the outgoing mayor of Rome Veltroni (by then secretary of the Italian *Partito Democratico*) resigned in order to run as candidate in the general elections. The centre-left candidate was Francesco Rutelli (again supported by a wide coalition ranging from the left-wing *Sinistra Arcobaleno* to the moderate

Table A3a Municipal elections in Rome, 2006

	Candidate	Party lists	Vote %	Coalition programme	Tot. %
Mainstream left coalition	**Walter Veltroni**	L'Ulivo*	33.8%	Walter Veltroni, Il sindaco di tutti	**61.4%**
		Civica Veltroni*	6.2%		
		Rifondazione Comunista*	5.4%		
		Verdi*	4.8%		
		Moderati*	4.4%		
		Di Pietro – Italia dei Valori*	2.3%		
		La Rosa nel Pugno*	2.0%		
		Comunisti Italiani*	1.5%		
		Roma Arcobaleno	0.6%		
		Lista Consumatori	0.2%		
		Consumatori Uniti	0.1%		
		Socialdemocrazia	0.1%		
Mainstream right coalition	**Giovanni Alemanno**	Alleanza Nazionale*	19.4%	In nome del Popolo Romano	**37%**
		Forza Italia*	10.2%		
		Unione Di Centro*	4.3%		
		Amore per Roma	0.8%		
		Az. Sociale Mussolini	0.6%		
		Dem.Cr. per Autonomie	0.6%		
		Nuovo PSI	0.4%		
		Forza Roma	0.3%		
		Partito Rep. Italiano	0.2%		
		Avanti Lazio	0.1%		
		Mida	0.1%		
		Pensione case lavoro	0.1%		
		Nuova Generazione	0.1%		
		Partito Real Democratico	0.1%		
Other	All other candidates below 1%				

Source: Italian Ministry of Internal Affairs – Electoral Archive (http://elezionistorico.interno.it).

* Indicates whether parties obtained seats in the city council.

Source: *Archivio Storico delle Elezioni, Ministero dell'Interno* (http://elezionistorico.interno.it/).

centrists of *Lista Moderati per Roma*), who was already mayor of Rome from 1993 to 2001. Gianni Alemanno was again the candidate of *PDL* and a centre-right coalition encompassing radical right *(Popolo della Vita)* as well as centrist lists *(Alleanza per il Sud)*. Yet, Alemanno was unable to secure an alliance with the newly-born radical right cartel of *La Destra-Fiamma Tricolore,* who presented Francesco Storace as their independent candidate. Similarly, the centrists who did not join the *Popolo delle Libertà* presented their autonomous candidate, who ran independently from the mainstream right coalition. Although the polling

Table A3b Municipal elections in Rome, 2008

	Candidate	Party lists	Vote %	Coalition programme	Tot. %	2nd Round
Mainstream right coalition	**Giovanni Alemanno**	Popolo delle Libertà*	36.6%	Roma Cambia	**40.7%**	**53.7%**
		Lista Civica Sindaco Alemmanno*	1.22%			
		Lista Civica il Popolo della Vita	0.7%			
		Movimento per le Autonomie, Allenza per il Sud	0.6%			
		Lista Civica la Voce dei Consumatori	0.3%			
		Partito Repubblicano Italiano	0.2%			
Mainstream left coalition	**Francesco Rutelli**	Partito Democratico*	34.0%	La Nostra Idea di Roma	**45.8%**	**46.3%**
		Sinistra Arcobaleno*	4.5%			
		Di Pietro – IDV*	3.3%			
		Lista Civica per Rutelli*	2.7%			
		Lista Civica under 30	0.8%			
		Lista Bonino-Radicali	0.7%			
		Moderati per Roma	0.5%			
		Unione Democratica per i Consumatori	0.2%			
Other	**Francesco Storace**	La DestraFiamma Tricolore*	3.8%	Programma La Destra	**3.8%**	
Other	**Luciano Ciocchetti**	Unione di Centro*	3.3%	Programma UDC	**3.3%**	
Other	All other candidates below 3%					

Source: Italian Ministry of Internal Affairs – Electoral Archive (http://elezionistorico.interno.it).

* Indicates whether parties obtained seats in the city council.

Source: *Archivio Storico delle Elezioni, Ministero dell'Interno* (http://elezionistorico.interno.it/).

were in favour of Rutelli, Alemanno eventually won after the second round of consultations, taking advantage (among other things) of a number of crime stories that discredited the outgoing city administration, and benefiting from the support enjoyed by the newly elected centre-right government of Silvio Berlusconi.

Note

1 This is the result of the strategy of 'expansion' to the south of the party.

Appendix 3

Full codebook

Table A4 Full codebook

Level	Variable label (short)	Variable label (long)	Comments	Values
Sentence	obs	Number of observation	Unique identifier of each core sentence	
Election	city	City	City in which the election campaign was coded	Milan
				Rome
				Prato
Election	year	Year	Year of the election campaign	2004
				2006
				2008
				2009
				2011
Election	election	Electoral campaign	Identifier for each city and year of the election campaign coded	
Election	ballottaggio	Ballottaggio	Identifier for second round of electoral campaigns	
Sentence	sen_type	Core sentence type	Type of core sentence	Actor-actor
				Actor-issue
				Actor-actor-issue
Sentence	proposal	Policy proposal	Identifier for claims proposing actual policy or policy changes	

Level	Variable label (short)	Variable label (long)	Comments	Values
Article	source_type	Type of data source (local newspaper articles, national newspaper articles, party manifestos)	Identifier for articles and manifestos. National newspapers were coded for all election except for the ones in Prato.	National newspaper
				Local newspaper
				Party manifesto
Article	source_name	Name of data source	Name of news outlet used (La Repubblica, Il Messaggero, etc.)	
Article	title	Title of article	The first two words of the title of the article	
Article	date	Date of newspaper article	Date of publication	
Article	page	Page of publication	Page of publication (when available for newspapers; for party manifestos = ranking)	
Article	type	Type of article	It indicates whether it is a commentary, an interview or a reportage article	
Article	length	Length of article	It indicates the length of the article in n° of words	
Article	comments		Any additional comments on article	
Article	art_ID	Article identification number	Unique identifier among the articles published on the same day of publication in the same news outlet	

(*Continued*)

Level	Variable label (short)	Variable label (long)	Comments	Values
Sentence	text	Grammatical sentence	When available, text of the grammatical sentence that was reduced to core sentence (for recoding and correction)	
Sentence	subject	Subject actor as coded	Mainly names of organizations (parties, interest groups)	
Sentence	subjectname	Second-level subject actor	When available, names of persons if mentioned in the document/ article	
Sentence	party	Party family of subject actor	If applicable, party family of the subject actor (e.g., social democrats, right-wing populists)	
Sentence	coalition	Coalition of subject actor	If applicable, the coalition to which subject actor belongs	
Sentence	incumbent	Incumbent or challenger	Whether subject actor is within incumbent or challenger coalition groups at local level	
Sentence	subj_direction	Relationship for actor-actor sentences	Direction of the relationship between subject and object	(−1, −0.5, 0, 0.5, 1)
Sentence	object	Object actor as coded	Mainly names of organizations (parties, interest groups)	
Sentence	objectname	Second-level object actor	When available, names of persons if mentioned in the document/ article	

Level	Variable label (short)	Variable label (long)	Comments	Values
Sentence	partyobj	Party family of object actor	If applicable, party family of the object actor	
Sentence	coalitionobj	Coalition of object actor	If applicable, the coalition to which object actor belongs	
Sentence	incumbentobj	Incumbent or challenger	Whether object actor is within incumbent or challenger coalition groups at local level	
Sentence	issue	Issue of reference of the core sentence	Coded for immigration sentences	
Sentence	dimension	Dimension of immigration	Dimensional issue categories	Dimensional issue categories
Sentence	direction	Relationship as coded	Direction of the relationship between subject and issue	(−1, −0.5, 0, 0.5, 1)
Frame	frame1	First-level frame of the immigration issue	Frame issue categories	
Frame	frame2	Second-level frame of the immigration issue	When available, additional frame issue categories	Frame issue categories
Frame	frame3	Third-level frame of the immigration issue	When available, additional frame issue categories	Frame issue categories

List of keywords

"immigra*", "migrant*", "stranier*", "extracomunitar*", "clandestin*", "vu compr*", "ambulant*", "Islam" "Musulman*", "Imam", "Moschea", "minaret*", "Jihad", "burqa", "maghrebin*", "magrebin*", "African*", "Albanes*", "Rumen*", "Romen*", "Rom" (excluded), "etnia+Rom", "zingar*", "nomad*", "cines*", "fabbrica-dormitor*", "capannon*", "Joan Rus", "La Storta", "Via Padova", "via Quaranta", "Macrolotto", "via Pistoiese", "Reggiani", "Piazza Vittorio", "Tor di Quinto", "sicurezza", "decoro", "camp*+abusiv*", "Neamtu", "Mailat", "tendopoli", "accampament*", "baracc*", "Lampedusa", "CIE", "CPT", "basist*", "scafist*", "rifugiat*", "barcon*", "Ponte Galeria", "ondata", "asilo", "richiedent*", "Bossi-Fini", "Turco-Napolitano", "Decreto flussi", "sanatori*", "soggiorno", "visto", "cittadinanza", "nazionalità", "Razzis*", "discrimina*", "multicultur*", "assimila*", "integraz, "xenofob*"

Appendix 4

Dimensions and frames for content analysis

Table A5 Dimensions and frames for content analysis

Dimension	Frame	Pro-immigration arguments	Anti-immigration arguments
Socioeconomic	Economic prosperity	Economic growth Immigrants necessary in specific sectors of labour market	Economic decay Illegal economic activities
	Labour and security	Immigrants as taxpayers and welfare contributors	Immigrants as welfare receivers Tradeoff employment with immigrants Black market and unfair labour competition
Cultural and religious	Multiculturalism	Multiculturalism Religious equality Political rights	Failure of multiculturalism Incompatibility of religions and cultures Political rights for Italian diaspora rather than immigrants
	Nationalism	Nationalism (-) Evolution of national identity citizenship (+)	Protection of national identity Communitarian-differentialism (-)
Law and order	Roma issues Urban issues	Citizenship and EU frame Banlieues and decency (+)	Security frame Banlieues and decency (-)
	Emergency issues	Refugee and shelter Amnesty and regularization	Urban violence Illegal entry and residence Terrorism and Islam

Appendix 5

Regression results

Table A6 Regression results for Model D – salience of the immigration issue (by dimension)

Salience of immigration

	Socioec	Cult	L&O
Intercept	6.22	4.15	3.14
	(1.938)	(0.680)	(0.945)
Centre-left	−1.22	−1 47**	−0.14
	(1.147)	(0.418)	(2.327)
Centre-right	0.21	−0.45	2.73
	(0.954)	(0.828)	(2.660)
CL challenger	1.101	0.80	−0.99
	(0.668)	(1.073)	(2.327)
CR challenger	−2.21	−0.81	−2.32
	(1.587)	(0.982)	(2.031)
Radical right	6.58***	−1.56**	2.38
	(1.053)	(0.730)	(3.016)
Time (ref. t1)	0.21	1.65	3.69**
	(1.059)	(1.050)	(1.566)
Rome (ref. Prato)	−3.66***	−2.57**	2.87**
	(0.34)	(0.591)	(1.45)
Milan (ref. Prato)	−5.51***	−1.01	−1.24
	(1.424)	(1.213)	(2.38)
R-squared	0.61	0.37	0.23
No. observations	31	31	31

Note: Standard errors are reported in parentheses.

*, **, *** indicate significance at the 90%, 95% and 99% levels.

Source: Author's data.

Table A7 Regression results for Model D – position on the immigration issue (by dimension)

Position on immigration	Coef.		
	Socioec	Cult	L&O
Intercept	0.48	0.35	−0.31
	(0.350)	(0.385)	(0.389)
Centre-left	0.62***	0.54	0.21
	(0.194)	(0.304)	(0.227)
Centre-right	−0.68***	−0.64	−0.38
	(0.143)	(0.356)	(0.233)
CL challenger	−0.43**	0.03	0.23
	(0.140)	(0.282)	(0.216)
CR challenger	−0.32*	−0.42	−0.15
	(0.171)	(0.356)	(0.339)
Radical right	−0.86*	−1.192***	−0.49**
	(0.260)	(0.359)	(0.204)
Time (ref. t1)	−0.36*	−0.09	0.03
	(0.189)	(0.396)	(0.211)
Salience	−0.04	−0.04	−0.18
	(0.037)	(0.070)	(0.016)
Rome (ref. Prato)	0.16	0.12	0.02
	(0.193)	(0.173)	(0.138)
Milan (ref. Prato)	0.25	0.05	0.46
	(0.252)	(0.396)	(0.353)
R-squared	0.78	0.54	0.46
No. observations	24	28	27

Note: Standard errors are reported in parentheses.

*, **, *** indicate significance at the 90%, 95% and 99% levels.

Source: Author's data.

References

ADS (2010) *Media Mobile Diffusione Stampa Luglio 2009 — Giugno 2010*. Rome: Accertamento Diffusione Stampa.

Baldini, G. (2002) 'The Direct Election of Mayors: an Assessment of the Institutional Reform Following the Italian Municipal Elections of 2001', *Journal of Modern Italian Studies*, 7(3), pp. 364–379.

Chiaramonte, A. (2007) 'Il nuovo sistema partitico italiano tra bipolarismo e frammentazione'. In: D'Alimonte, R. and Chiaramonte, A. eds. *Proporzionale ma non solo. Le elezioni politiche del 2006*. Bologna: Il Mulino, pp. 369–406.

Cotta, M. and Verzichelli, L. (2008) *Il sistema politico Italiano*. Bologna: Il Mulino.

Fabbrini, S. (2009) 'The Transformation of Italian Democracy', *Bulletin of Italian Politics*, 1(1), pp. 29–47.

Helbling, M. and Tresch, A. (2011) 'Measuring Party Positions and Issue Salience from Media Coverage: Discussing and Cross Validating New Indicators', *Electoral Studies*, 30, pp. 174–183.

Janda, K., Harmel, R., Edens, C. and Goff, P. (1995) 'Changes in Party Identity: Evidence from Party Manifestos', *Party Politics*, 1(2), pp. 171–196.

Kriesi, H., Grande, E., Dolezal, M., Helbling, M., Höglinger, D., Hutter, S. and Wuest, B. (2012) *Political Conflict in Western Europe*. Cambridge/New York: Cambridge University Press.

Kriesi, H., Grande, E., Lachat, R., Dolezal, M., Bornschier, S. and Frey, T. (2008) *West European Politics in the Age of Globalization*. Cambridge: Cambridge University Press.

McDonnell, D. (2013) 'Silvio Berlusconi's Personal Parties: From Forza Italia to the Popolo della Libertà', *Political Studies,* 61(S1), pp. 217–233.

Newell, J.L. and Bull, M. (1997) 'Party Organisations and Alliances in Italy in the 1990s: A Revolution of Sorts', *West European Politics*, 20(1), pp. 81–109.

Pasquino, G. (2001) 'Le elezioni locali nella transizione italiana: la creazione della leadership', *Teoria Politica,* 17(1), pp. 91–106.

Schuck, A., Xezonakis, G., Banducci, S. and de Vreese, C.H. (2010) *EES (2009) Media Study Data Advance Release Documentation*. Amsterdam and Exeter: PIREDEU.

Index

Note: figures and tables are denoted with italicized page numbers; end note information is denoted with an n and note number following the page number.